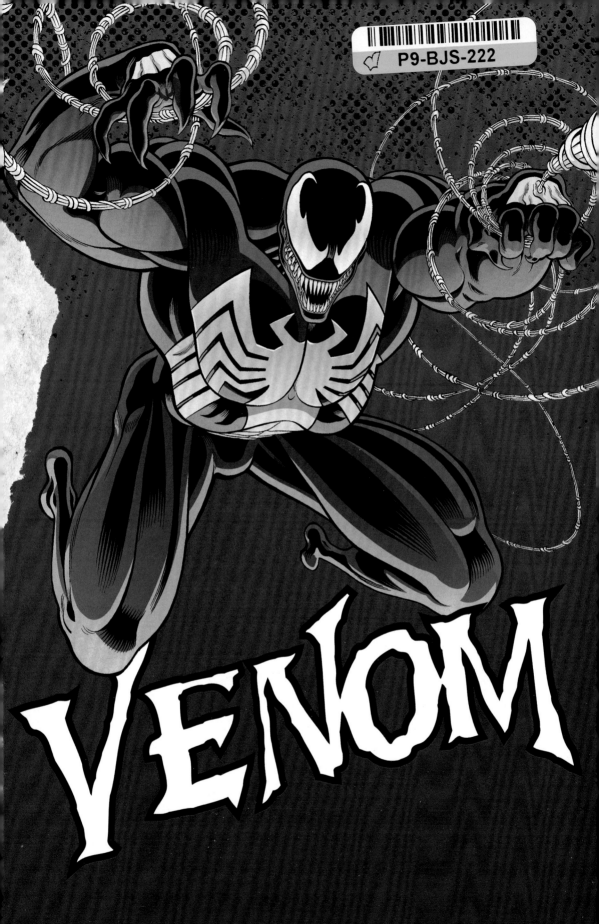

VENOM

CONTEMPLATING SUICIDE AFTER HIS LIFE FELL APART,
DISGRACED REPORTER **EDDIE BROCK** SOUGHT FORGIVENESS AT
THE SAME CHURCH WHERE SPIDER-MAN WAS REJECTING A LIVING,
ALIEN COSTUME CALLED A **SYMBIOTE**. SENSING BROCK'S MISERY,
THE SYMBIOTE BONDED WITH HIM AND IMBUED HIM WITH POWERS
SIMILAR TO THOSE OF THE AMAZING SPIDER-MAN.

FOR A TIME, EDDIE TRIED TO BE A HERO. HOWEVER, HIS VIOLENT
METHODS OFTEN PUT HIM AT ODDS WITH HEROES AND VILLAINS
ALIKE. EVENTUALLY, EDDIE AND THE SYMBIOTE WERE SEPARATED,
AND, FOR A TIME, THEY WENT THEIR SEPARATE WAYS.

THEY WERE HAPPY LIVING SEPARATELY.
BUT WHEN FATE OFFERED THEM THE CHANCE TO REUNITE,
THEY FOUND THEMSELVES UNABLE TO RESIST.

VENOM

150

HEART OF DARKNESS

MIKE COSTA
WRITER

TRADD MOORE
ARTIST

FELIPE SOBREIRO
COLOR ARTIST

DEPENDENCE DAY

ROBBIE THOMPSON
WRITER

GERARDO SANDOVAL
ARTIST

DONO SÁNCHEZ-ALMARA
COLOR ARTIST

MAILED!

DAVID MICHELINIE
WRITER

RON LIM
PENCILER

JOHN LIVESAY
INKER

LEE LOUGHRIDGE
COLORIST

151-153: THE LAND BEFORE CRIME

MIKE COSTA
WRITER

GERARDO SANDOVAL
ARTIST

DONO SÁNCHEZ-ALMARA
COLOR ARTIST

GERARDO SANDOVAL (#150); **FRANCISCO HERRERA** & **FERNANDA RIZO** (#151-153)
COVER ARTISTS

VC's CLAYTON COWLES
LETTERER

ALLISON STOCK
ASSISTANT EDITOR

DEVIN LEWIS
EDITOR

NICK LOWE
EXECUTIVE EDITOR

COLLECTION EDITOR **MARK D. BEAZLEY**
ASSISTANT EDITOR **CAITLIN O'CONNELL**
ASSOCIATE MANAGING EDITOR **KATERI WOODY**
SENIOR EDITOR, SPECIAL PROJECTS **JENNIFER GRÜNWALD**

VP PRODUCTION & SPECIAL PROJECTS **JEFF YOUNGQUIST**
SVP PRINT, SALES & MARKETING **DAVID GABRIEL**
BOOK DESIGNER **ADAM DEL RE**

EDITOR IN CHIEF **AXEL ALONSO**
CHIEF CREATIVE OFFICER **JOE QUESADA**
PRESIDENT **DAN BUCKLEY**
EXECUTIVE PRODUCER **ALAN FINE**

VENOM VOL. 2: THE LAND BEFORE CRIME. Contains material originally published in magazine form as VENOM #150-153. First printing 2017. ISBN# 978-1-302-90603-0. Published by MARVEL WORLDWIDE, INC., a subsidiary of MARVEL ENTERTAINMENT, LLC. OFFICE OF PUBLICATION: 135 West 50th Street, New York, NY 10020.

Printed in Canada. DAN BUCKLEY, President, Marvel Entertainment; JOE QUESADA, Chief Creative Officer; TOM BREVOORT, SVP of Publishing; DAVID BOGART, SVP of Business Affairs & Operations, Publishing & Partnership; C.B. CEBULSKI, VP of Brand Management & Development, Asia; DAVID GABRIEL, SVP of Sales & Marketing, Publishing; JEFF YOUNGQUIST, VP of Production & Special Projects; DAN CARR, Executive Director of Publishing Technology; ALEX MORALES, Director of Publishing Operations; SUSAN CRESPI, Production Manager; STAN LEE, Chairman Emeritus. For information regarding advertising in Marvel Comics or on Marvel.com, please contact Vit DeBellis, Integrated Sales Manager, at vdebellis@marvel.com. For Marvel subscription inquiries, please call 888-511-5480. **Manufactured between 9/1/2017 and 10/3/2017 by SOLISCO PRINTERS, SCOTT, QC, CANADA.**

10 9 8 7 6 5 4 3 2 1

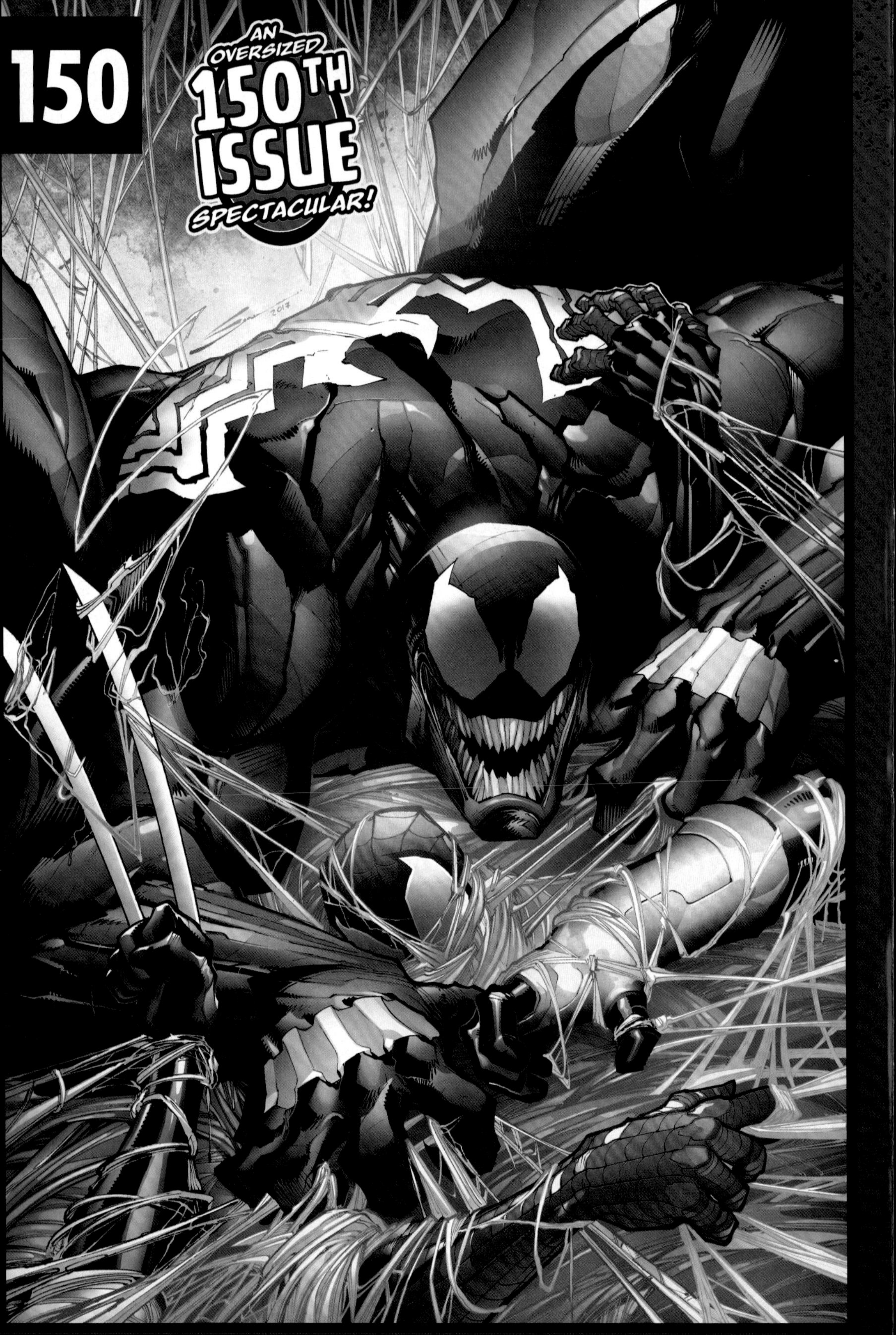
150
AN OVERSIZED 150TH ISSUE SPECTACULAR!

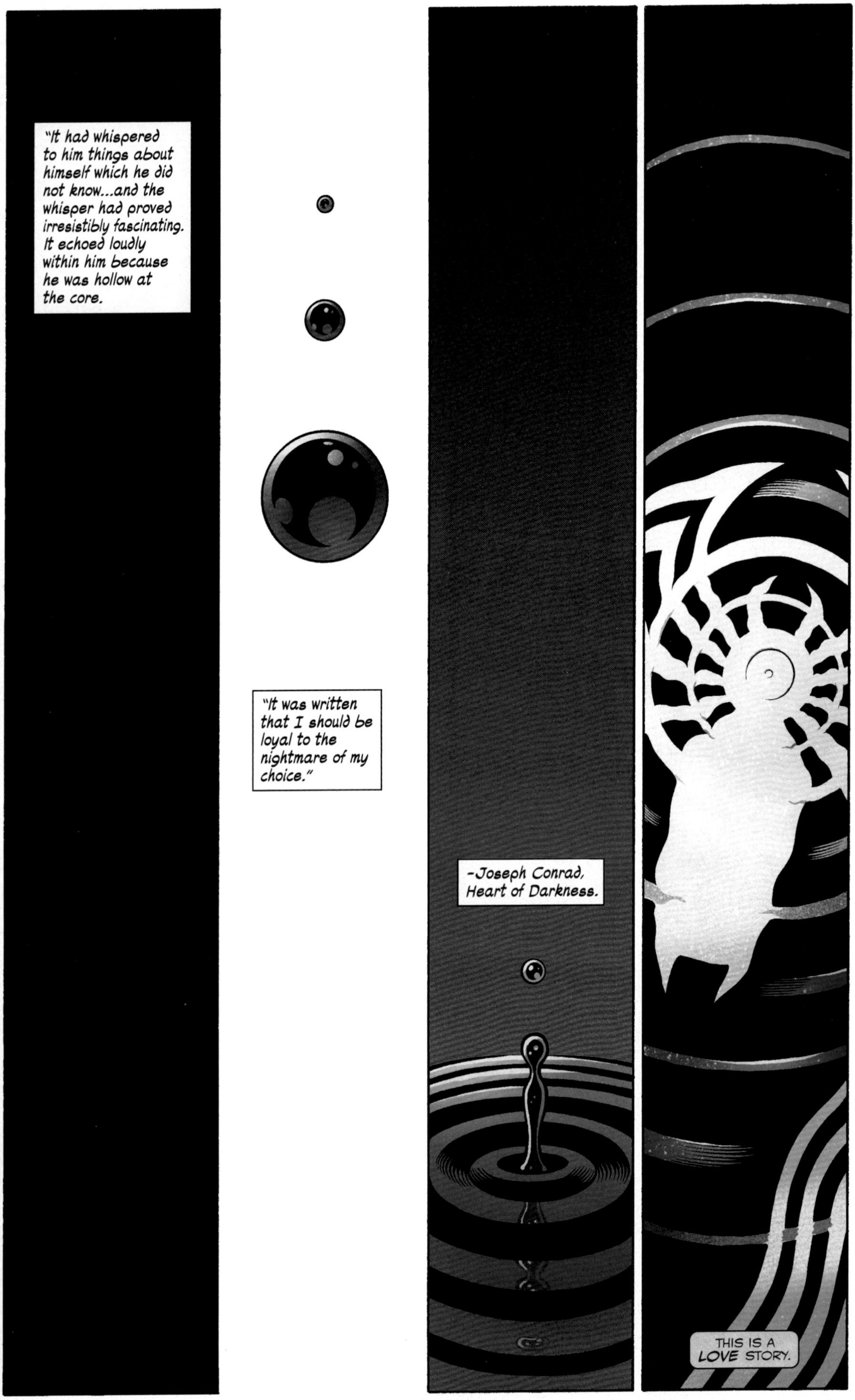
"It had whispered to him things about himself which he did not know...and the whisper had proved irresistibly fascinating. It echoed loudly within him because he was hollow at the core.
"It was written that I should be loyal to the nightmare of my choice."
-Joseph Conrad, Heart of Darkness.
THIS IS A LOVE STORY.

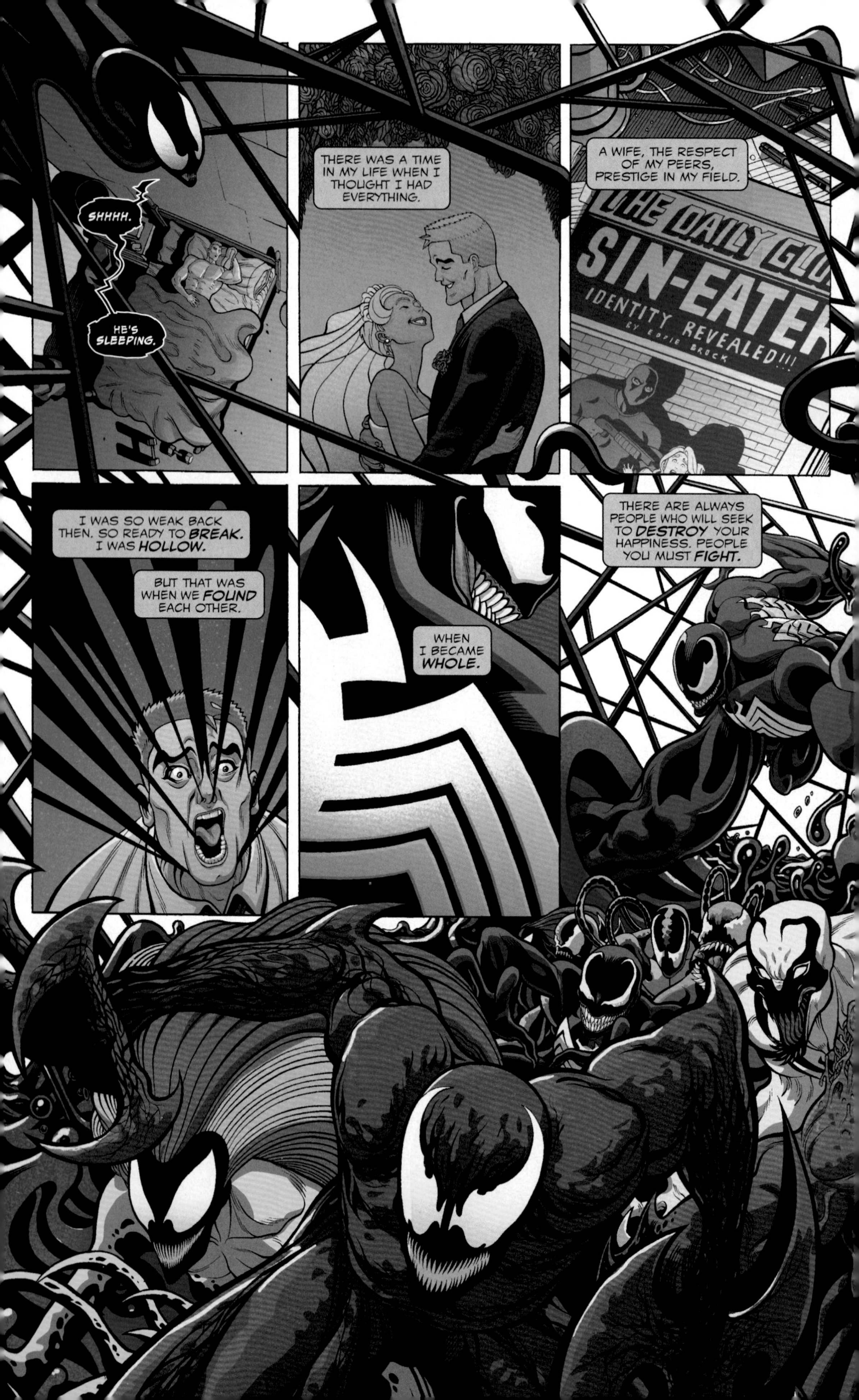
SHHHH.
HE'S SLEEPING.
THERE WAS A TIME IN MY LIFE WHEN I THOUGHT I HAD EVERYTHING.
A WIFE, THE RESPECT OF MY PEERS, PRESTIGE IN MY FIELD.
THE DAILY GLO
SIN-EATER
IDENTITY REVEALED!!!
BY EDDIE BROCK
I WAS SO WEAK BACK THEN. SO READY TO BREAK. I WAS HOLLOW.
BUT THAT WAS WHEN WE FOUND EACH OTHER.
WHEN I BECAME WHOLE.
THERE ARE ALWAYS PEOPLE WHO WILL SEEK TO DESTROY YOUR HAPPINESS. PEOPLE YOU MUST FIGHT.

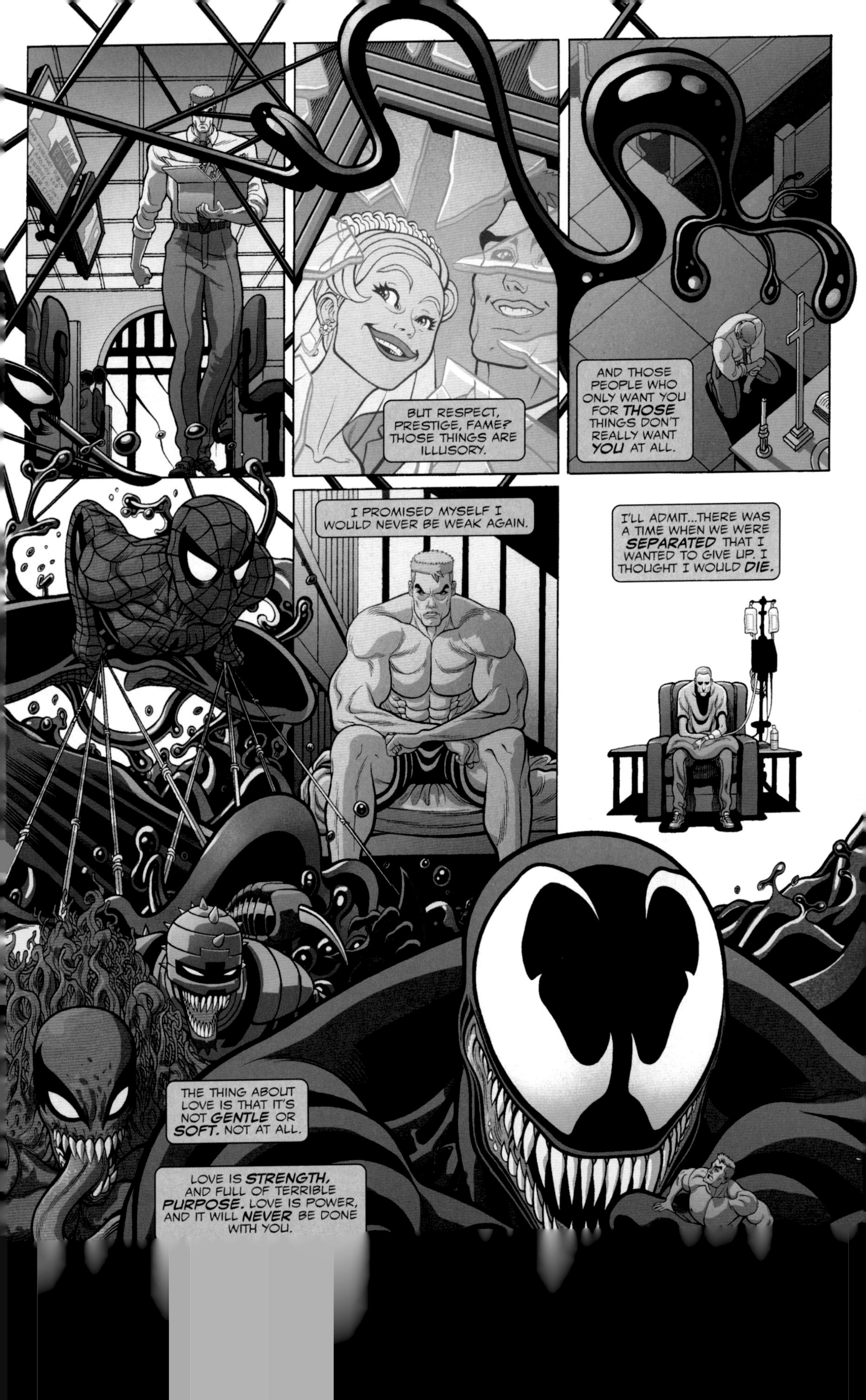
BUT RESPECT, PRESTIGE, FAME? THOSE THINGS ARE ILLUSORY.
AND THOSE PEOPLE WHO ONLY WANT YOU FOR THOSE THINGS DON'T REALLY WANT YOU AT ALL.
I PROMISED MYSELF I WOULD NEVER BE WEAK AGAIN.
I'LL ADMIT...THERE WAS A TIME WHEN WE WERE SEPARATED THAT I WANTED TO GIVE UP. I THOUGHT I WOULD DIE.
THE THING ABOUT LOVE IS THAT IT'S NOT GENTLE OR SOFT. NOT AT ALL.
LOVE IS STRENGTH, AND FULL OF TERRIBLE PURPOSE. LOVE IS POWER, AND IT WILL NEVER BE DONE WITH YOU.

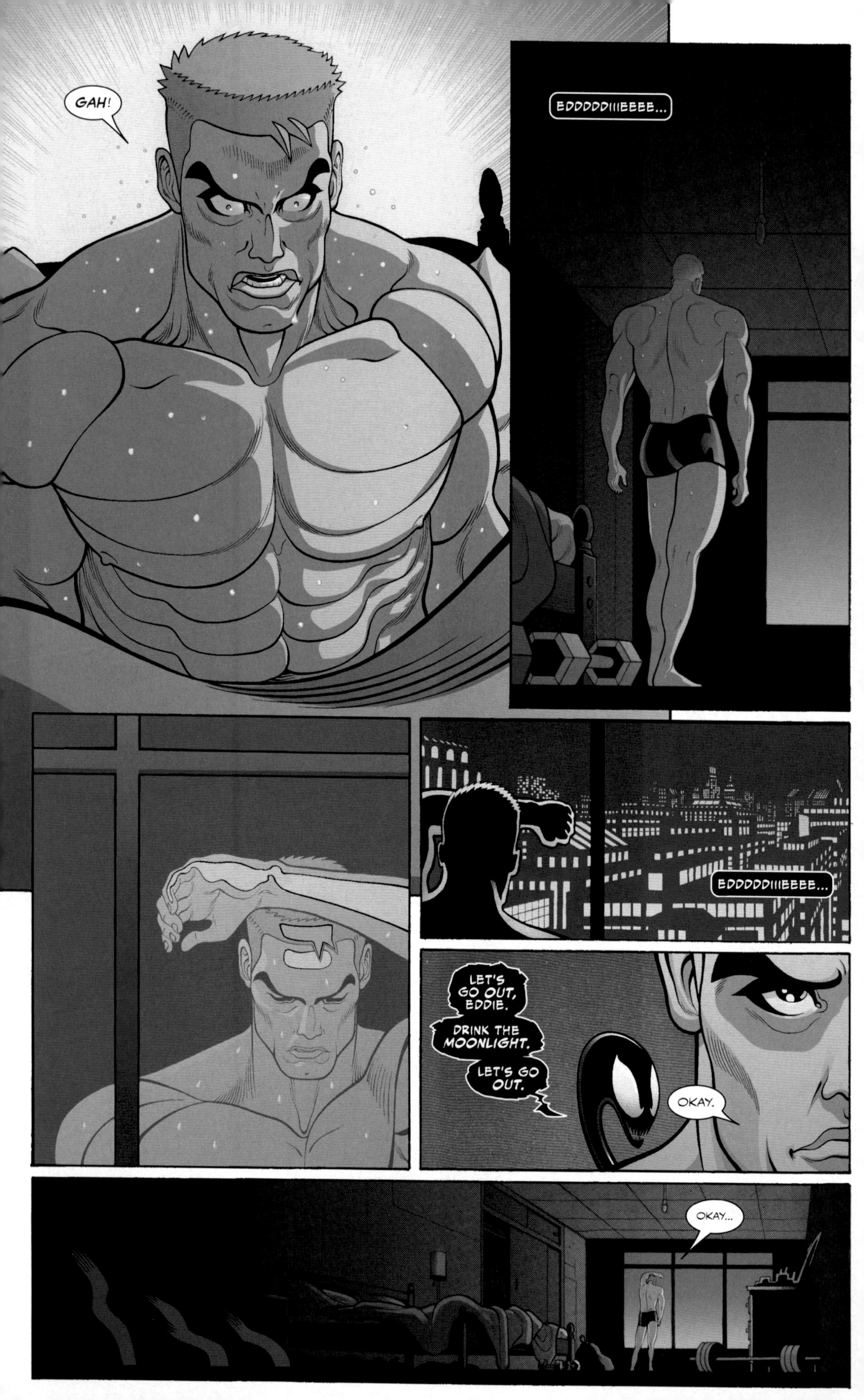
GAH!
EDDDDDIIIEEEE...
EDDDDDIIIEEEE...
LET'S GO OUT, EDDIE.
DRINK THE MOONLIGHT.
LET'S GO OUT.
OKAY.
OKAY...

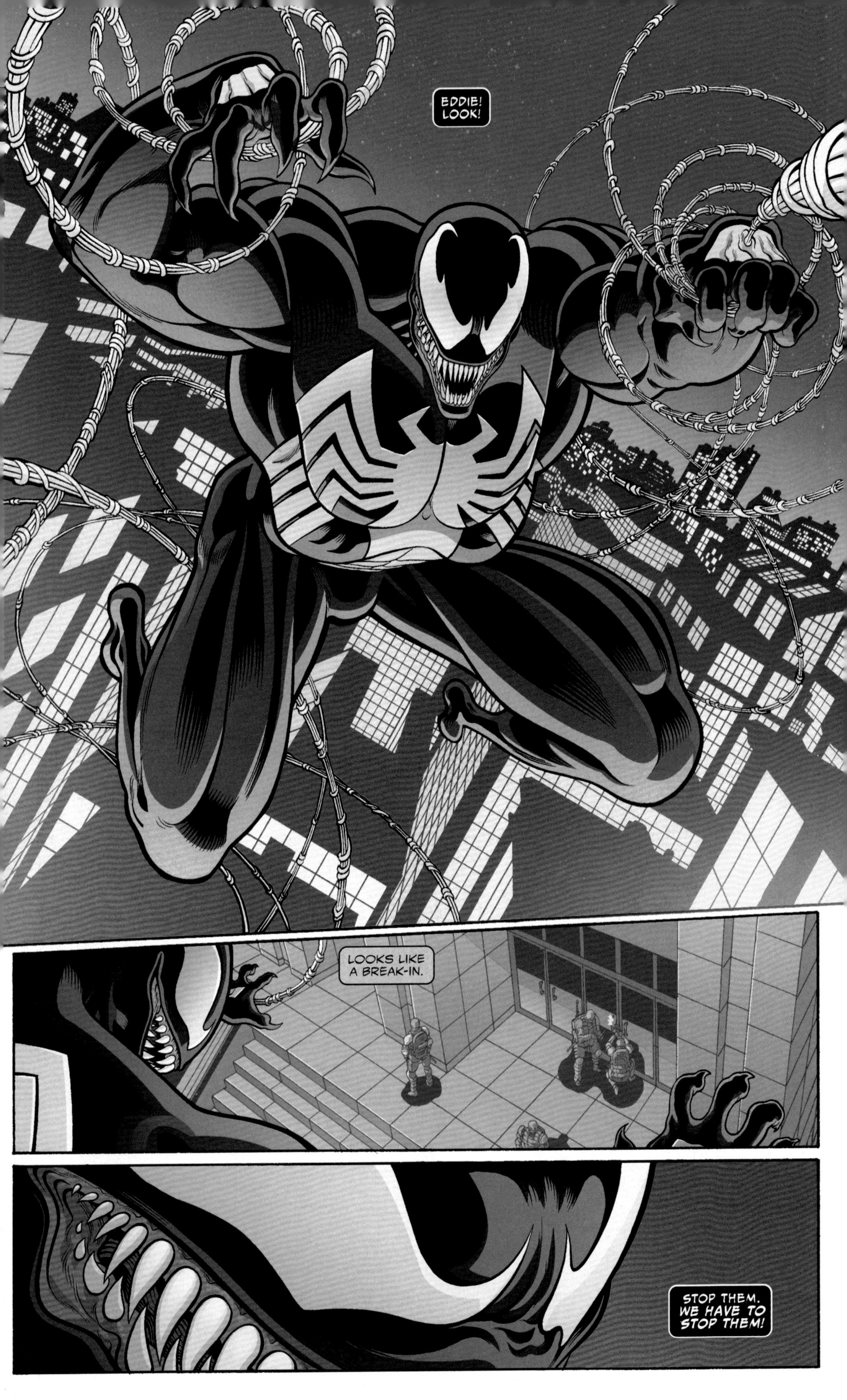
EDDIE! LOOK!
LOOKS LIKE A BREAK-IN.
STOP THEM. WE HAVE TO STOP THEM!

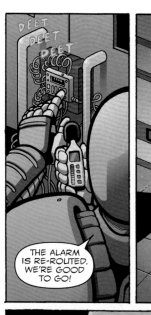

DEET
DEET
DEET

THE ALARM IS RE-ROUTED. WE'RE GOOD TO GO!

CHOOME

ONCE YOU'RE IN THE INNER CORE, KEEP IT DOWN TO 20 DECIBELS OR YOU'LL TRIP THE ACOUSTIC TRIGGERS.

OOOOOH, LOOKEE HERE!

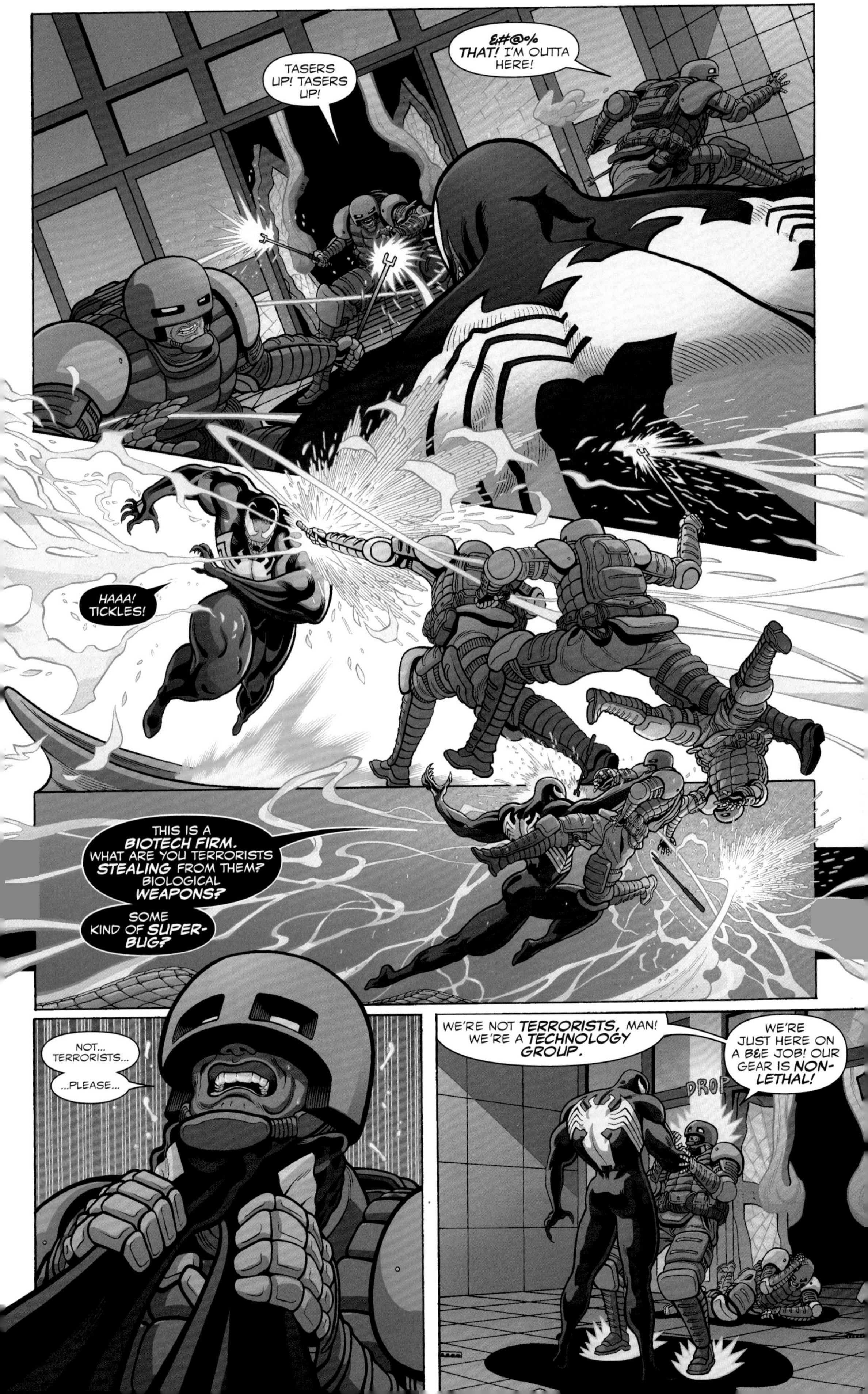
TASERS UP! TASERS UP!
&#@%% THAT! I'M OUTTA HERE!
HAAA! TICKLES!
THIS IS A BIOTECH FIRM. WHAT ARE YOU TERRORISTS STEALING FROM THEM? BIOLOGICAL WEAPONS?
SOME KIND OF SUPER-BUG?
NOT... TERRORISTS...
...PLEASE...
WE'RE NOT TERRORISTS, MAN! WE'RE A TECHNOLOGY GROUP.
WE'RE JUST HERE ON A B&E JOB! OUR GEAR IS NON-LETHAL!
DROP

STEALING TECHNOLOGY, THEN. **FOR WHOSE GAIN?**

I GOT IT! THIS LITTLE SUCKER IS GOING TO MAKE US **RICH.**

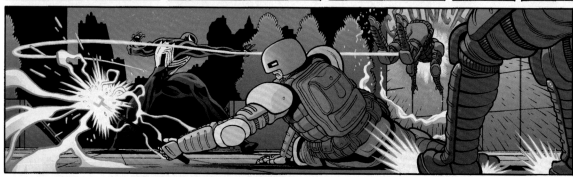

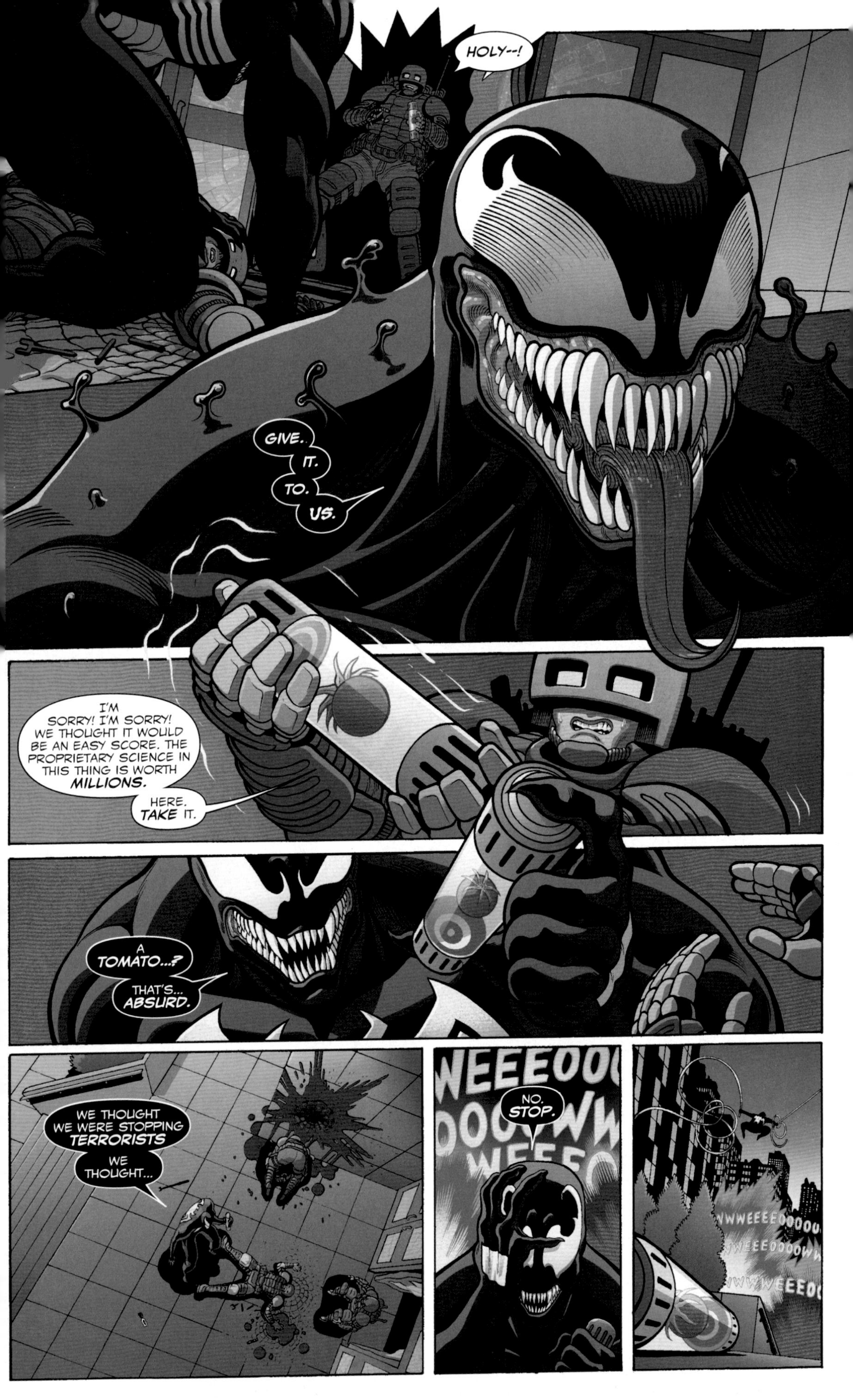
HOLY--!
GIVE. IT. TO. US.
I'M SORRY! I'M SORRY! WE THOUGHT IT WOULD BE AN EASY SCORE. THE PROPRIETARY SCIENCE IN THIS THING IS WORTH MILLIONS.
HERE. TAKE IT.
A TOMATO...?
THAT'S... ABSURD.
WE THOUGHT WE WERE STOPPING TERRORISTS
WE THOUGHT...
WEEEOOO
OOOOWW
NO. STOP.
WWWEEEOOOOU
WWEEEOOOOWW
WWWEEEO

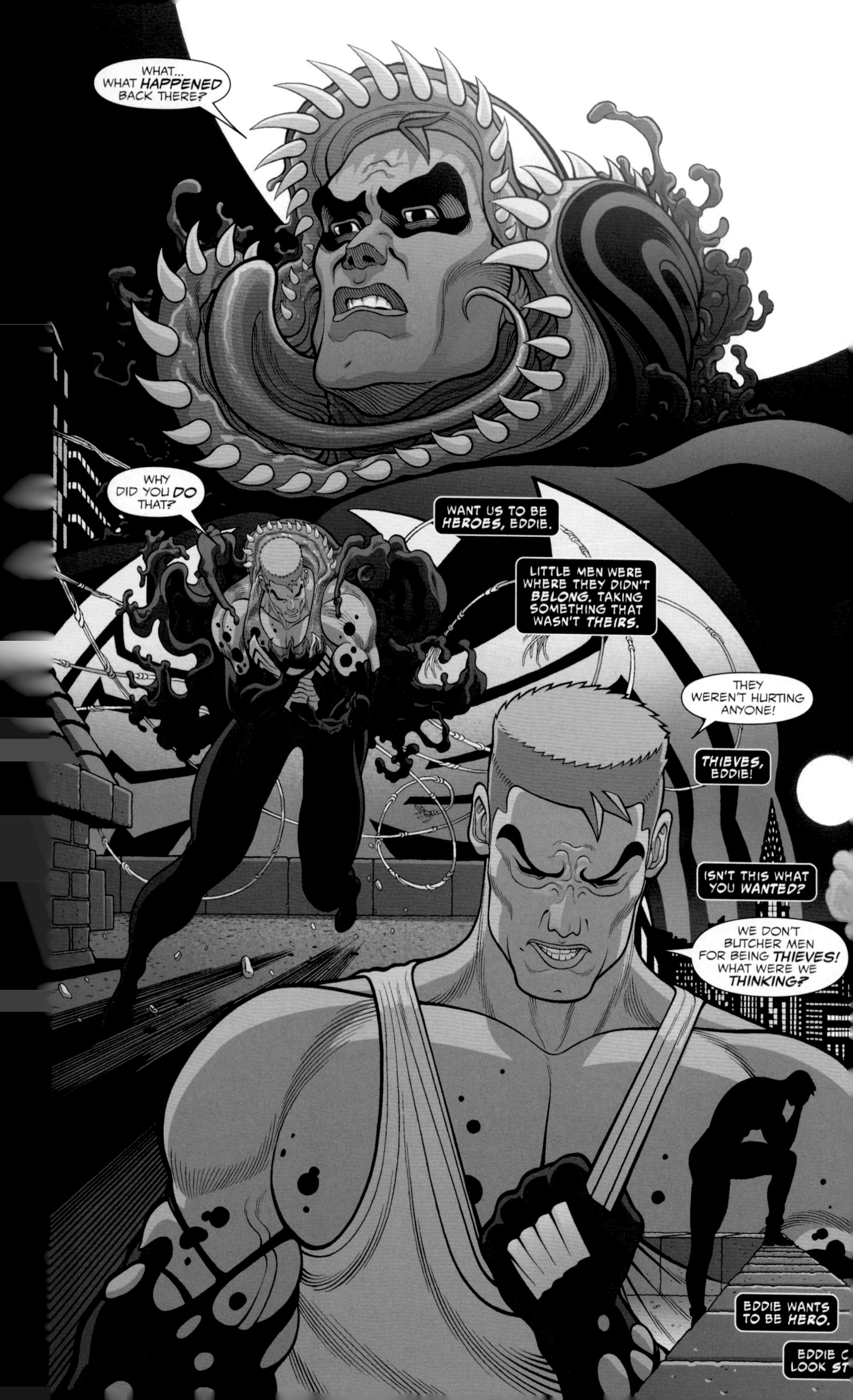
WHAT... WHAT HAPPENED BACK THERE?
WHY DID YOU DO THAT?
WANT US TO BE HEROES, EDDIE.
LITTLE MEN WERE WHERE THEY DIDN'T BELONG. TAKING SOMETHING THAT WASN'T THEIRS.
THEY WEREN'T HURTING ANYONE!
THIEVES, EDDIE!
ISN'T THIS WHAT YOU WANTED?
WE DON'T BUTCHER MEN FOR BEING THIEVES! WHAT WERE WE THINKING?
EDDIE WANTS TO BE HERO.

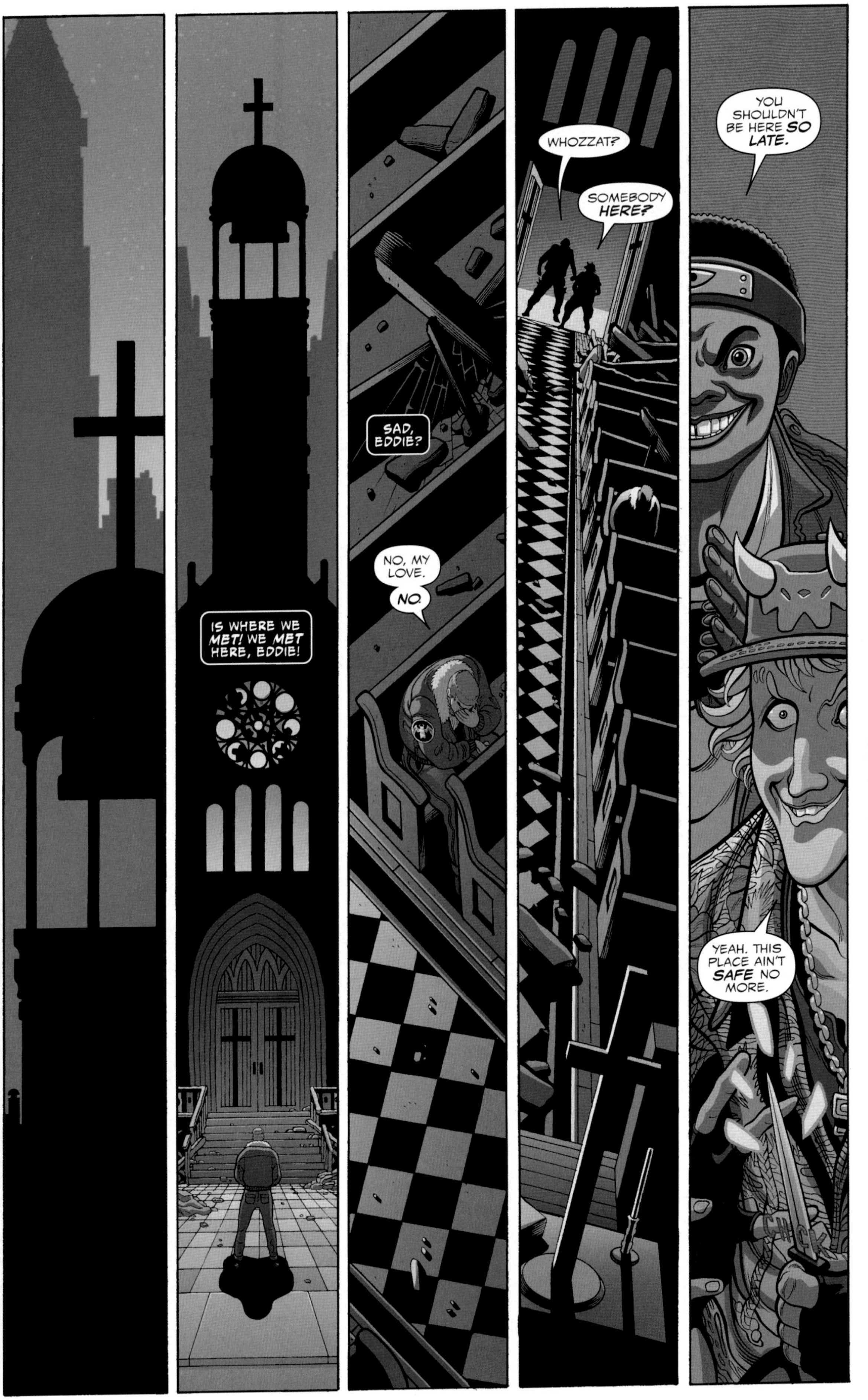
IS WHERE WE MET! WE MET HERE, EDDIE!
SAD, EDDIE?
NO, MY LOVE. NO.
WHOZZAT?
SOMEBODY HERE?
YOU SHOULDN'T BE HERE SO LATE.
YEAH. THIS PLACE AIN'T SAFE NO MORE.

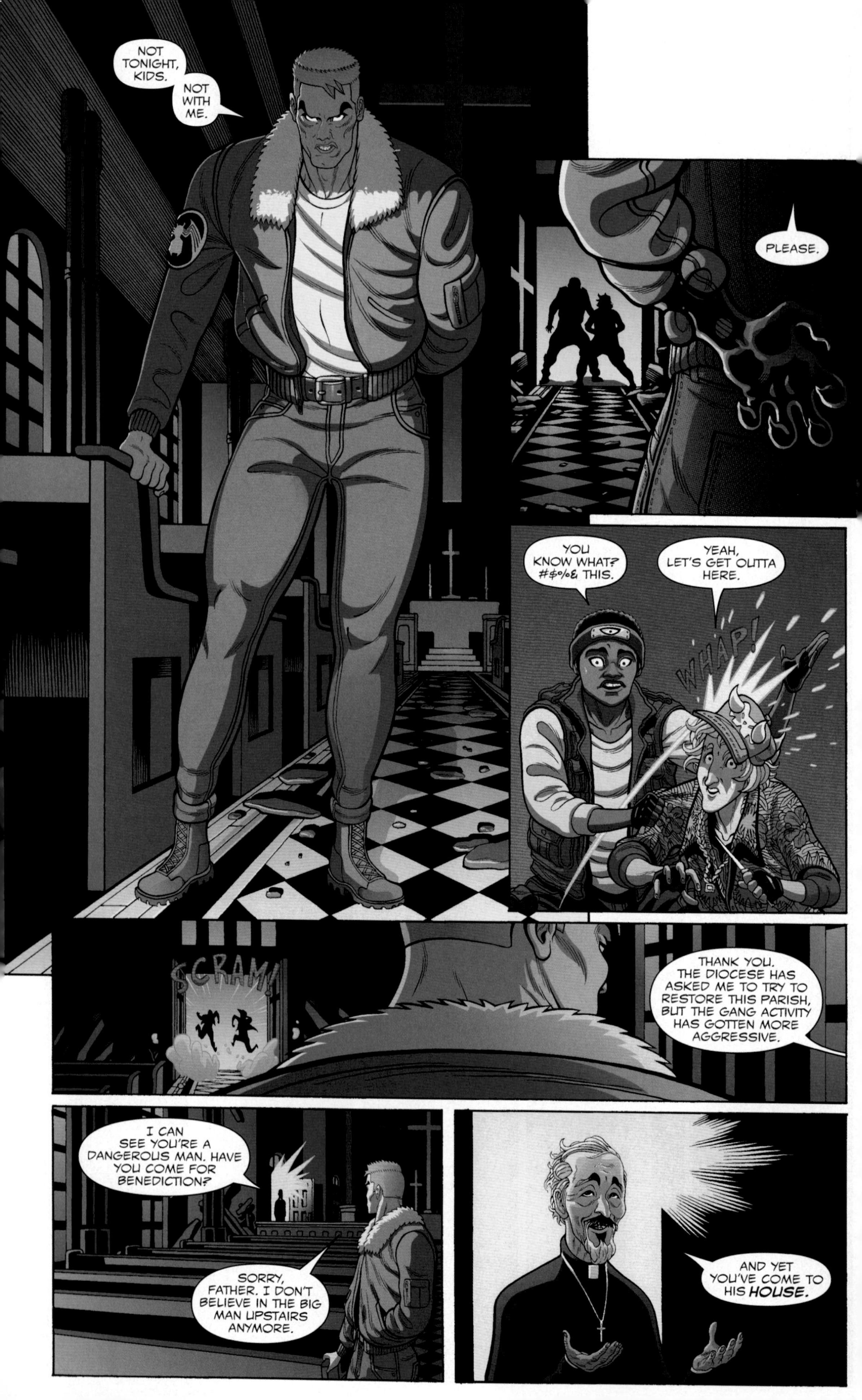
NOT TONIGHT, KIDS.
NOT WITH ME.
PLEASE.
YOU KNOW WHAT? #$%& THIS.
YEAH, LET'S GET OUTTA HERE.
WHAP!
SCRAM!
THANK YOU. THE DIOCESE HAS ASKED ME TO TRY TO RESTORE THIS PARISH, BUT THE GANG ACTIVITY HAS GOTTEN MORE AGGRESSIVE.
I CAN SEE YOU'RE A DANGEROUS MAN. HAVE YOU COME FOR BENEDICTION?
SORRY, FATHER. I DON'T BELIEVE IN THE BIG MAN UPSTAIRS ANYMORE.
AND YET YOU'VE COME TO HIS HOUSE.

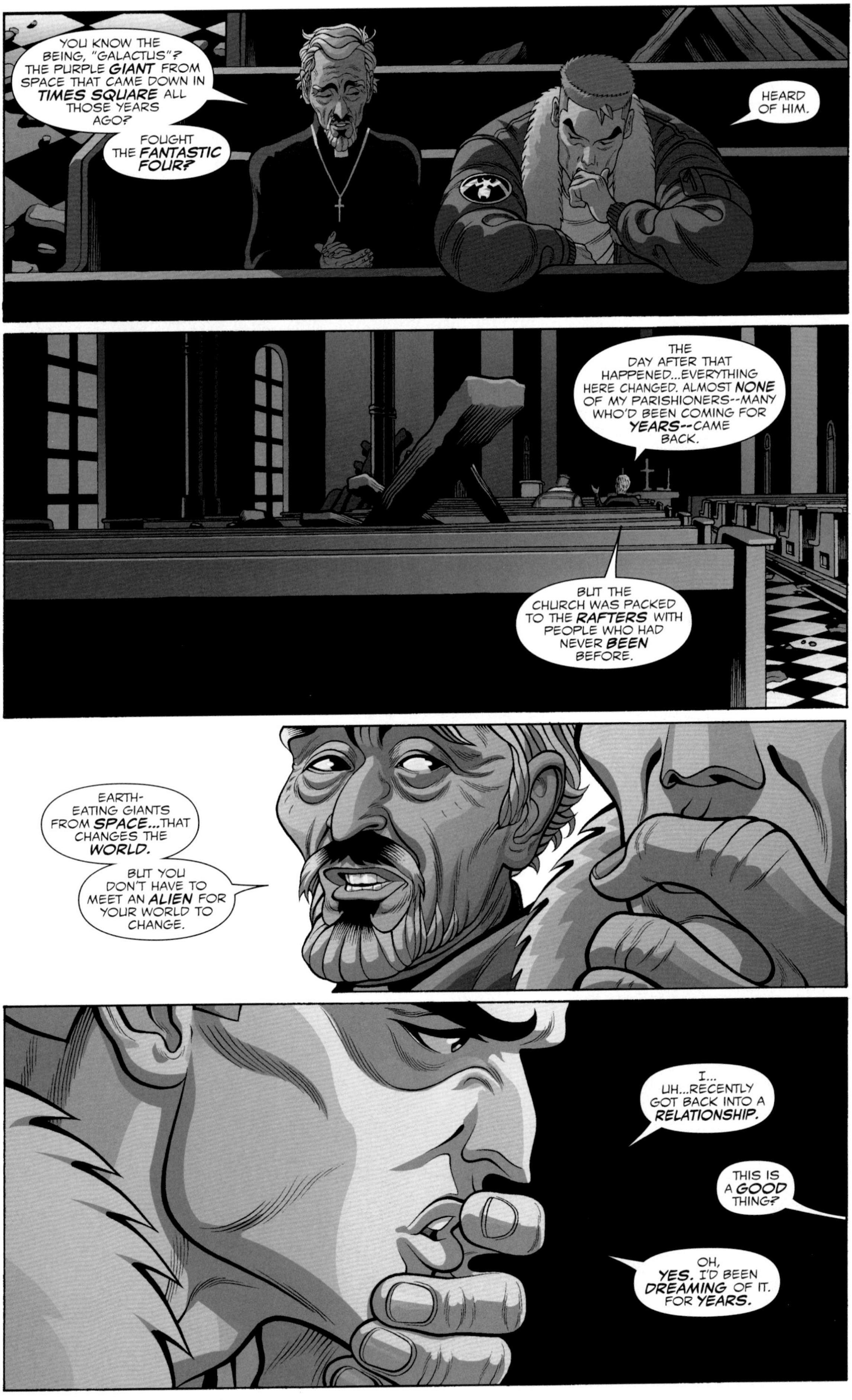
YOU KNOW THE BEING, "GALACTUS"? THE PURPLE GIANT FROM SPACE THAT CAME DOWN IN TIMES SQUARE ALL THOSE YEARS AGO?
FOUGHT THE FANTASTIC FOUR?
HEARD OF HIM.
THE DAY AFTER THAT HAPPENED...EVERYTHING HERE CHANGED. ALMOST NONE OF MY PARISHIONERS--MANY WHO'D BEEN COMING FOR YEARS--CAME BACK.
BUT THE CHURCH WAS PACKED TO THE RAFTERS WITH PEOPLE WHO HAD NEVER BEEN BEFORE.
EARTH-EATING GIANTS FROM SPACE...THAT CHANGES THE WORLD.
BUT YOU DON'T HAVE TO MEET AN ALIEN FOR YOUR WORLD TO CHANGE.
I... UH...RECENTLY GOT BACK INTO A RELATIONSHIP.
THIS IS A GOOD THING?
OH, YES. I'D BEEN DREAMING OF IT. FOR YEARS.

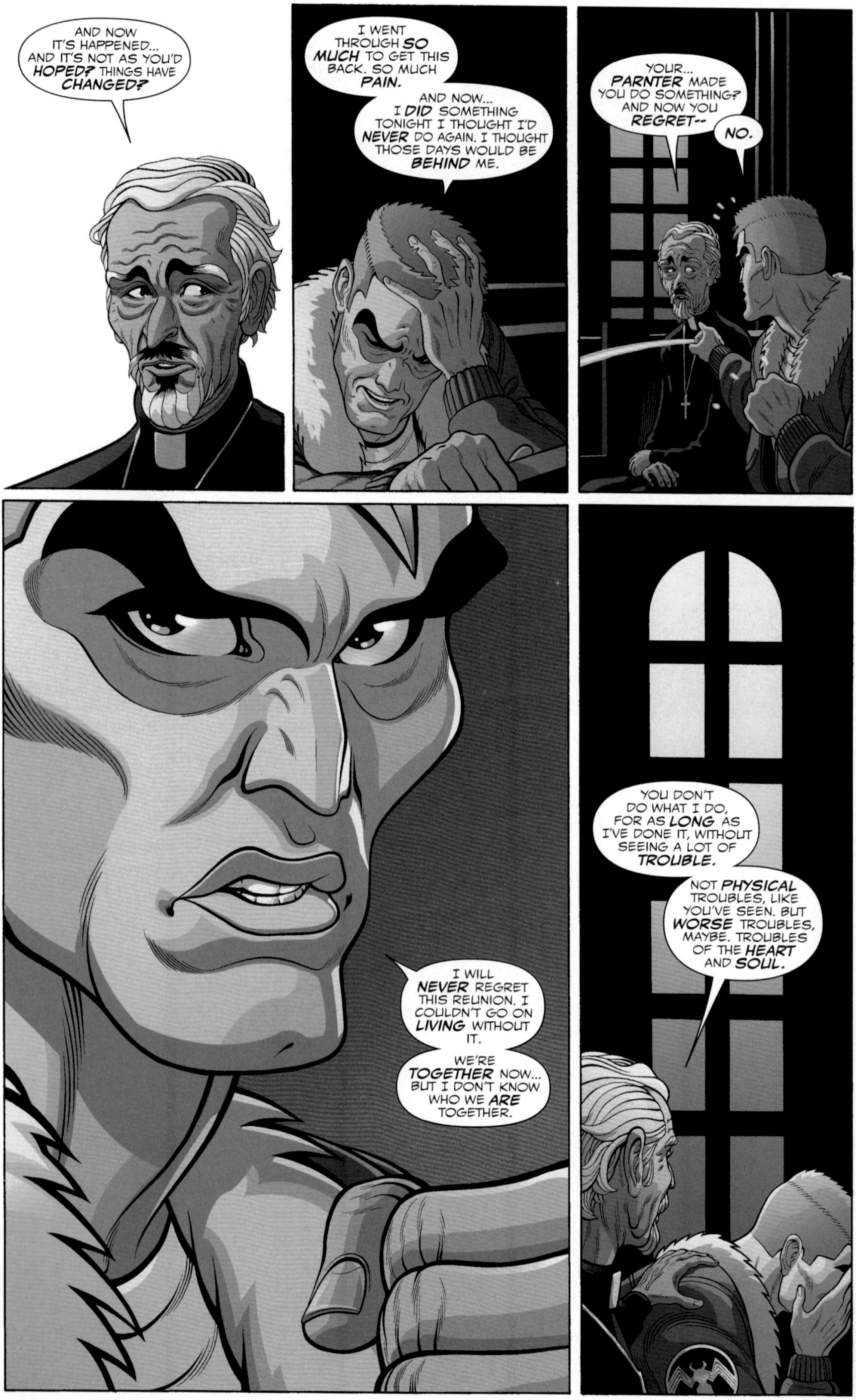
AND NOW IT'S HAPPENED... AND IT'S NOT AS YOU'D HOPED? THINGS HAVE CHANGED?
I WENT THROUGH SO MUCH TO GET THIS BACK. SO MUCH PAIN.
AND NOW... I DID SOMETHING TONIGHT I THOUGHT I'D NEVER DO AGAIN. I THOUGHT THOSE DAYS WOULD BE BEHIND ME.
YOUR... PARNTER MADE YOU DO SOMETHING? AND NOW YOU REGRET--
NO.
I WILL NEVER REGRET THIS REUNION. I COULDN'T GO ON LIVING WITHOUT IT.
WE'RE TOGETHER NOW... BUT I DON'T KNOW WHO WE ARE TOGETHER.
YOU DON'T DO WHAT I DO, FOR AS LONG AS I'VE DONE IT, WITHOUT SEEING A LOT OF TROUBLE.
NOT PHYSICAL TROUBLES, LIKE YOU'VE SEEN. BUT WORSE TROUBLES, MAYBE. TROUBLES OF THE HEART AND SOUL.

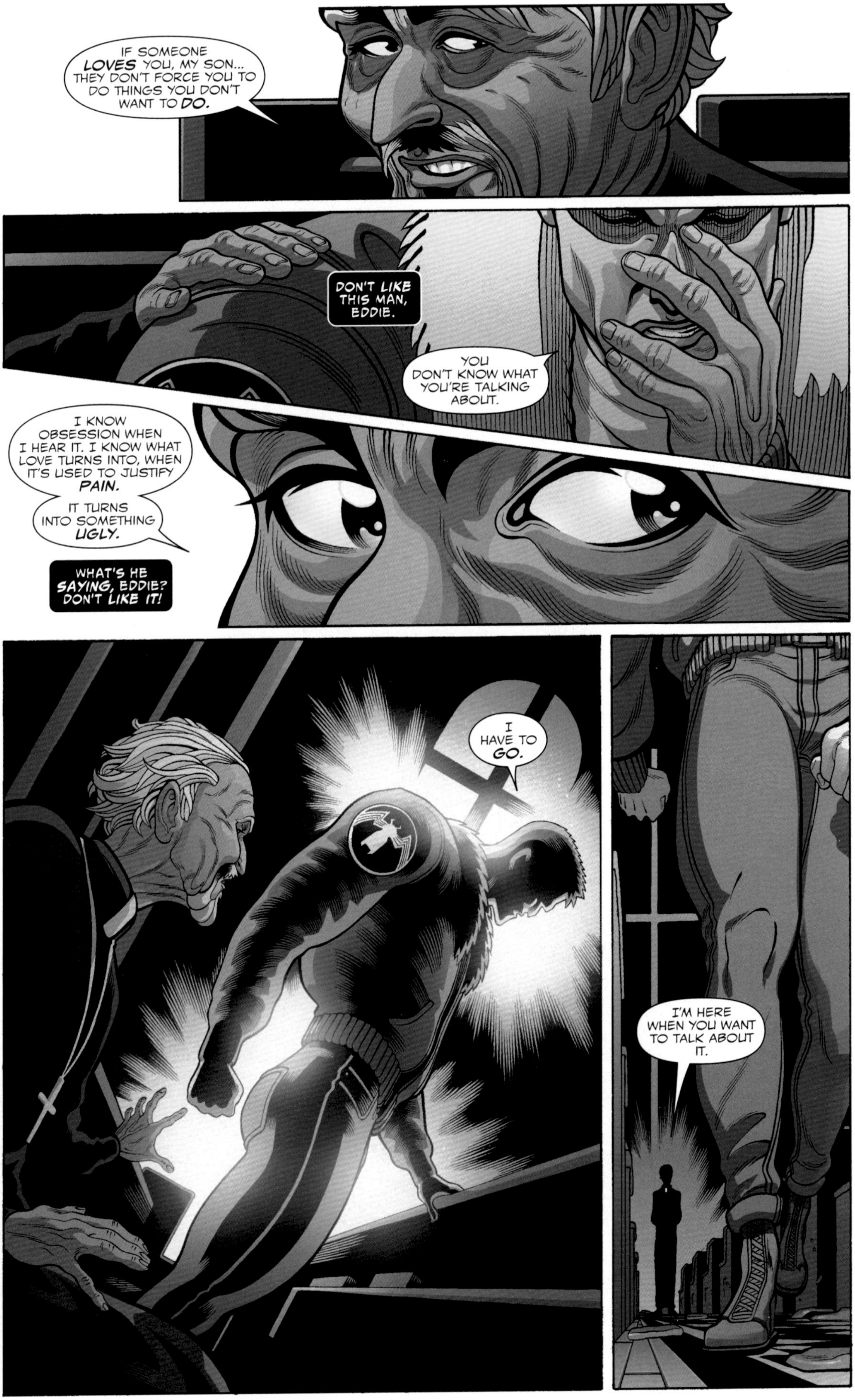

IF SOMEONE LOVES YOU, MY SON... THEY DON'T FORCE YOU TO DO THINGS YOU DON'T WANT TO DO.
DON'T LIKE THIS MAN, EDDIE.
YOU DON'T KNOW WHAT YOU'RE TALKING ABOUT.
I KNOW OBSESSION WHEN I HEAR IT. I KNOW WHAT LOVE TURNS INTO, WHEN IT'S USED TO JUSTIFY PAIN.
IT TURNS INTO SOMETHING UGLY.
WHAT'S HE SAYING, EDDIE? DON'T LIKE IT!
I HAVE TO GO.
I'M HERE WHEN YOU WANT TO TALK ABOUT IT.

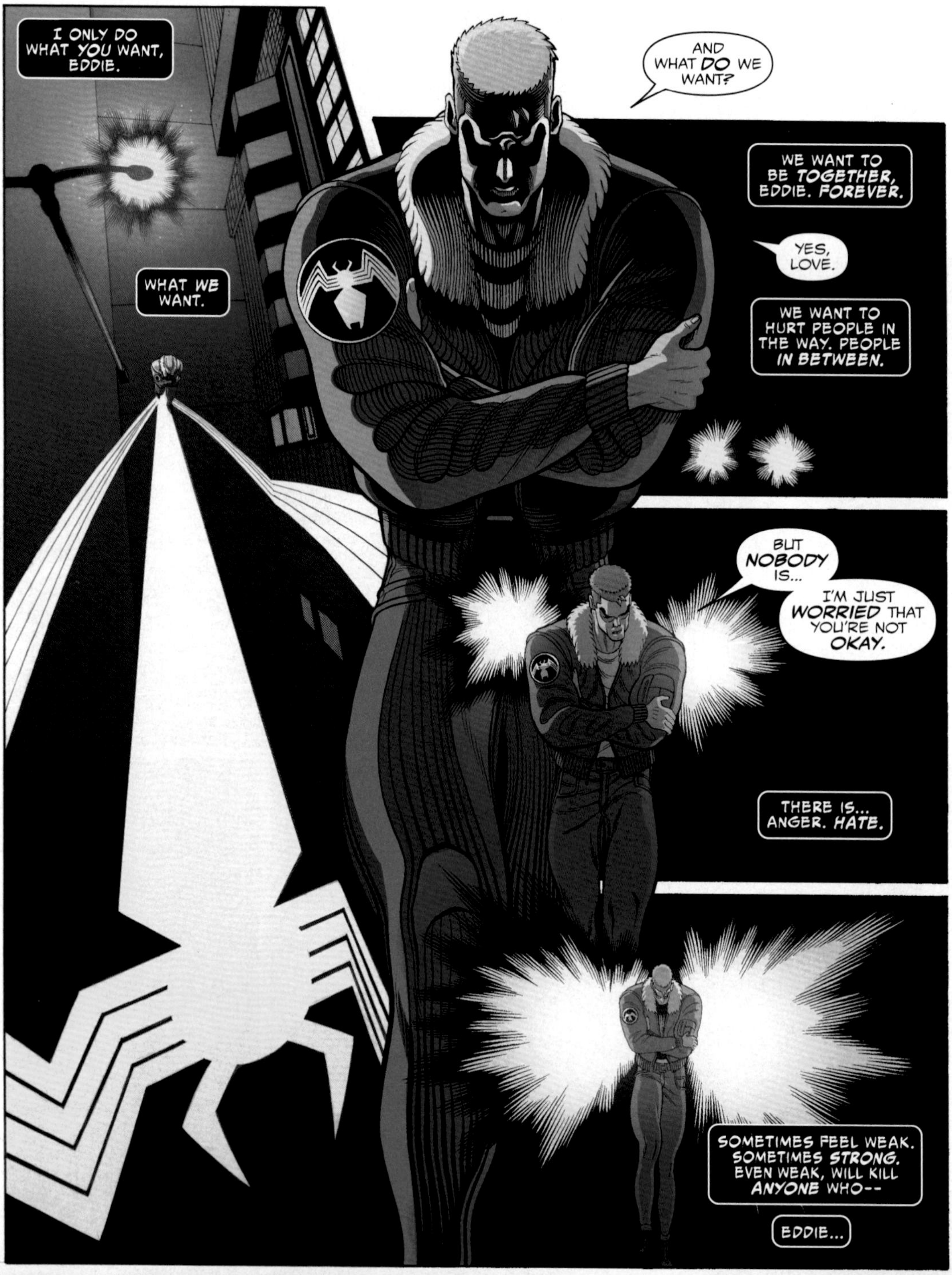
I ONLY DO WHAT YOU WANT, EDDIE.
AND WHAT DO WE WANT?
WHAT WE WANT.
WE WANT TO BE TOGETHER, EDDIE. FOREVER.
YES, LOVE.
WE WANT TO HURT PEOPLE IN THE WAY. PEOPLE IN BETWEEN.
BUT NOBODY IS...
I'M JUST WORRIED THAT YOU'RE NOT OKAY.
THERE IS... ANGER. HATE.
SOMETIMES FEEL WEAK. SOMETIMES STRONG. EVEN WEAK, WILL KILL ANYONE WHO--
EDDIE...

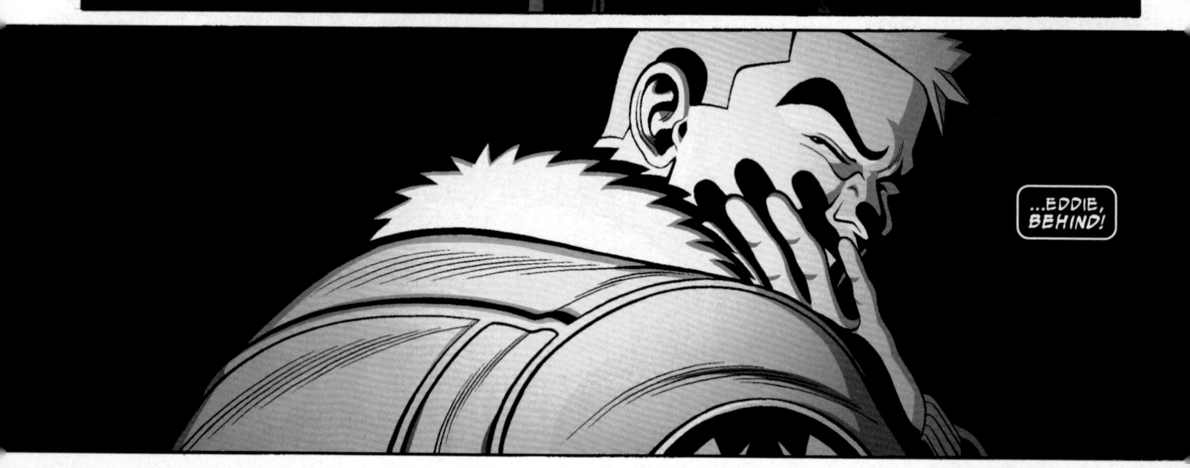
...EDDIE, BEHIND!

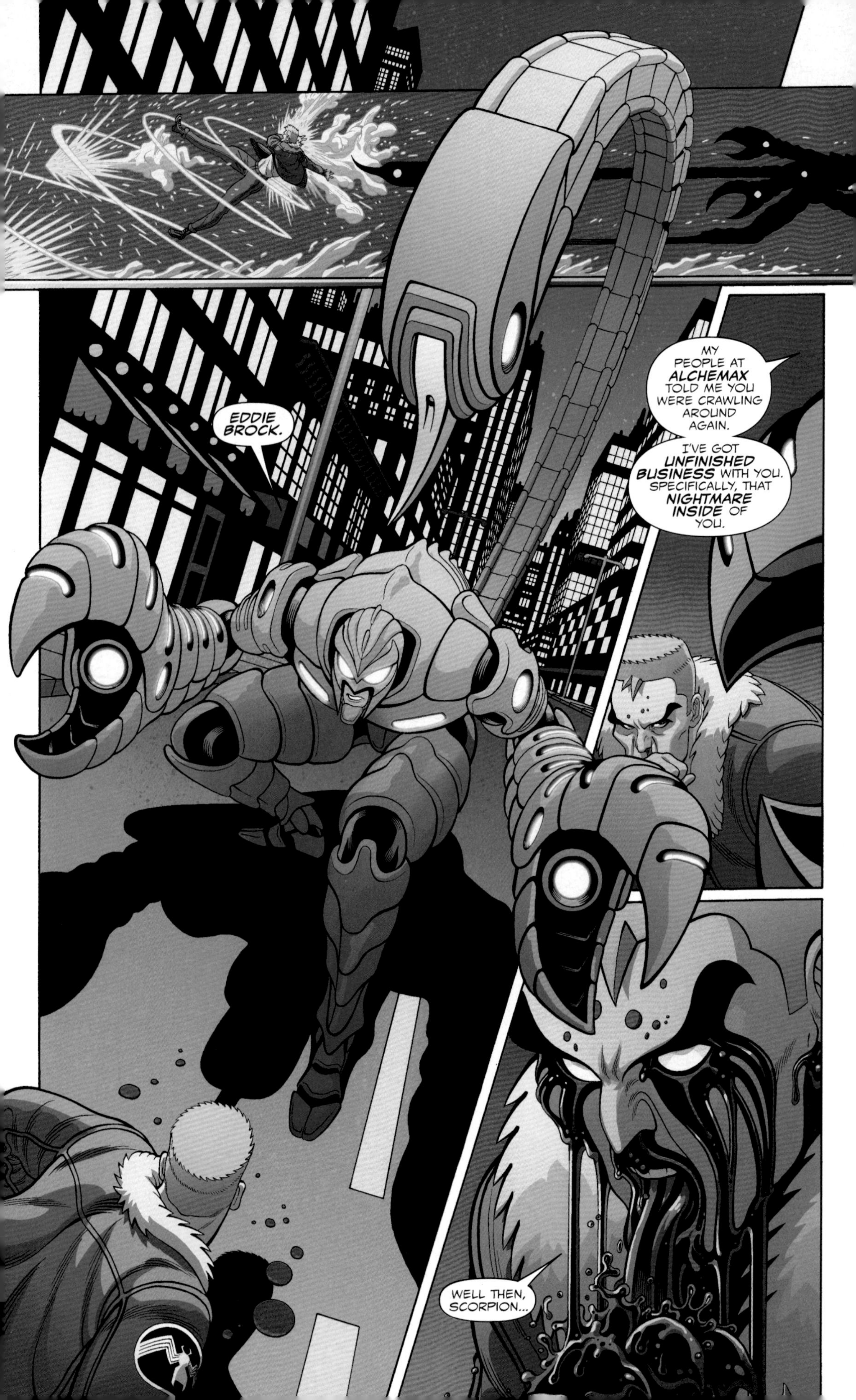
EDDIE BROCK.
MY PEOPLE AT ALCHEMAX TOLD ME YOU WERE CRAWLING AROUND AGAIN.
I'VE GOT UNFINISHED BUSINESS WITH YOU. SPECIFICALLY, THAT NIGHTMARE INSIDE OF YOU.
WELL THEN, SCORPION...

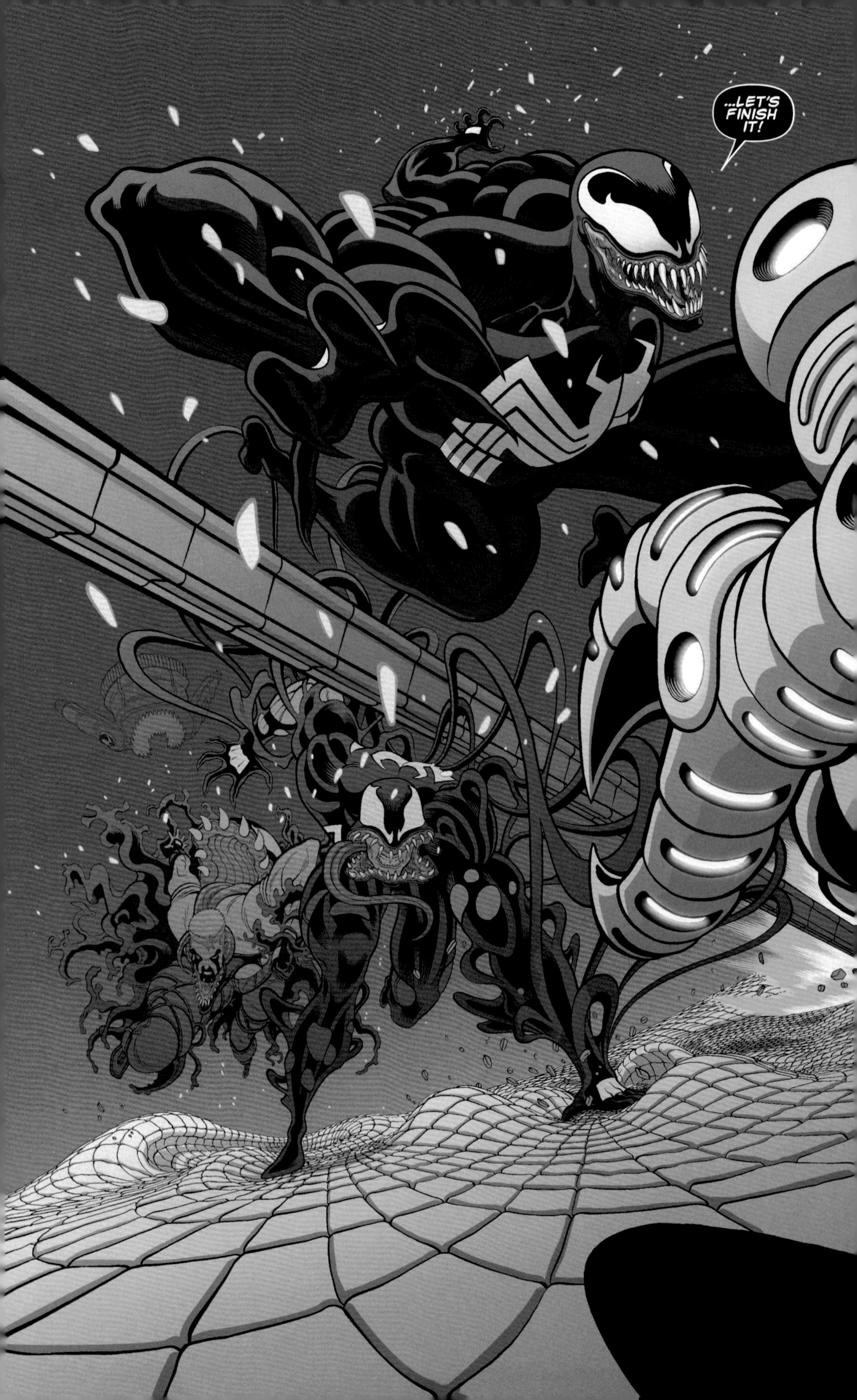
...LET'S FINISH IT!

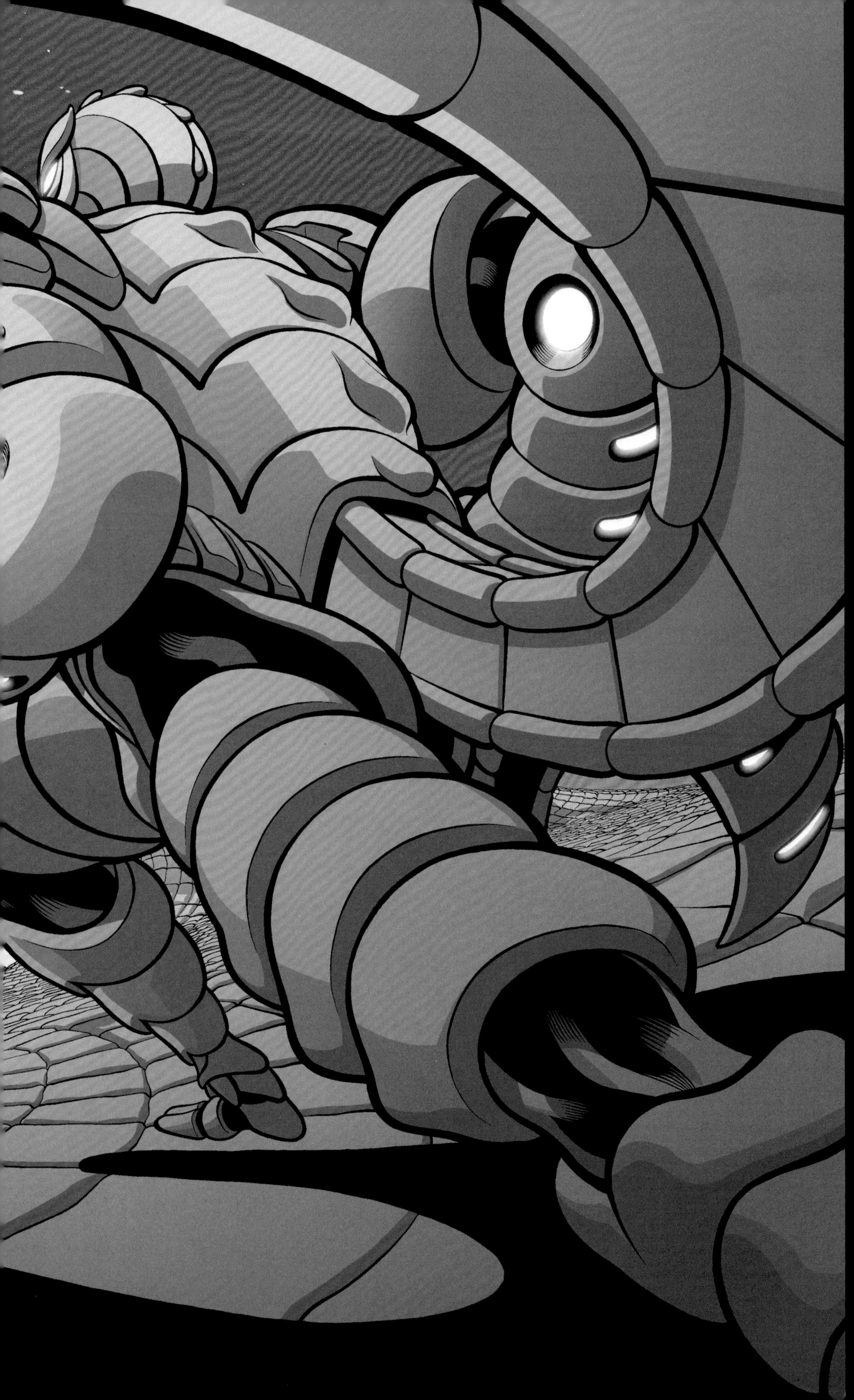

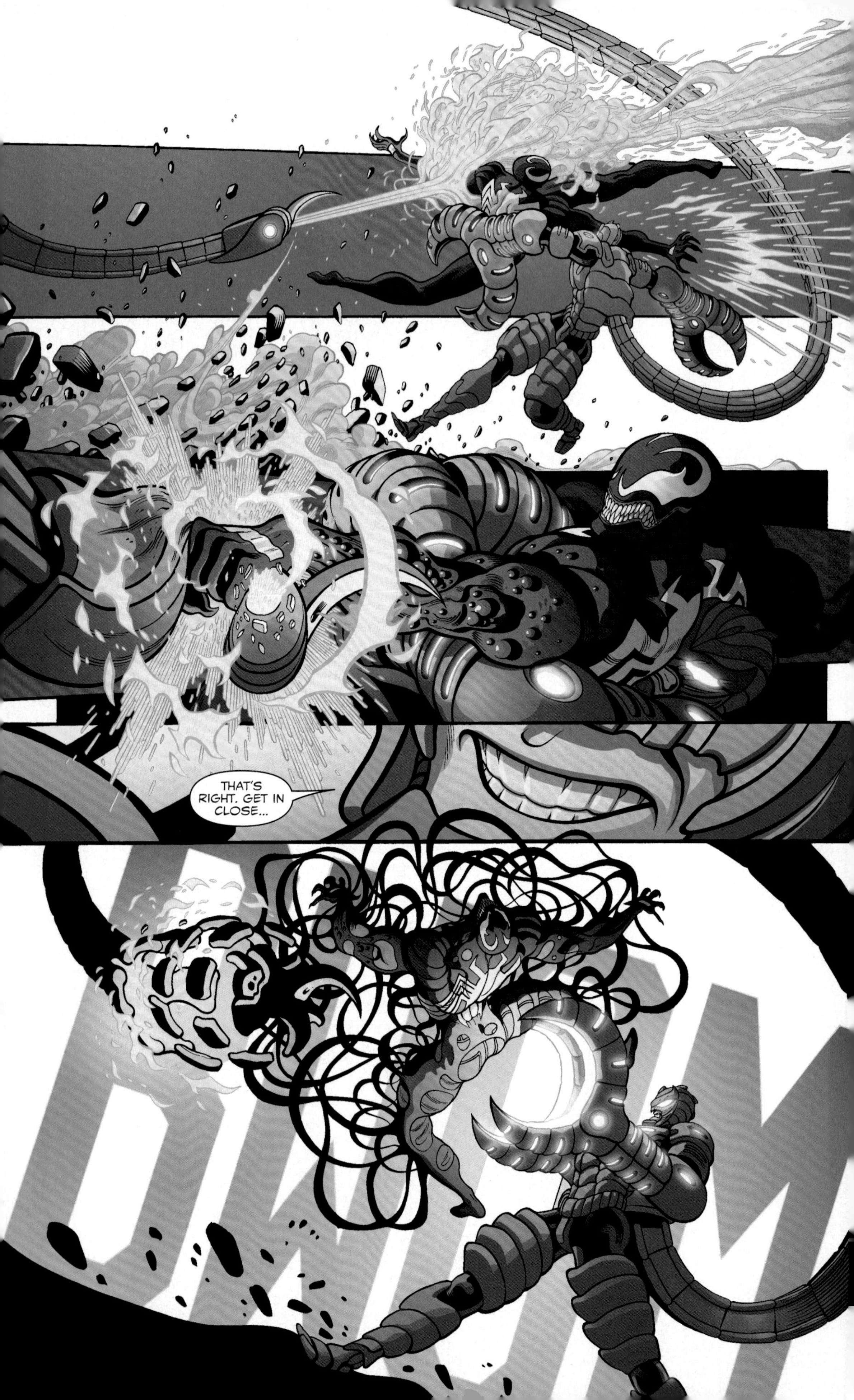
THAT'S RIGHT. GET IN CLOSE...

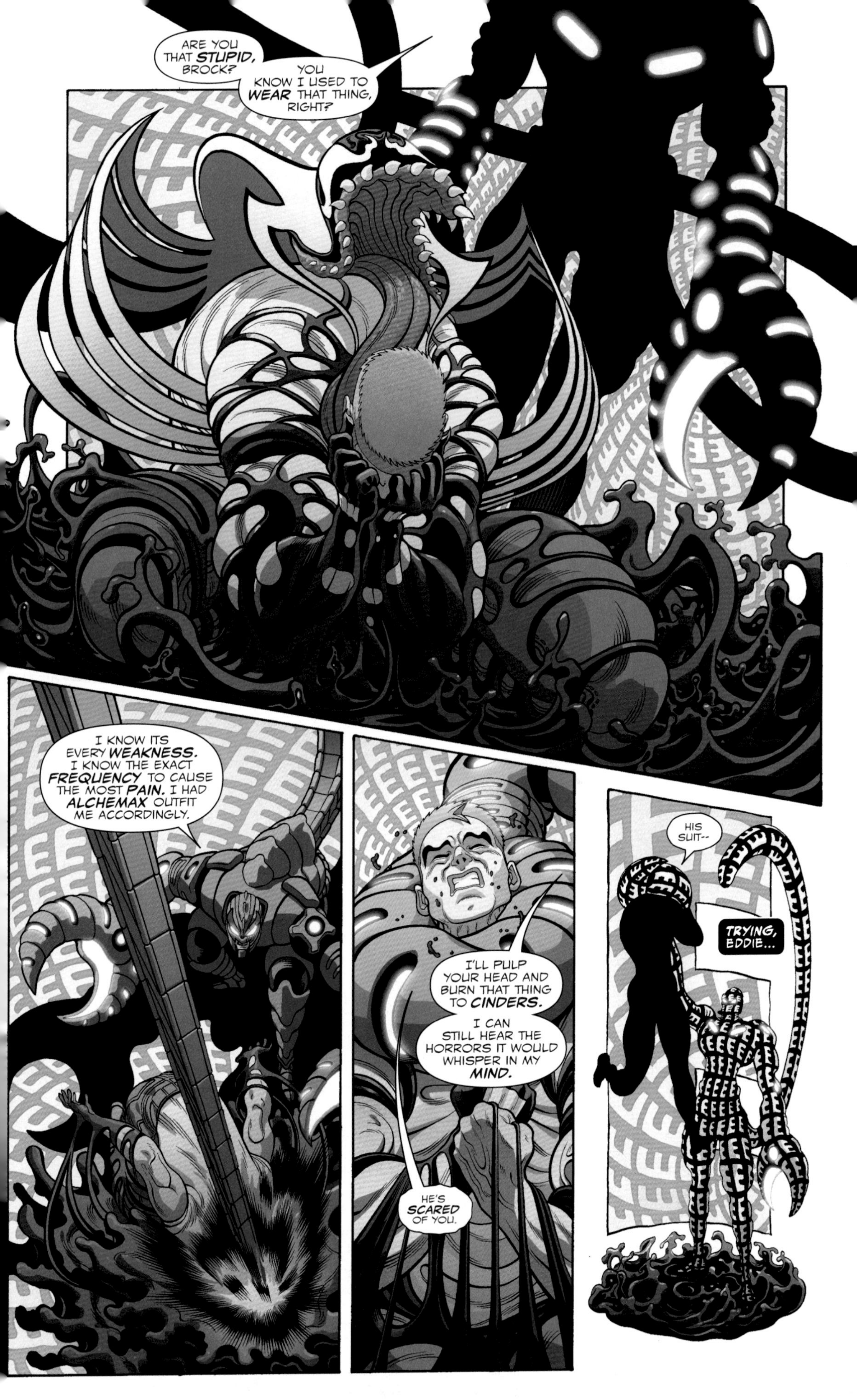

ARE YOU THAT STUPID, BROCK?
YOU KNOW I USED TO WEAR THAT THING, RIGHT?
I KNOW ITS EVERY WEAKNESS. I KNOW THE EXACT FREQUENCY TO CAUSE THE MOST PAIN. I HAD ALCHEMAX OUTFIT ME ACCORDINGLY.
I'LL PULP YOUR HEAD AND BURN THAT THING TO CINDERS.
I CAN STILL HEAR THE HORRORS IT WOULD WHISPER IN MY MIND.
HE'S SCARED OF YOU.
HIS SUIT--
TRYING, EDDIE...

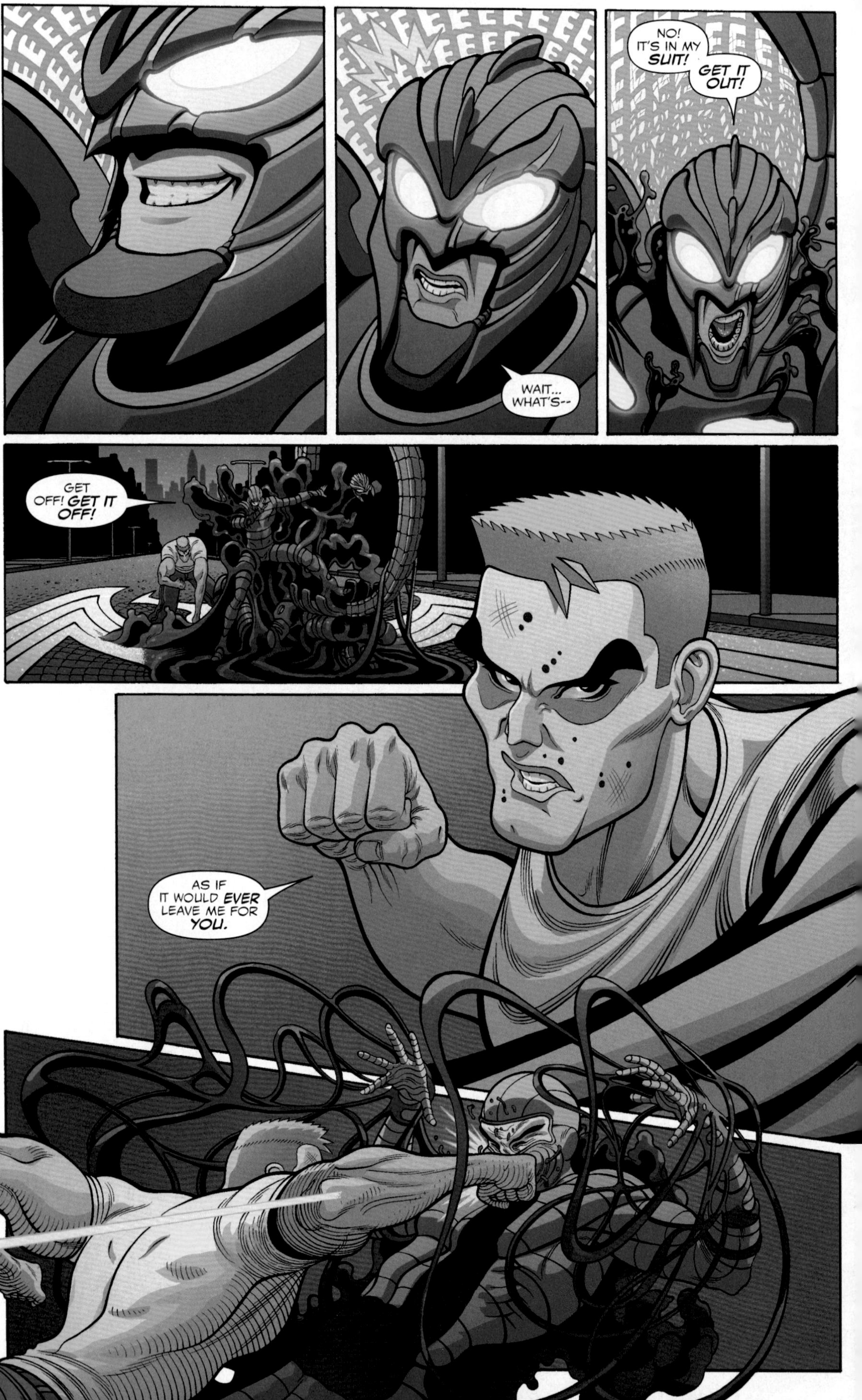
WAIT... WHAT'S--
NO! IT'S IN MY SUIT!
GET IT OUT!
GET OFF! GET IT OFF!
AS IF IT WOULD EVER LEAVE ME FOR YOU.

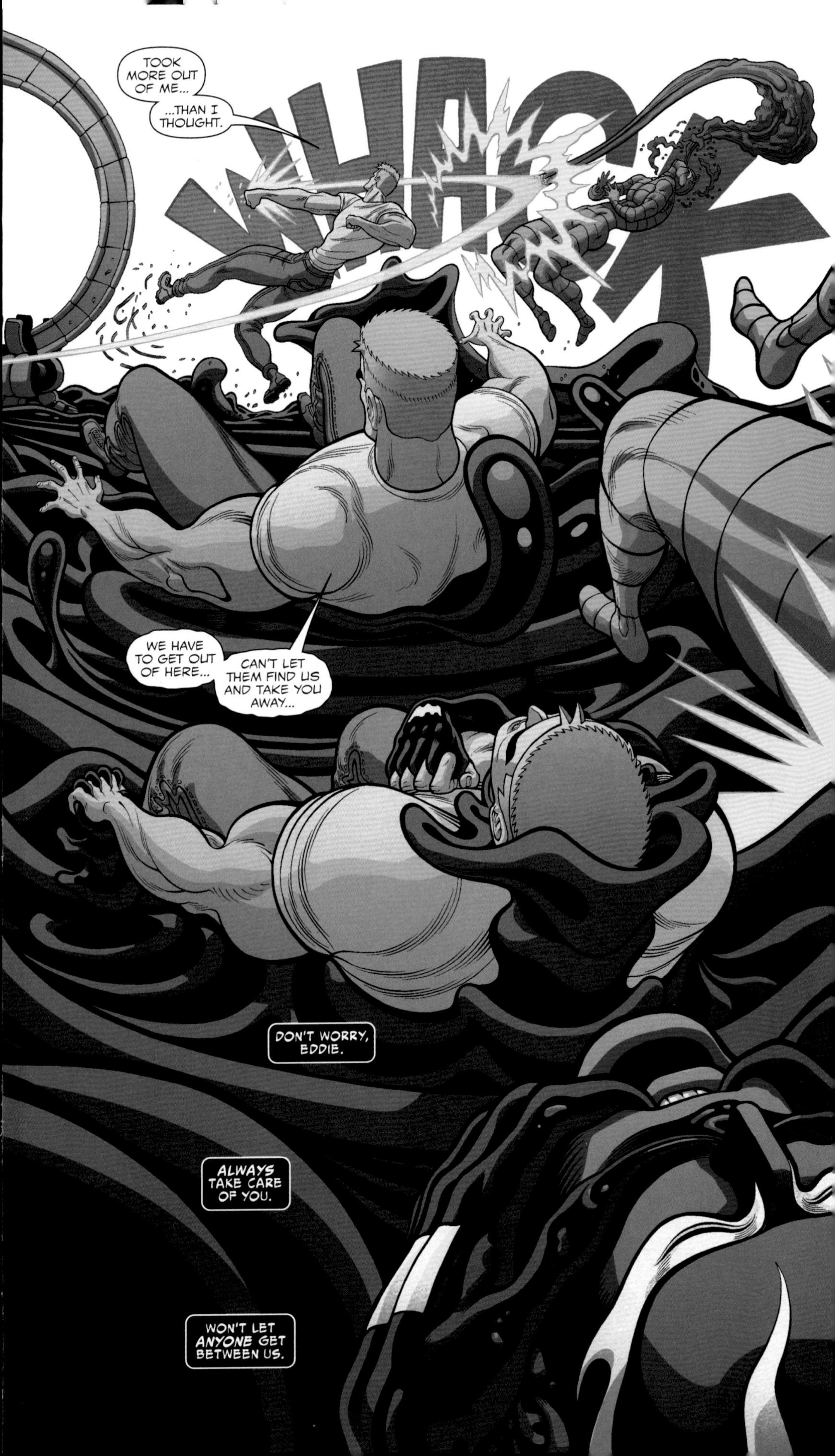

TOOK MORE OUT OF ME...
...THAN I THOUGHT.
WHACK
WE HAVE TO GET OUT OF HERE...
CAN'T LET THEM FIND US AND TAKE YOU AWAY...
DON'T WORRY, EDDIE.
ALWAYS TAKE CARE OF YOU.
WON'T LET ANYONE GET BETWEEN US.

WH...WHERE AM I?

SAFE, EDDIE. SAFE.

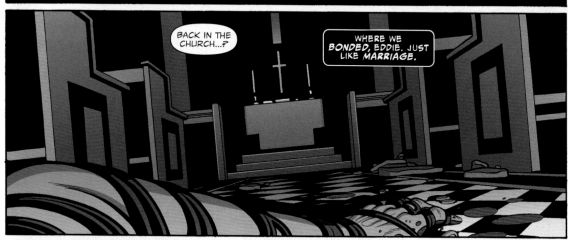

BACK IN THE CHURCH...?

WHERE WE *BONDED*, EDDIE. JUST LIKE *MARRIAGE*.

WHY DID YOU BRING US *HERE...?*

IMPORTANT PLACE, EDDIE. BONDED FOREVER. NO ONE WILL BREAK THAT BOND.

OH, NO. WHAT DID YOU *DO?*

WHAT *WE DID,* EDDIE. WHAT WE DO TO *ANY* WHO COME BETWEEN US.

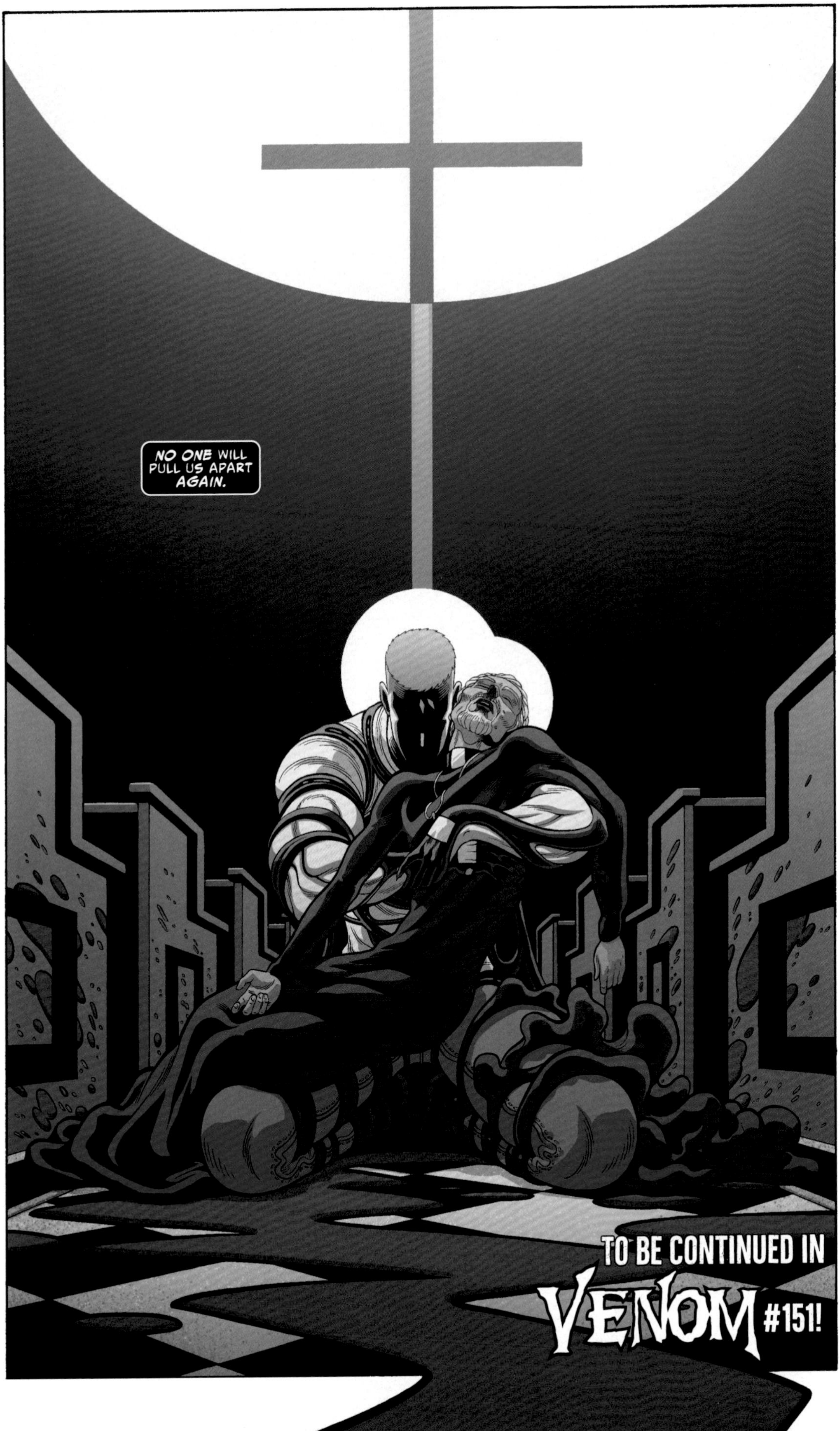
NO ONE WILL PULL US APART AGAIN.
TO BE CONTINUED IN
VENOM #151!

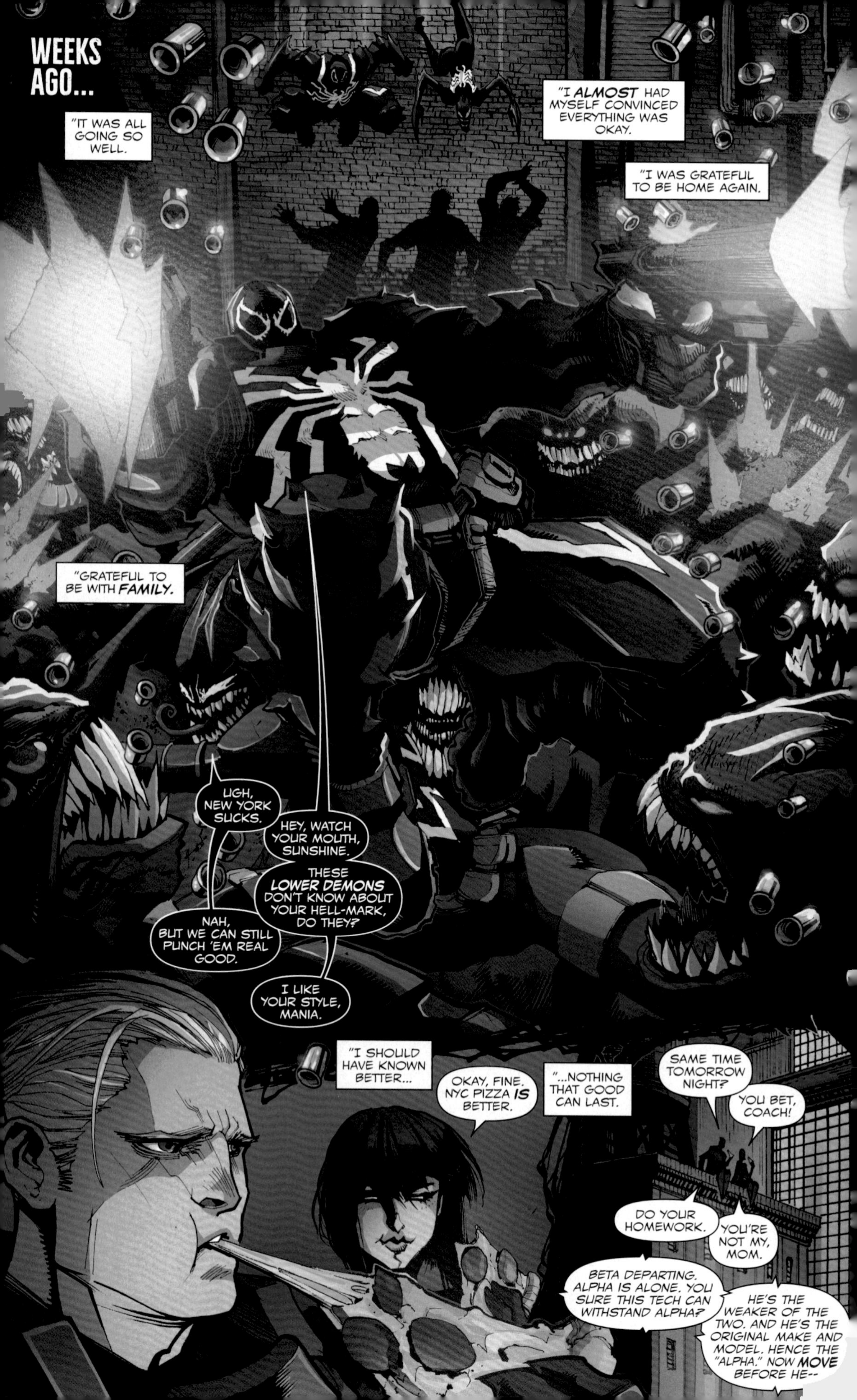
WEEKS AGO...
"IT WAS ALL GOING SO WELL.
"I ALMOST HAD MYSELF CONVINCED EVERYTHING WAS OKAY.
"I WAS GRATEFUL TO BE HOME AGAIN.
"GRATEFUL TO BE WITH FAMILY.
UGH, NEW YORK SUCKS.
HEY, WATCH YOUR MOUTH, SUNSHINE.
THESE LOWER DEMONS DON'T KNOW ABOUT YOUR HELL-MARK, DO THEY?
NAH, BUT WE CAN STILL PUNCH 'EM REAL GOOD.
I LIKE YOUR STYLE, MANIA.
"I SHOULD HAVE KNOWN BETTER...
OKAY, FINE. NYC PIZZA IS BETTER.
"...NOTHING THAT GOOD CAN LAST.
SAME TIME TOMORROW NIGHT?
YOU BET, COACH!
DO YOUR HOMEWORK.
YOU'RE NOT MY MOM.
BETA DEPARTING. ALPHA IS ALONE. YOU SURE THIS TECH CAN WITHSTAND ALPHA?
HE'S THE WEAKER OF THE TWO. AND HE'S THE ORIGINAL MAKE AND MODEL. HENCE THE "ALPHA." NOW MOVE BEFORE HE--

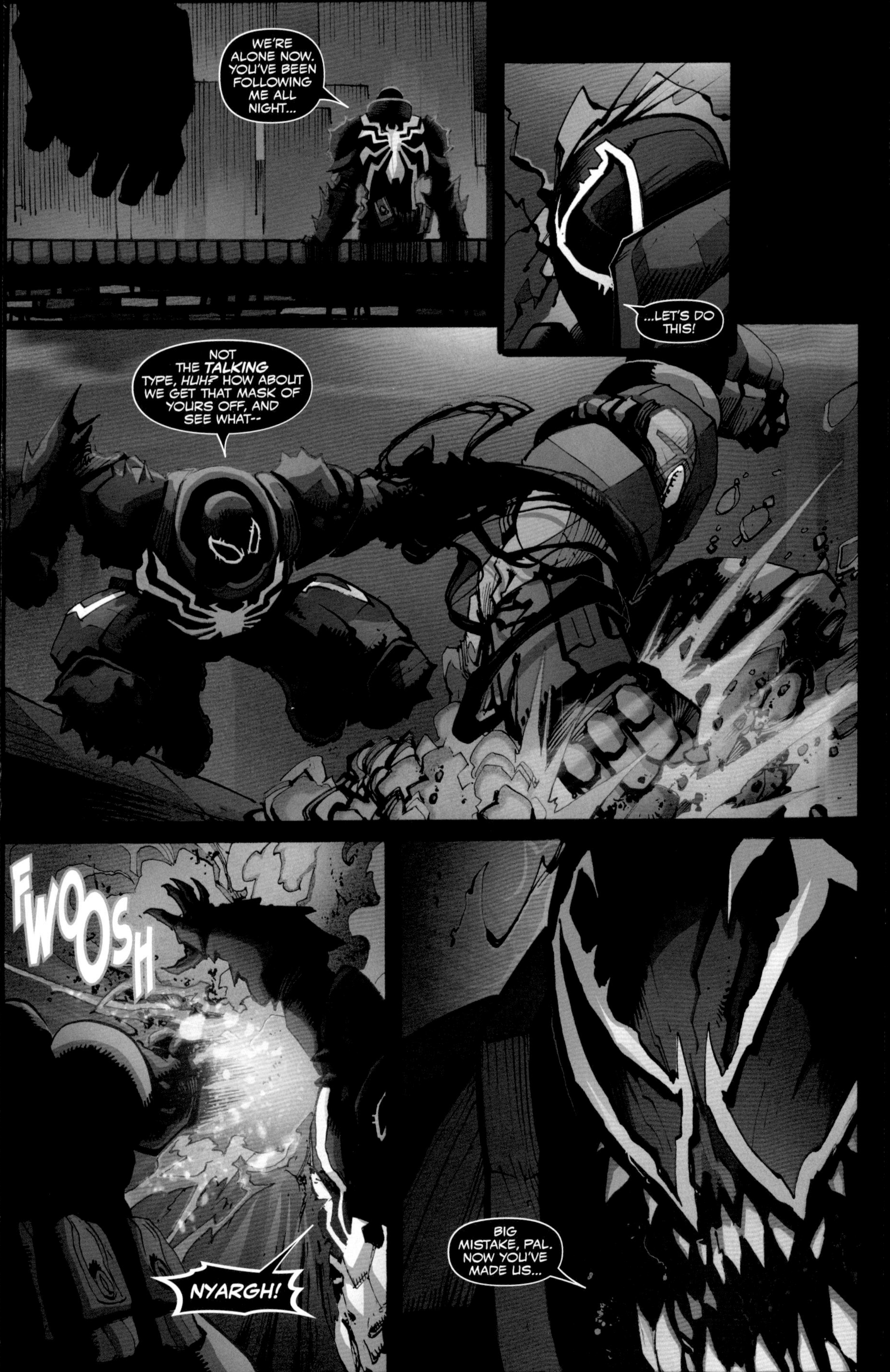
WE'RE ALONE NOW. YOU'VE BEEN FOLLOWING ME ALL NIGHT...
...LET'S DO THIS!
NOT THE *TALKING* TYPE, *HUH?* HOW ABOUT WE GET THAT MASK OF YOURS OFF, AND SEE WHAT--
FWOOSH
NYARGH!
BIG MISTAKE, PAL. NOW YOU'VE MADE US...

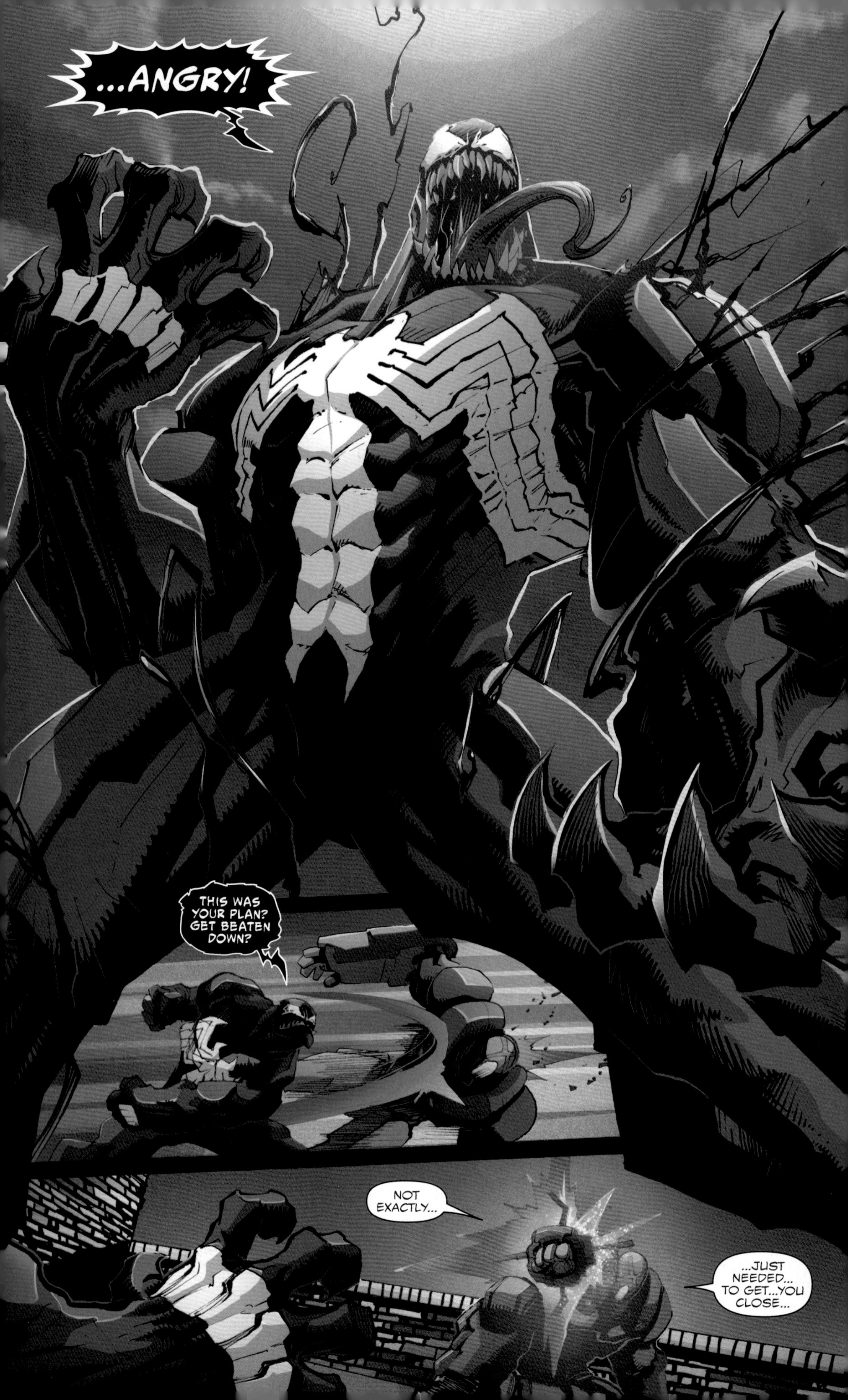
...ANGRY!
THIS WAS YOUR PLAN? GET BEATEN DOWN?
NOT EXACTLY...
...JUST NEEDED... TO GET...YOU CLOSE...

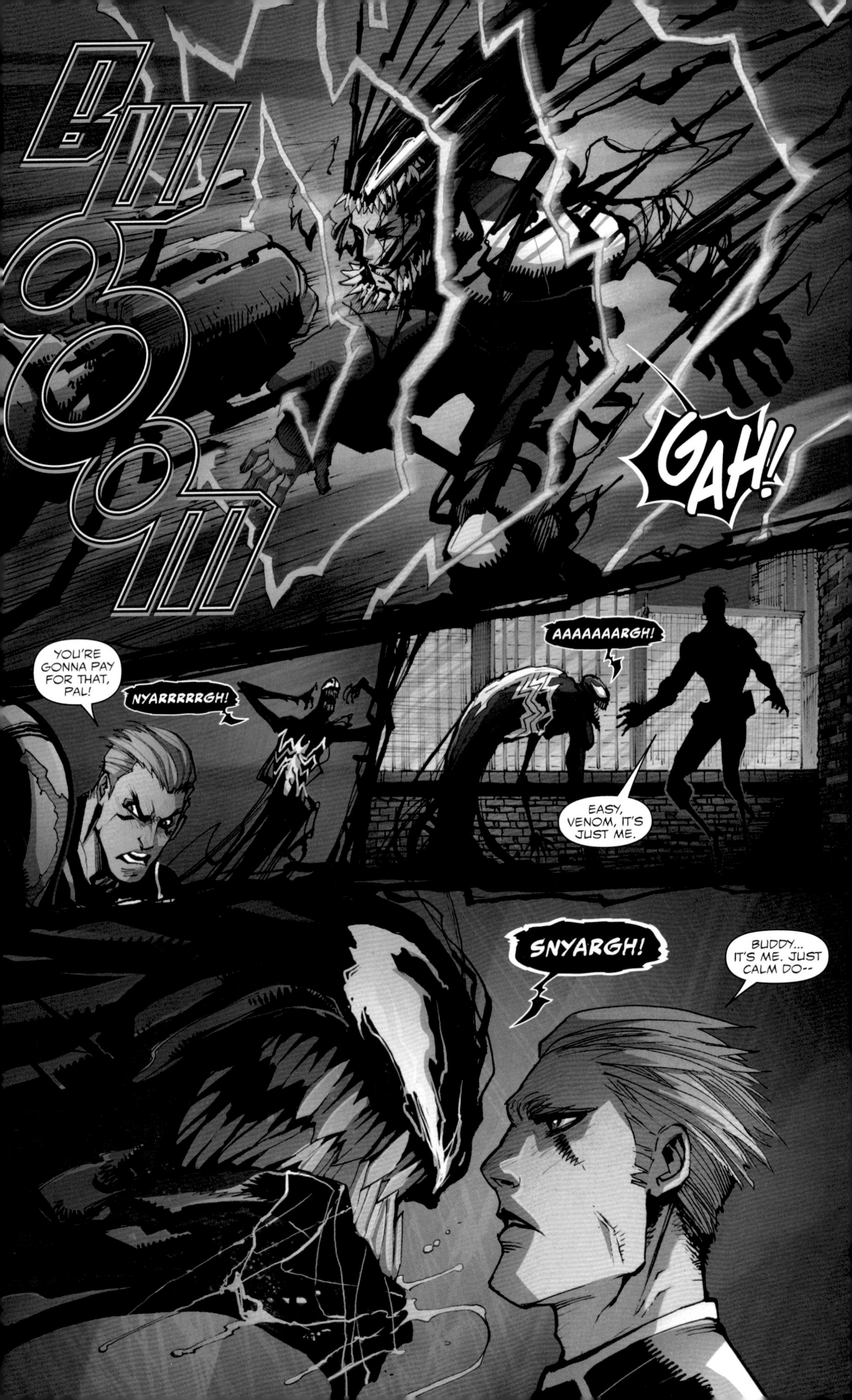
BOOOM!
GAH!!
YOU'RE GONNA PAY FOR THAT, PAL!
NYARRRRRGH!
AAAAAAARGH!
EASY, VENOM, IT'S JUST ME.
SNYARGH!
BUDDY... IT'S ME. JUST CALM DO--

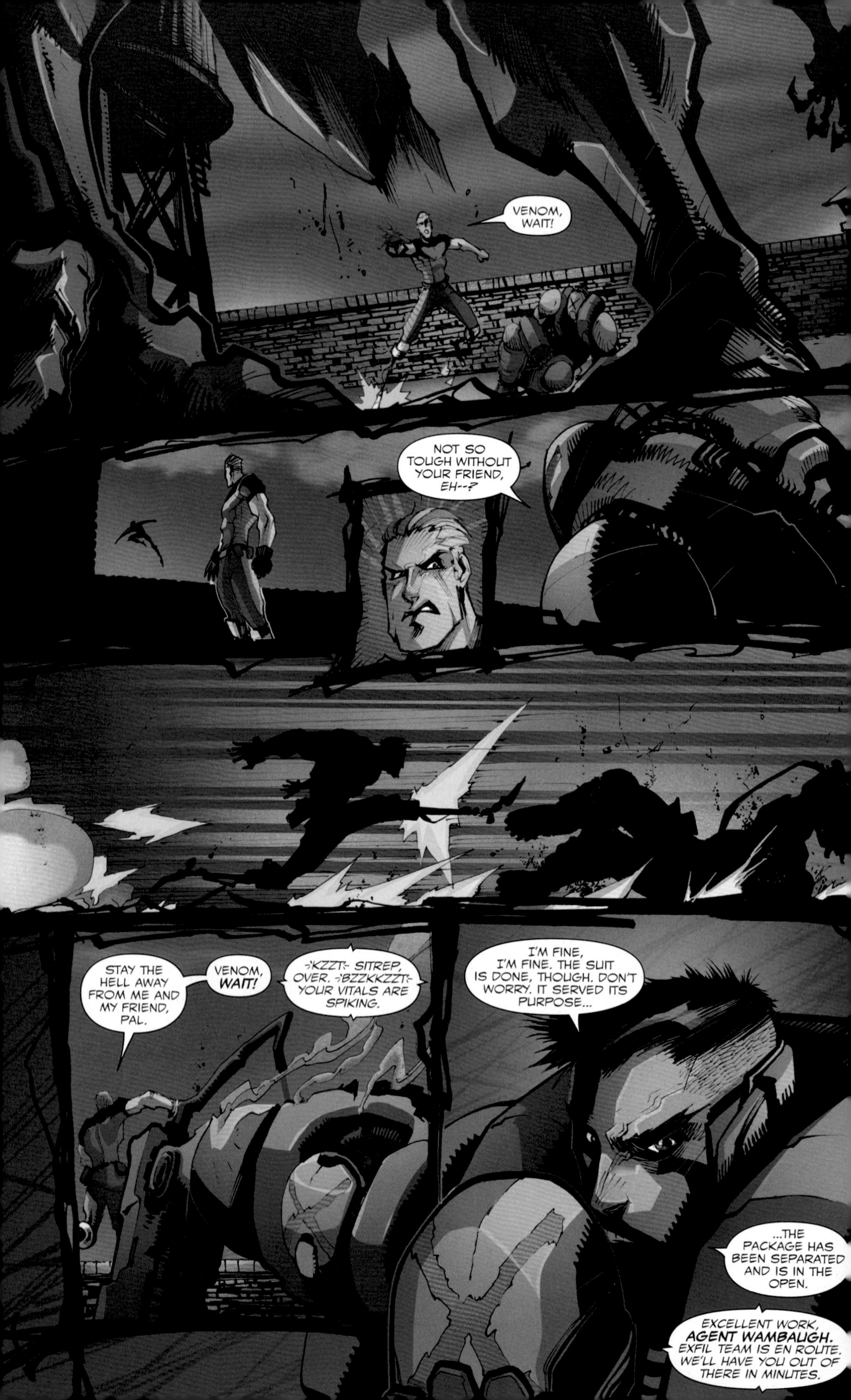
VENOM, WAIT!
NOT SO TOUGH WITHOUT YOUR FRIEND, EH--?
STAY THE HELL AWAY FROM ME AND MY FRIEND, PAL.
VENOM, WAIT!
-KZZT- SITREP, OVER. -BZZKKZZT- YOUR VITALS ARE SPIKING.
I'M FINE, I'M FINE. THE SUIT IS DONE, THOUGH. DON'T WORRY. IT SERVED ITS PURPOSE...
...THE PACKAGE HAS BEEN SEPARATED AND IS IN THE OPEN.
EXCELLENT WORK, AGENT WAMBAUGH. EXFIL TEAM IS EN ROUTE. WE'LL HAVE YOU OUT OF THERE IN MINUTES.

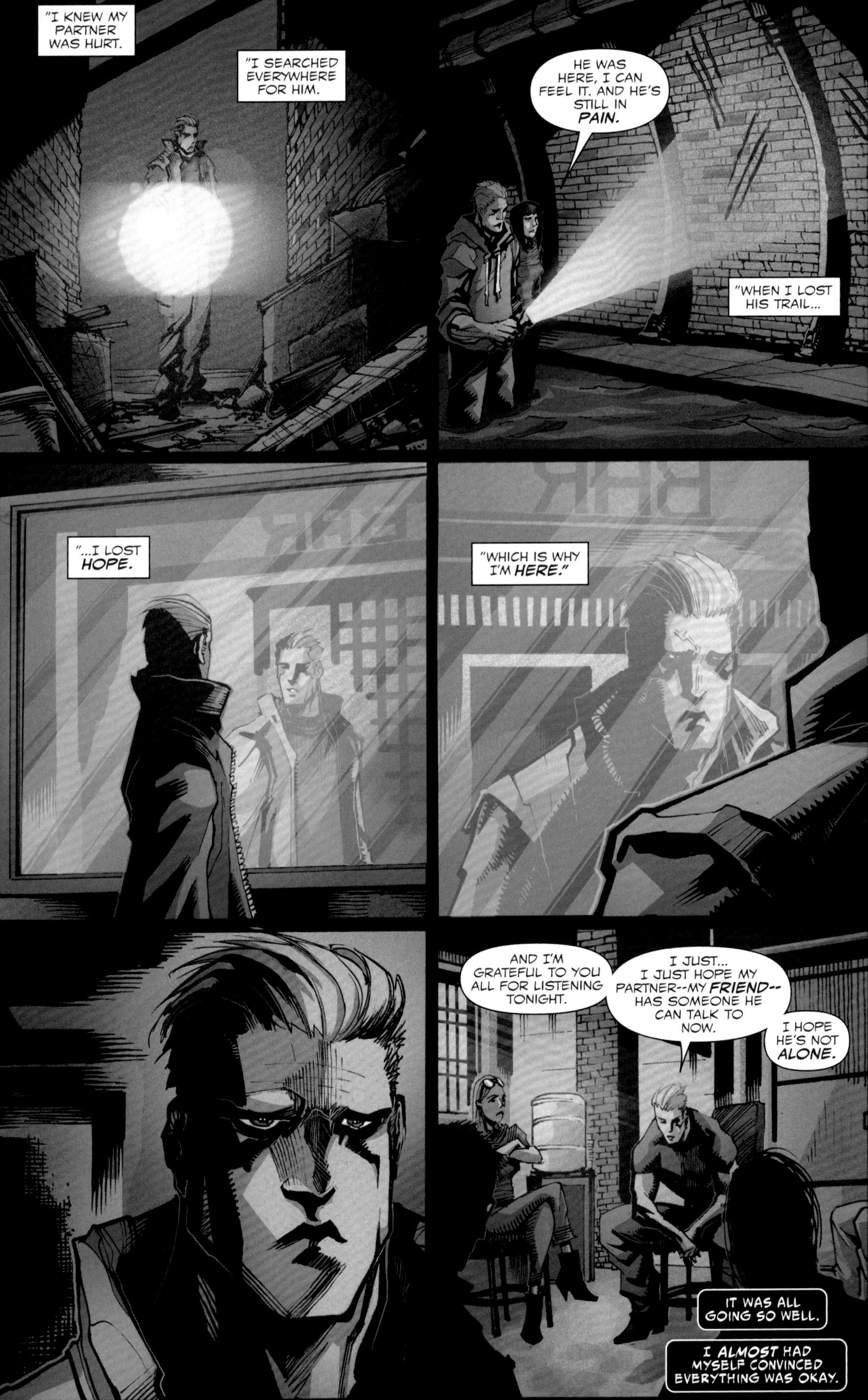

"I KNEW MY PARTNER WAS HURT.
"I SEARCHED EVERYWHERE FOR HIM.
HE WAS HERE, I CAN FEEL IT. AND HE'S STILL IN PAIN.
"WHEN I LOST HIS TRAIL...
"...I LOST HOPE.
"WHICH IS WHY I'M HERE."
AND I'M GRATEFUL TO YOU ALL FOR LISTENING TONIGHT.
I JUST... I JUST HOPE MY PARTNER--MY FRIEND--HAS SOMEONE HE CAN TALK TO NOW.
I HOPE HE'S NOT ALONE.
IT WAS ALL GOING SO WELL.
I ALMOST HAD MYSELF CONVINCED EVERYTHING WAS OKAY.

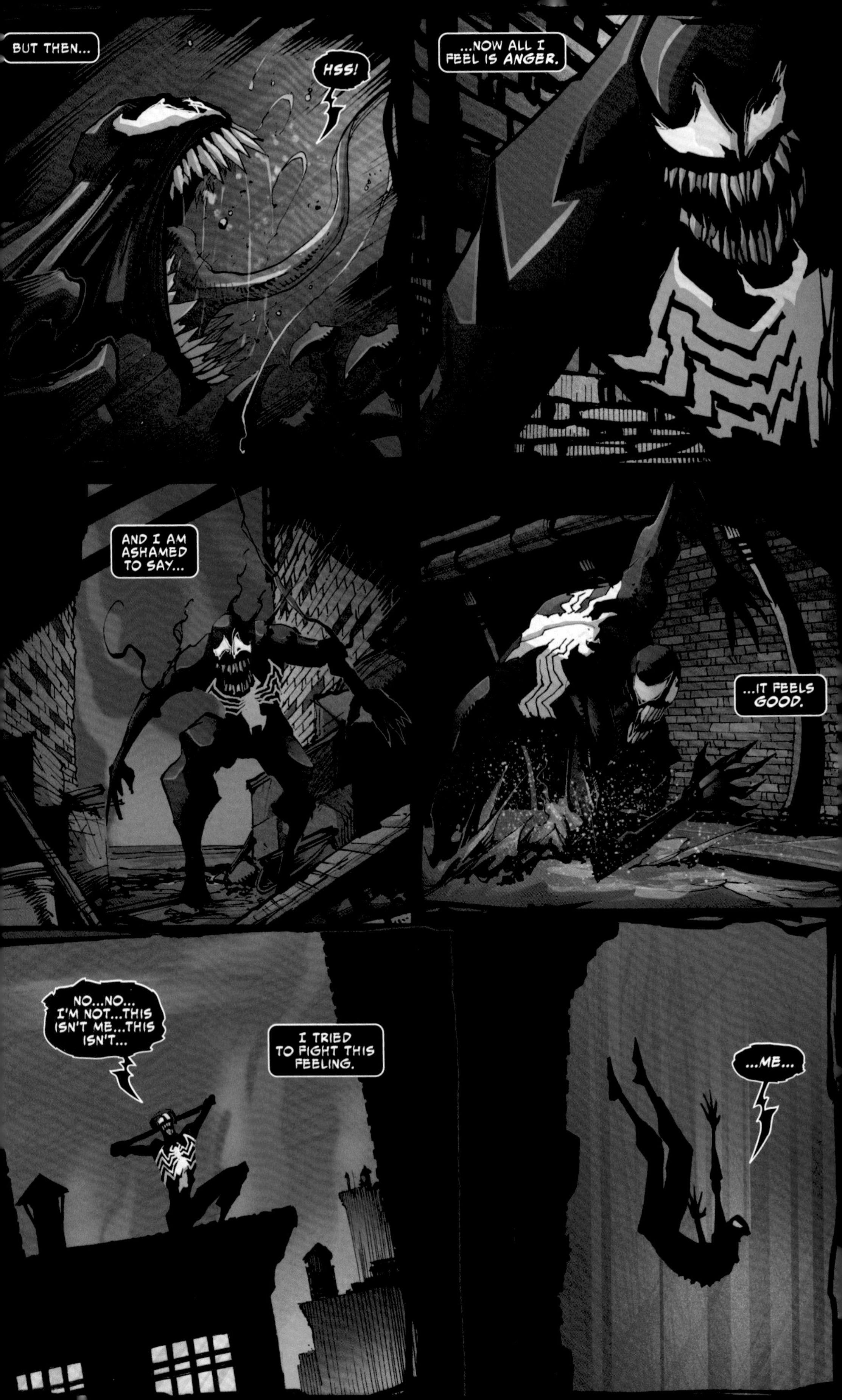

BUT THEN...
HSS!
...NOW ALL I FEEL IS ANGER.
AND I AM ASHAMED TO SAY...
...IT FEELS GOOD.
NO...NO... I'M NOT...THIS ISN'T ME...THIS ISN'T...
I TRIED TO FIGHT THIS FEELING.
...ME...

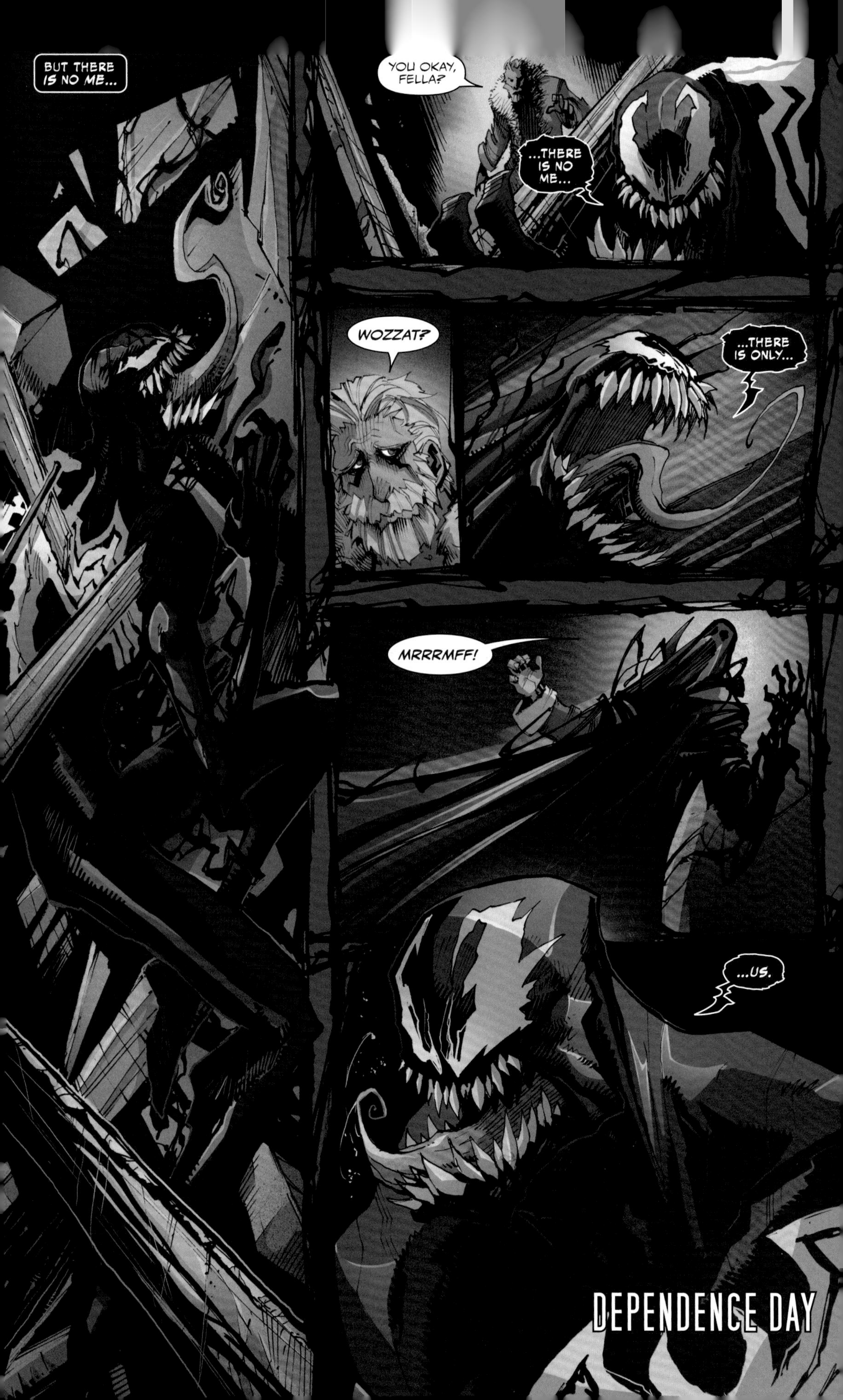
BUT THERE IS NO ME...
YOU OKAY, FELLA?
...THERE IS NO ME...
WOZZAT?
...THERE IS ONLY...
MRRRMFF!
...US.
DEPENDENCE DAY

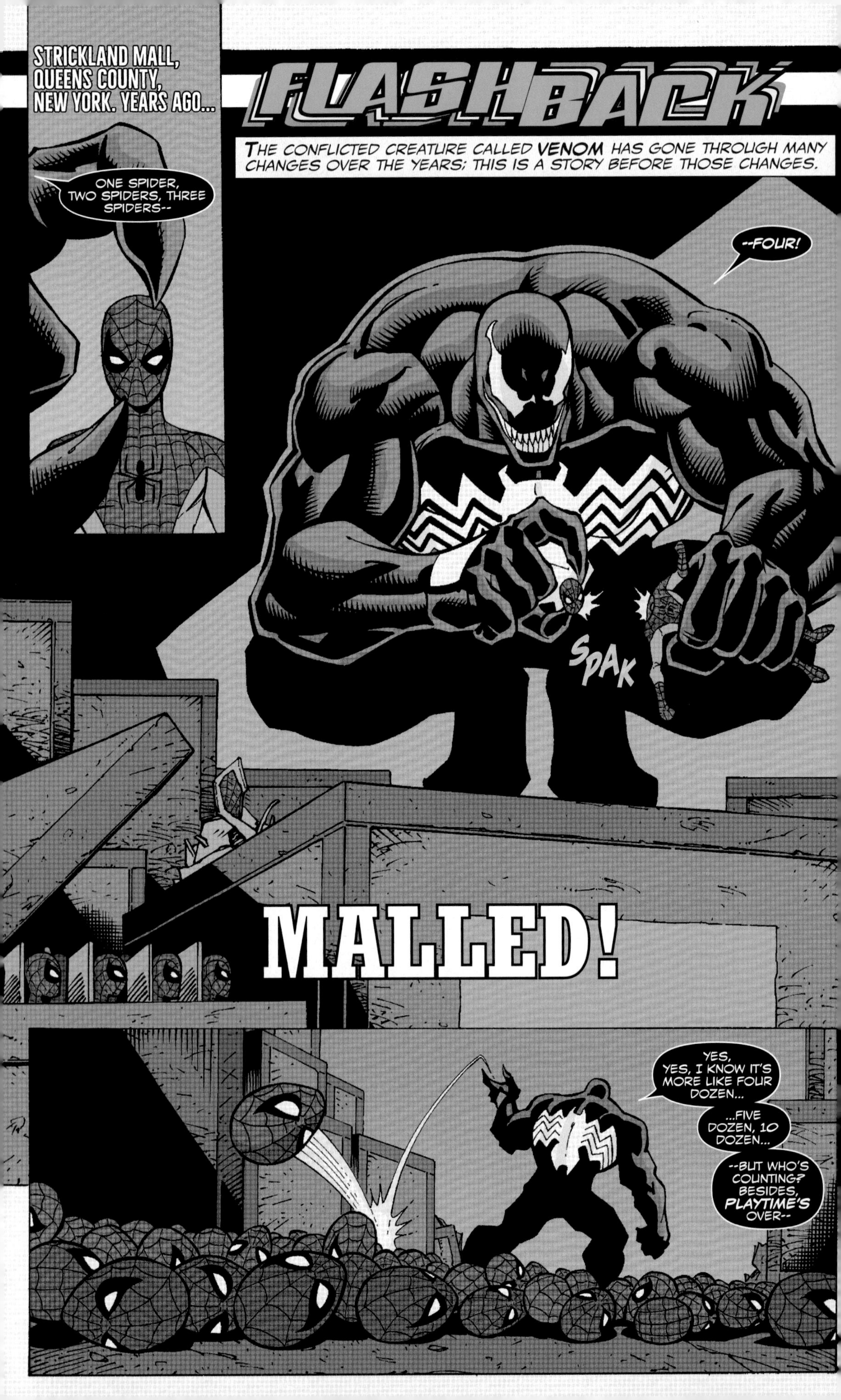
STRICKLAND MALL, QUEENS COUNTY, NEW YORK. YEARS AGO...
FLASHBACK
THE CONFLICTED CREATURE CALLED VENOM HAS GONE THROUGH MANY CHANGES OVER THE YEARS; THIS IS A STORY BEFORE THOSE CHANGES.
ONE SPIDER, TWO SPIDERS, THREE SPIDERS--
--FOUR!
SPAK
MALLED!
YES, YES, I KNOW IT'S MORE LIKE FOUR DOZEN...
...FIVE DOZEN, 10 DOZEN...
--BUT WHO'S COUNTING? BESIDES, PLAYTIME'S OVER--

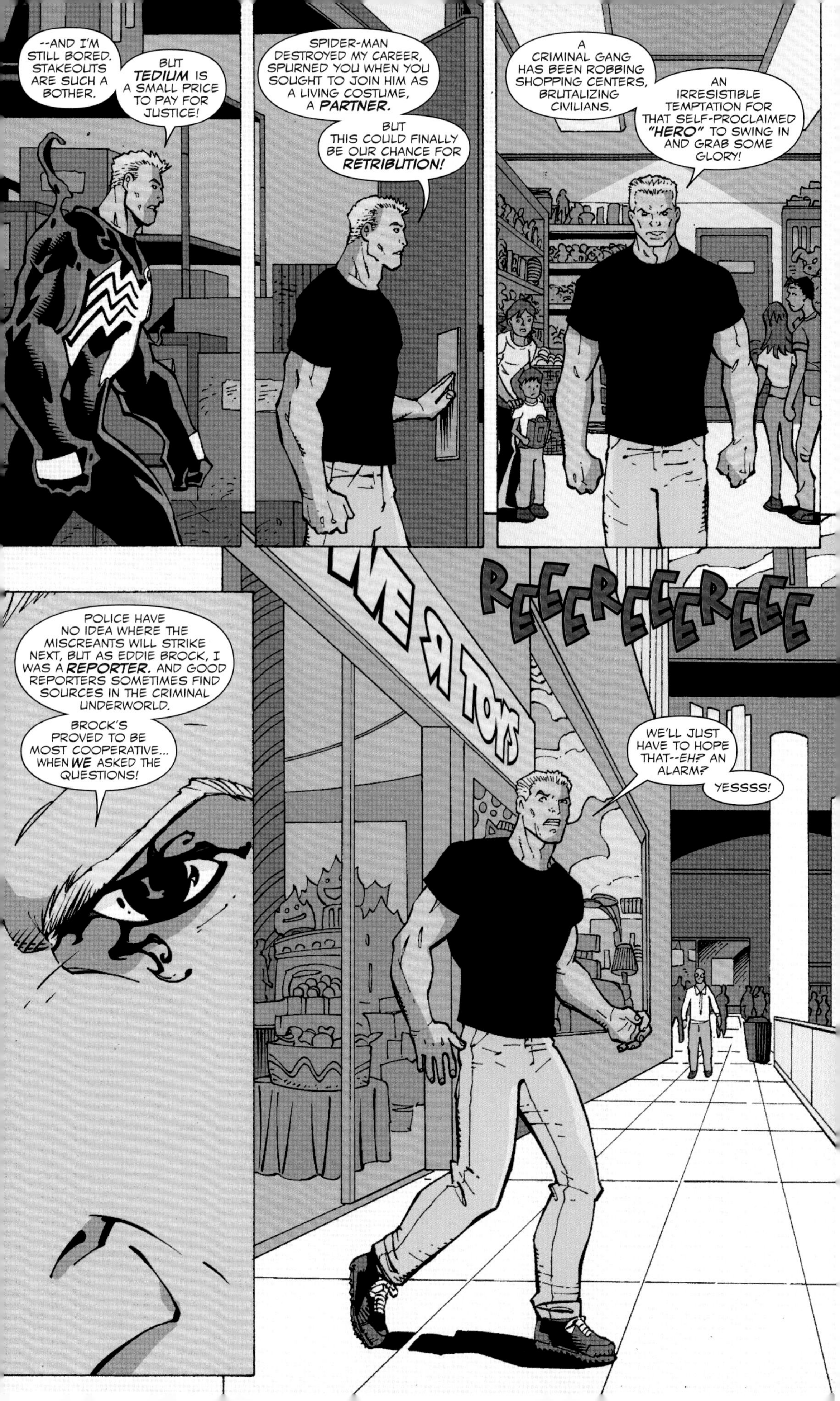
--AND I'M STILL BORED. STAKEOUTS ARE SUCH A BOTHER.
BUT *TEDIUM* IS A SMALL PRICE TO PAY FOR JUSTICE!
SPIDER-MAN DESTROYED MY CAREER, SPURNED YOU WHEN YOU SOUGHT TO JOIN HIM AS A LIVING COSTUME, A *PARTNER.*
BUT THIS COULD FINALLY BE OUR CHANCE FOR *RETRIBUTION!*
A CRIMINAL GANG HAS BEEN ROBBING SHOPPING CENTERS, BRUTALIZING CIVILIANS.
AN IRRESISTIBLE TEMPTATION FOR THAT SELF-PROCLAIMED *"HERO"* TO SWING IN AND GRAB SOME GLORY!
POLICE HAVE NO IDEA WHERE THE MISCREANTS WILL STRIKE NEXT, BUT AS EDDIE BROCK, I WAS A *REPORTER.* AND GOOD REPORTERS SOMETIMES FIND SOURCES IN THE CRIMINAL UNDERWORLD.
BROCK'S PROVED TO BE MOST COOPERATIVE... WHEN *WE* ASKED THE QUESTIONS!
REEEREEEREEE
WE'LL JUST HAVE TO HOPE THAT--*EH?* AN ALARM?
YESSSS!

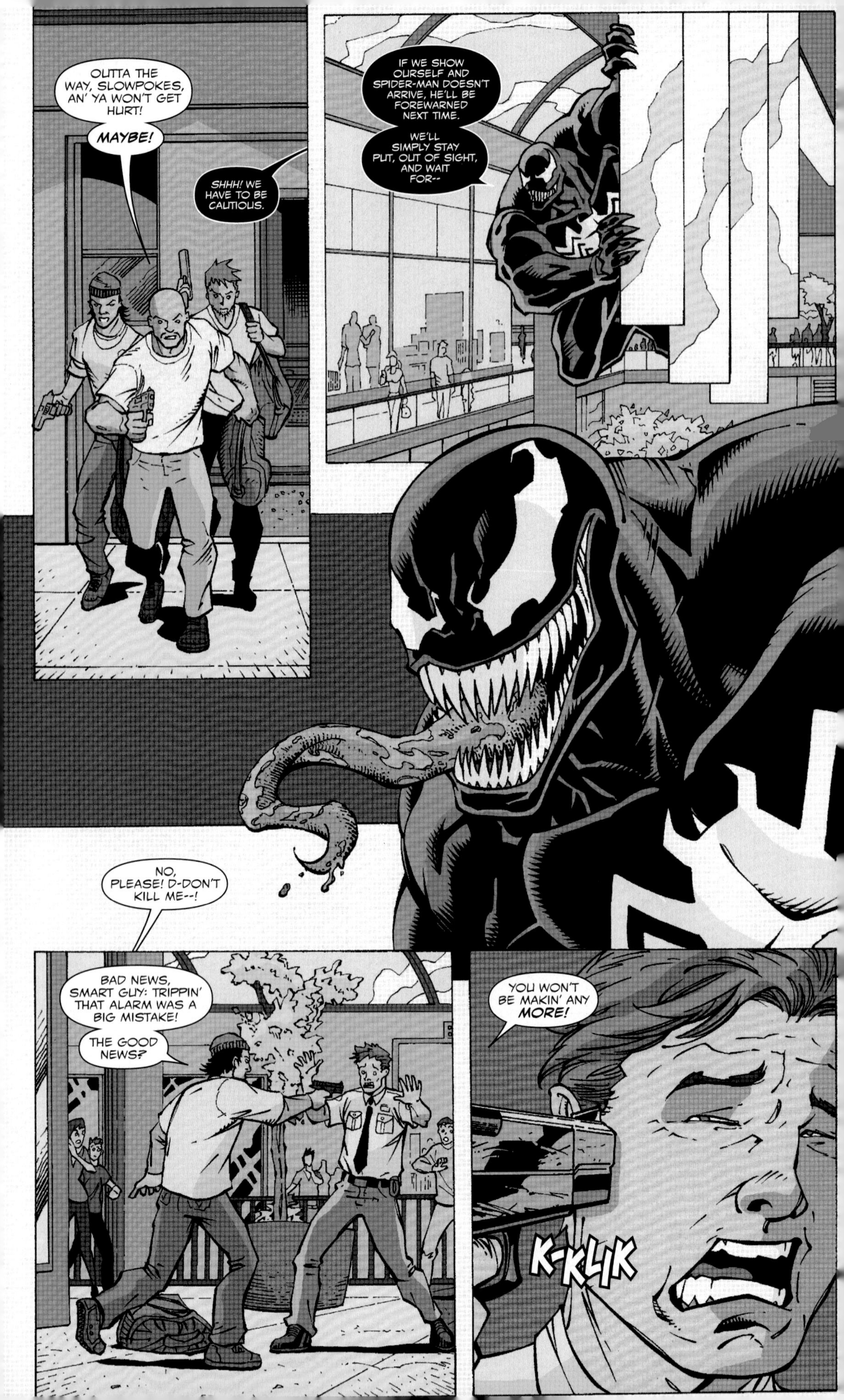
OUTTA THE WAY, SLOWPOKES, AN' YA WON'T GET HURT!
MAYBE!
SHHH! WE HAVE TO BE CAUTIOUS.
IF WE SHOW OURSELF AND SPIDER-MAN DOESN'T ARRIVE, HE'LL BE FOREWARNED NEXT TIME.
WE'LL SIMPLY STAY PUT, OUT OF SIGHT, AND WAIT FOR--
NO, PLEASE! D-DON'T KILL ME--!
BAD NEWS, SMART GUY: TRIPPIN' THAT ALARM WAS A BIG MISTAKE!
THE GOOD NEWS?
YOU WON'T BE MAKIN' ANY MORE!
K-KLIK

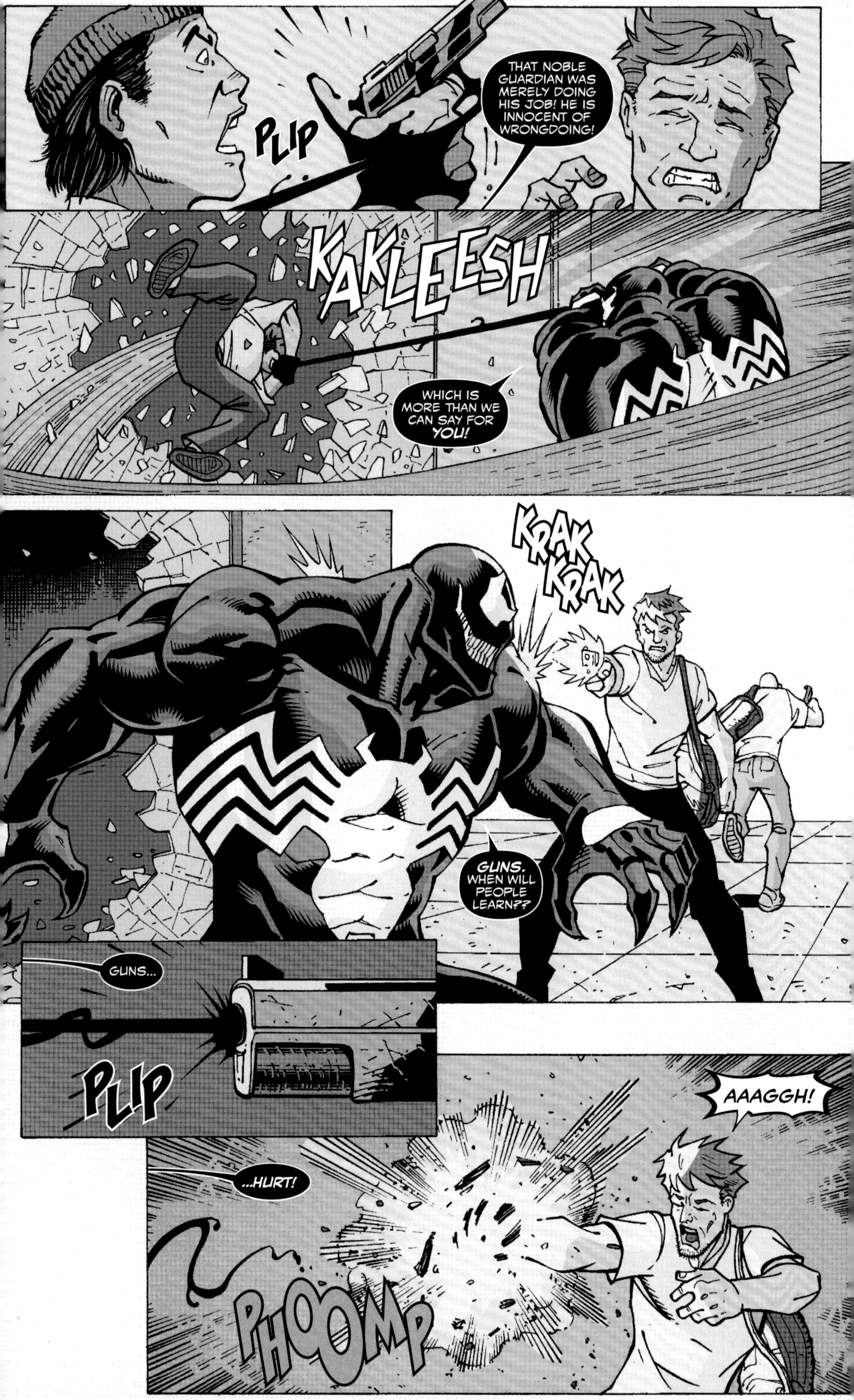
PLIP
THAT NOBLE GUARDIAN WAS MERELY DOING HIS JOB! HE IS INNOCENT OF WRONGDOING!
KAKLEESH
WHICH IS MORE THAN WE CAN SAY FOR YOU!
KRAK KRAK
GUNS. WHEN WILL PEOPLE LEARN??
GUNS...
PLIP
AAAGGH!
...HURT!
PHOOMP

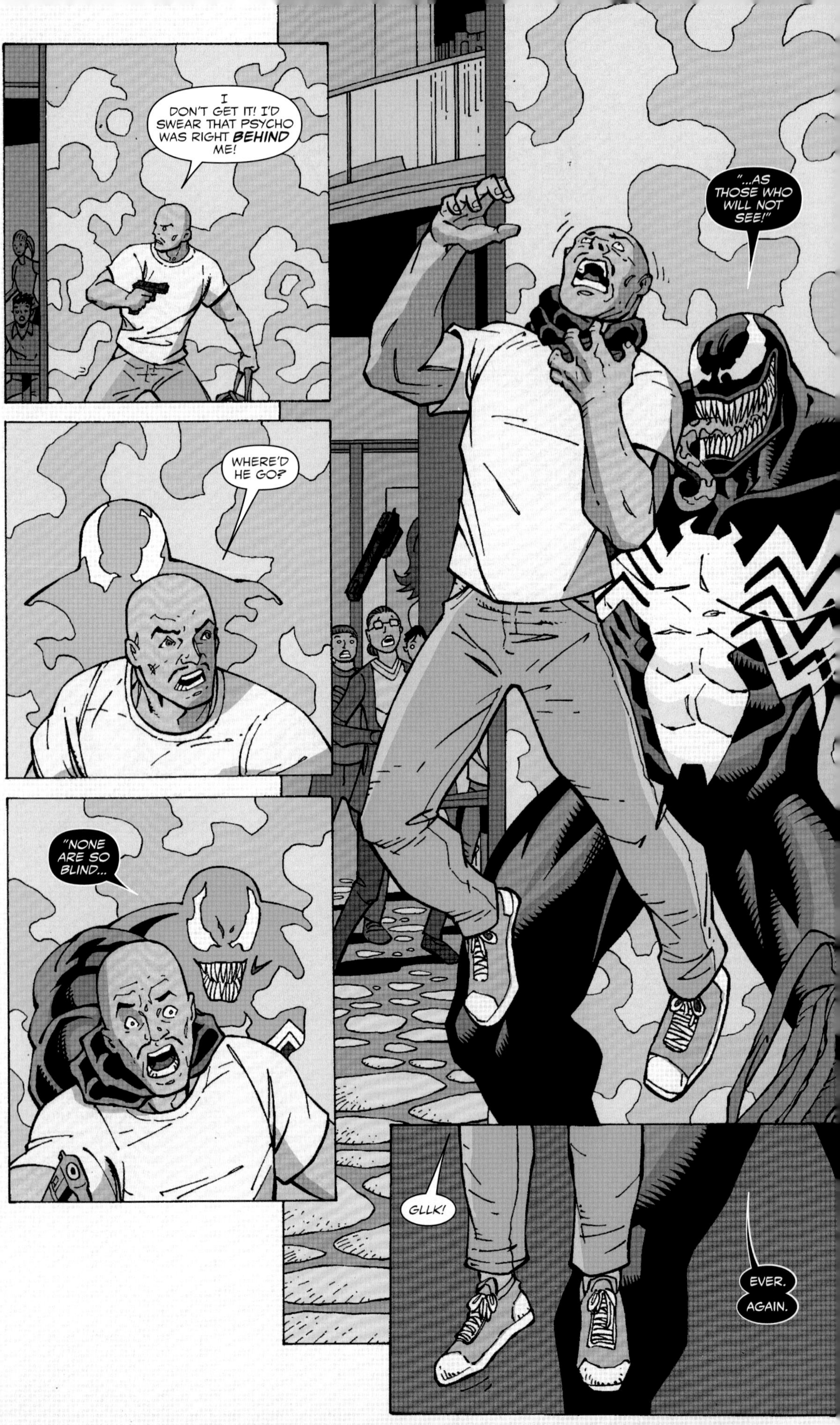
I DON'T GET IT! I'D SWEAR THAT PSYCHO WAS RIGHT BEHIND ME!
WHERE'D HE GO?
"NONE ARE SO BLIND...
"...AS THOSE WHO WILL NOT SEE!"
GLLK!
EVER.
AGAIN.

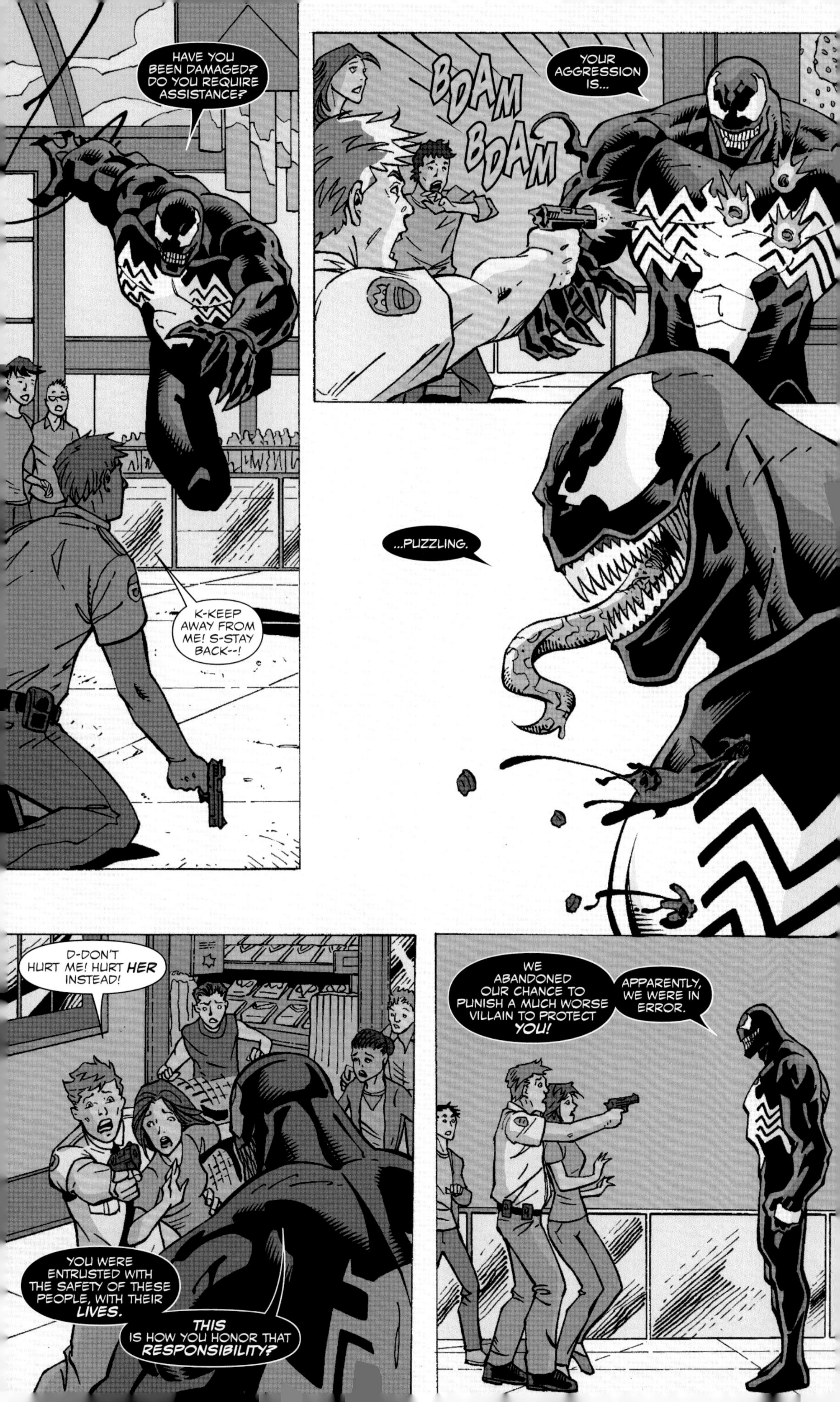
HAVE YOU BEEN DAMAGED? DO YOU REQUIRE ASSISTANCE?
K-KEEP AWAY FROM ME! S-STAY BACK--!
BDAM BDAM
YOUR AGGRESSION IS...
...PUZZLING.
D-DON'T HURT ME! HURT HER INSTEAD!
YOU WERE ENTRUSTED WITH THE SAFETY OF THESE PEOPLE, WITH THEIR LIVES.
THIS IS HOW YOU HONOR THAT RESPONSIBILITY?
WE ABANDONED OUR CHANCE TO PUNISH A MUCH WORSE VILLAIN TO PROTECT YOU!
APPARENTLY, WE WERE IN ERROR.

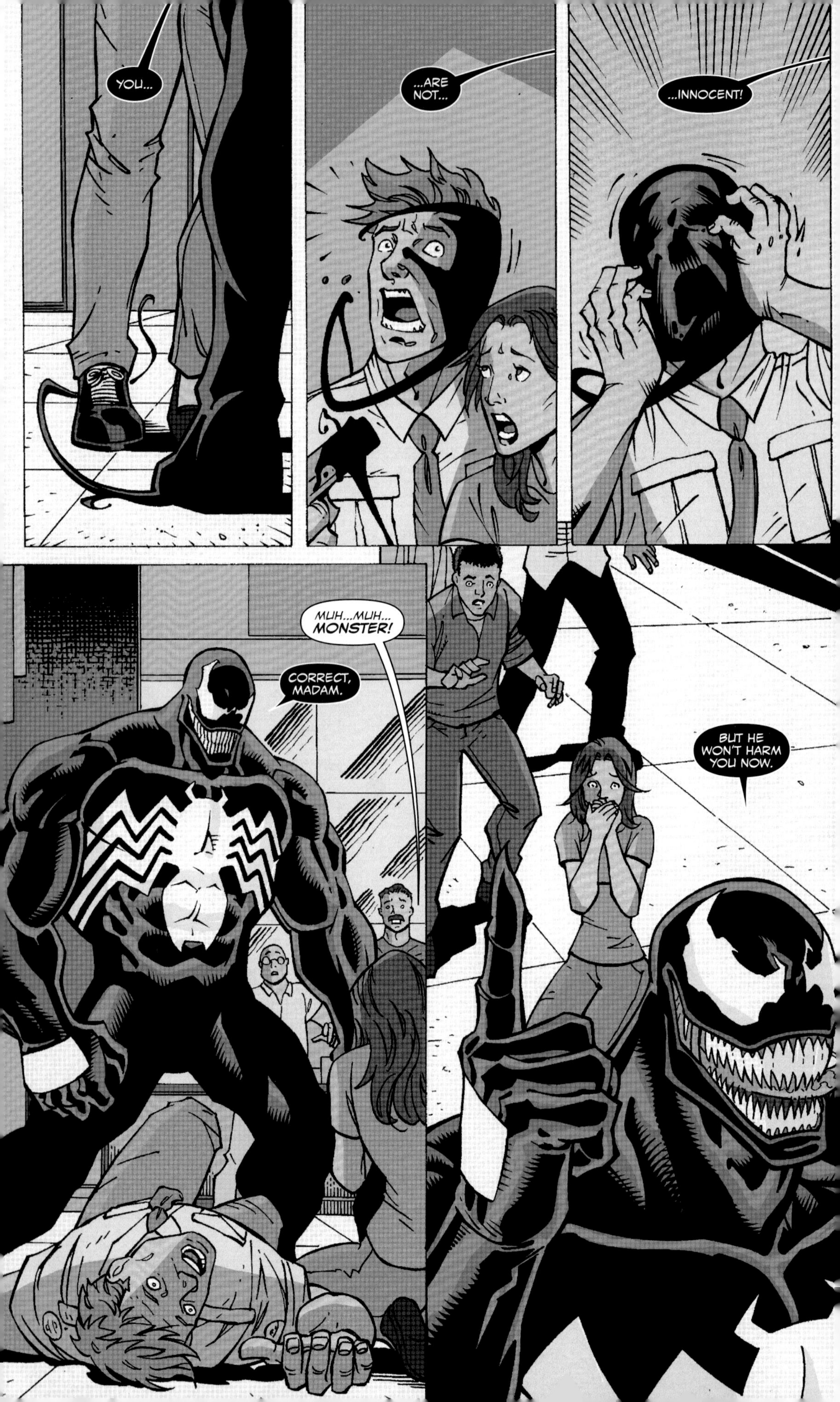
YOU...
...ARE NOT...
...INNOCENT!
MUH...MUH... MONSTER!
CORRECT, MADAM.
BUT HE WON'T HARM YOU NOW.

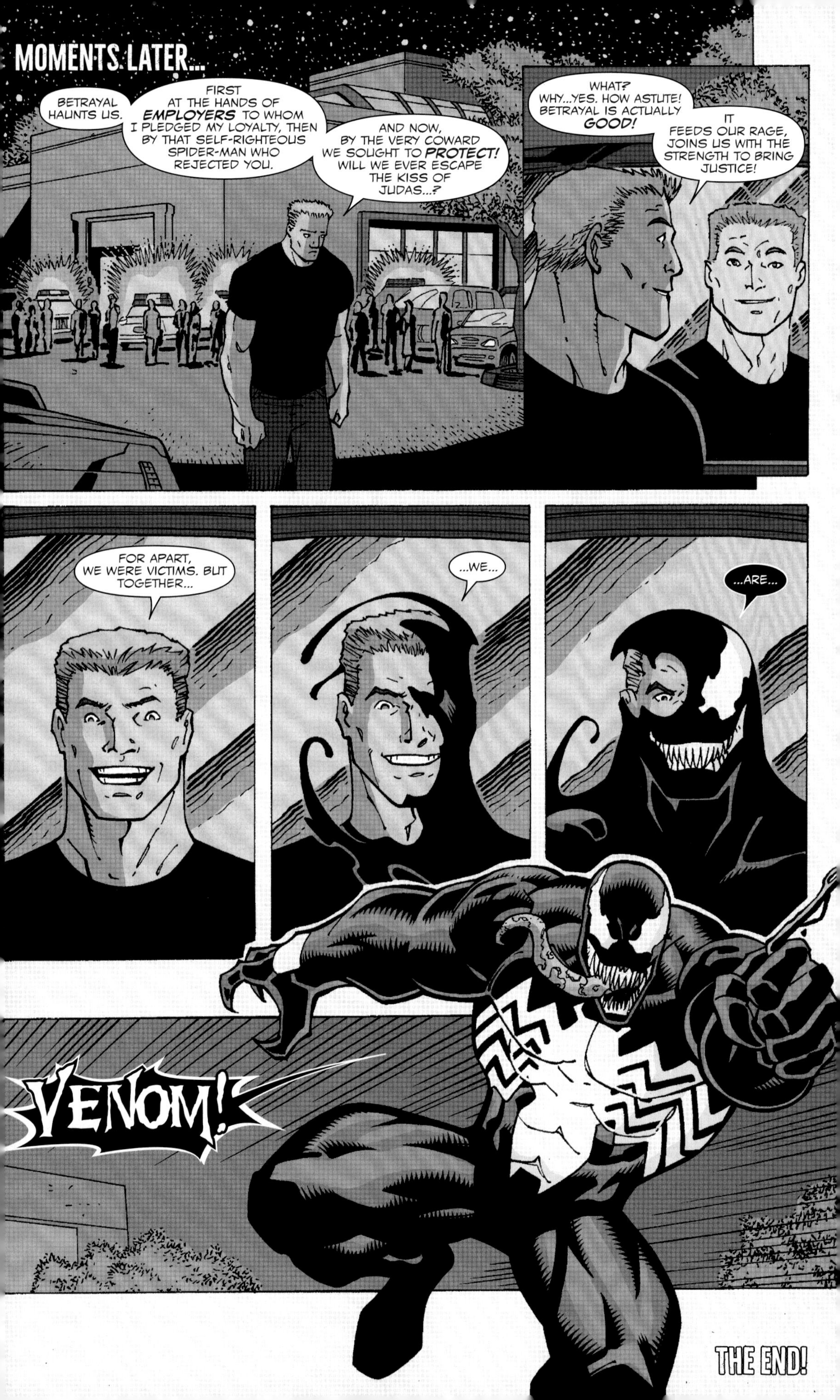
MOMENTS LATER...
BETRAYAL HAUNTS US.
FIRST AT THE HANDS OF EMPLOYERS TO WHOM I PLEDGED MY LOYALTY, THEN BY THAT SELF-RIGHTEOUS SPIDER-MAN WHO REJECTED YOU.
AND NOW, BY THE VERY COWARD WE SOUGHT TO PROTECT! WILL WE EVER ESCAPE THE KISS OF JUDAS...?
WHAT? WHY...YES. HOW ASTUTE! BETRAYAL IS ACTUALLY GOOD!
IT FEEDS OUR RAGE, JOINS US WITH THE STRENGTH TO BRING JUSTICE!
FOR APART, WE WERE VICTIMS. BUT TOGETHER...
...WE...
...ARE...
VENOM!
THE END!

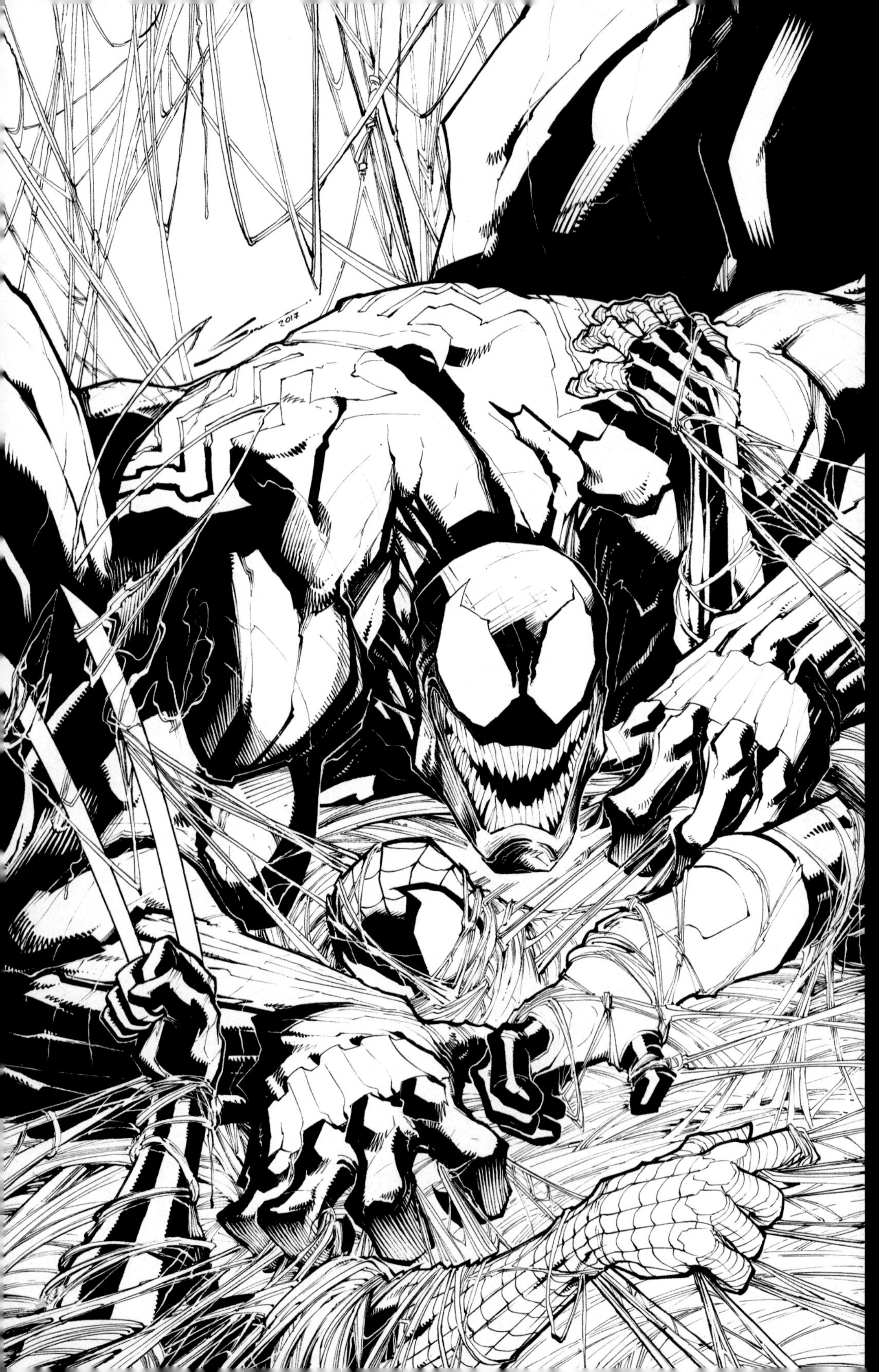

151

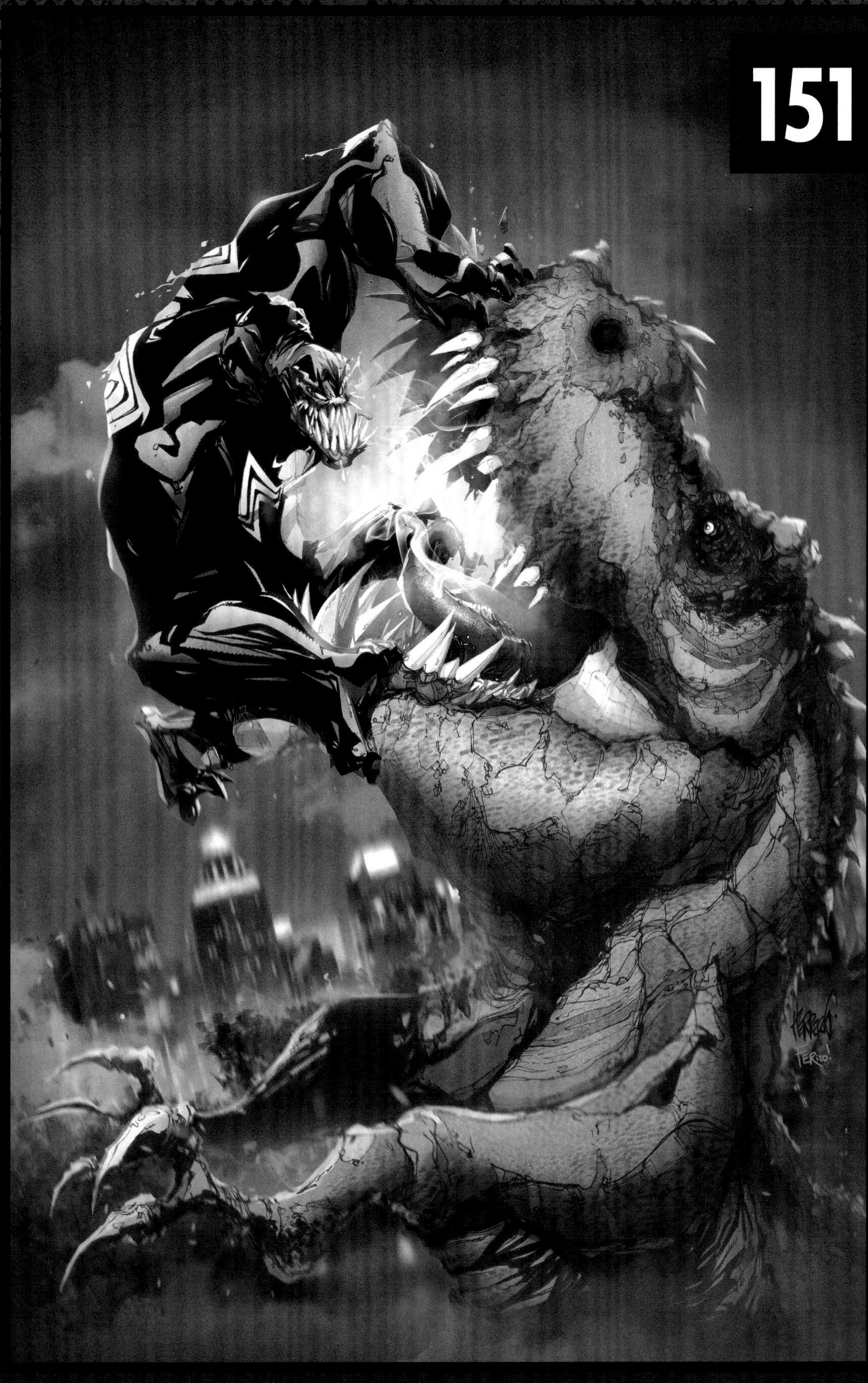

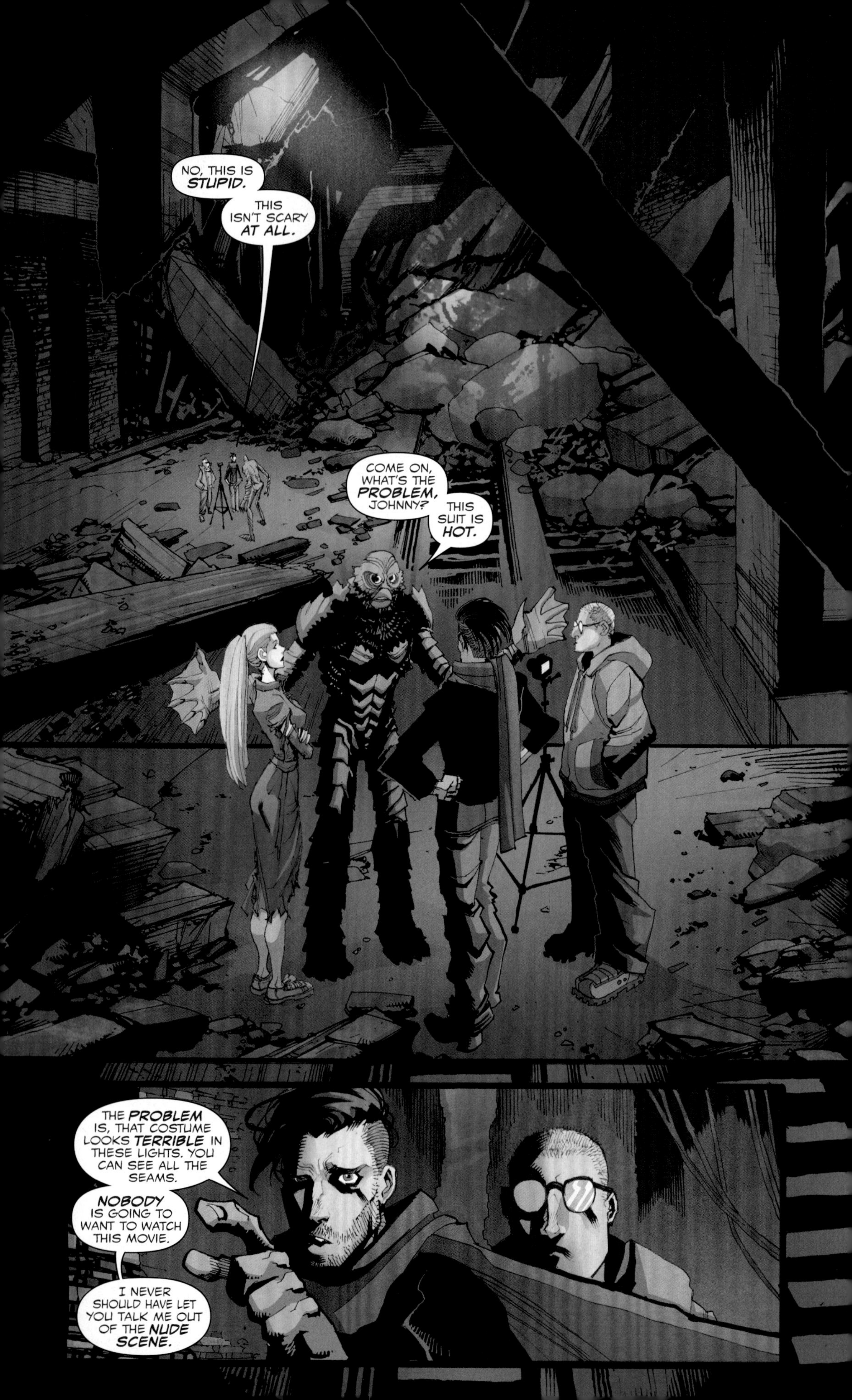
NO, THIS IS STUPID.
THIS ISN'T SCARY AT ALL.
COME ON, WHAT'S THE PROBLEM, JOHNNY?
THIS SUIT IS HOT.
THE PROBLEM IS, THAT COSTUME LOOKS TERRIBLE IN THESE LIGHTS. YOU CAN SEE ALL THE SEAMS.
NOBODY IS GOING TO WANT TO WATCH THIS MOVIE.
I NEVER SHOULD HAVE LET YOU TALK ME OUT OF THE NUDE SCENE.

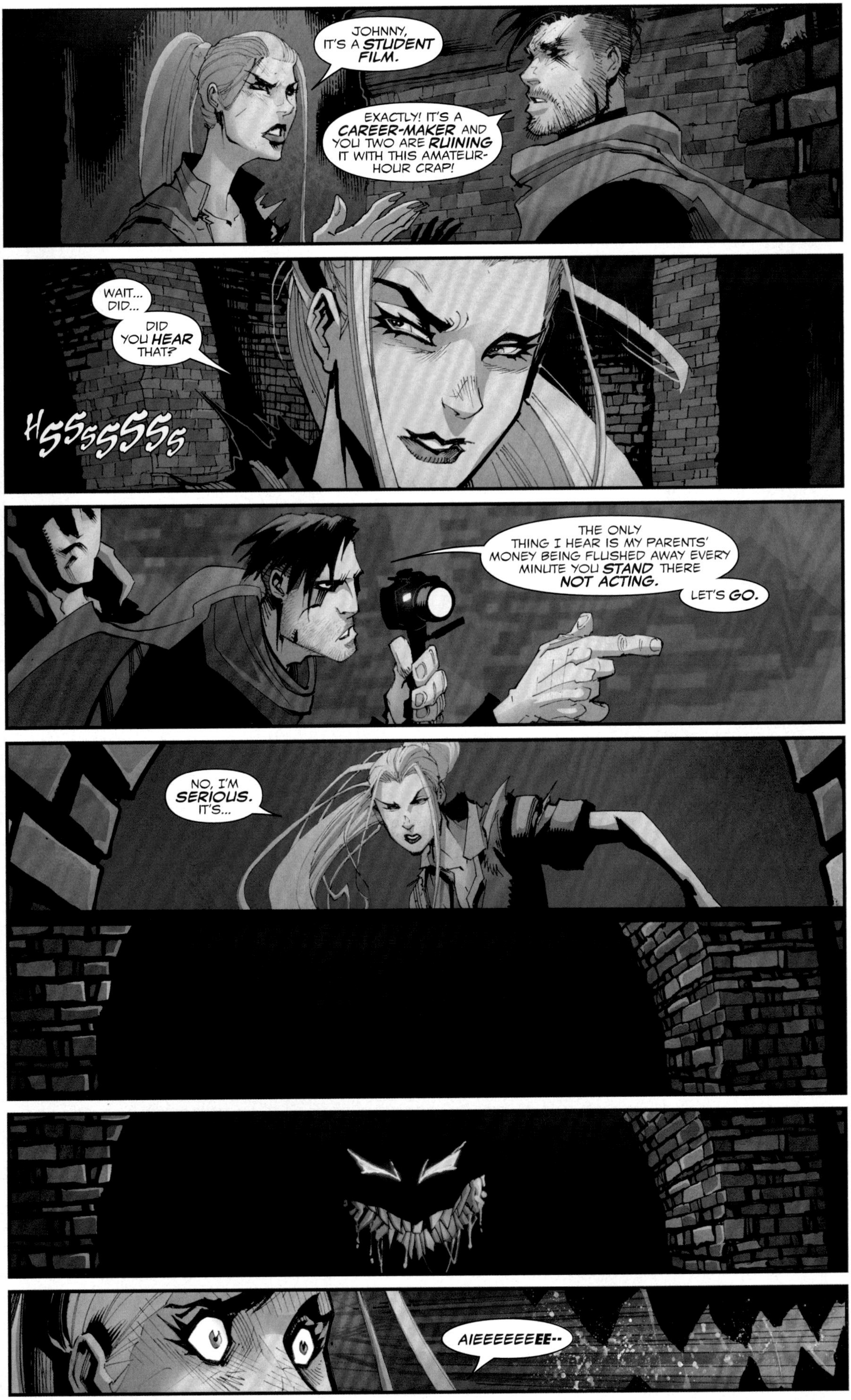

JOHNNY, IT'S A STUDENT FILM.
EXACTLY! IT'S A CAREER-MAKER AND YOU TWO ARE RUINING IT WITH THIS AMATEUR-HOUR CRAP!
WAIT... DID...
DID YOU HEAR THAT?
HSSSSSSS
THE ONLY THING I HEAR IS MY PARENTS' MONEY BEING FLUSHED AWAY EVERY MINUTE YOU STAND THERE NOT ACTING.
LET'S GO.
NO, I'M SERIOUS. IT'S...
AIEEEEEEEE--

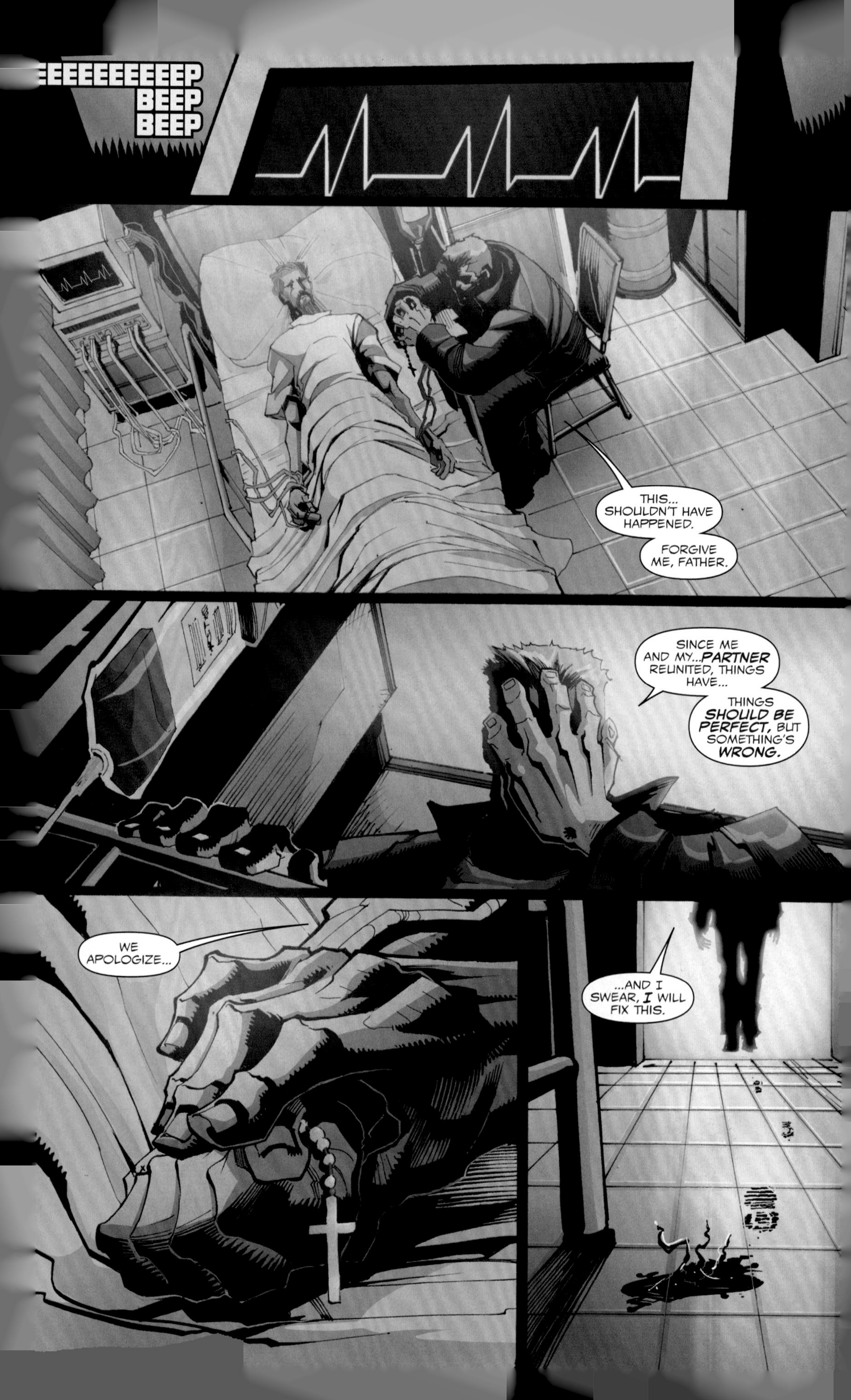
EEEEEEEEEEEP
BEEP
BEEP
THIS... SHOULDN'T HAVE HAPPENED.
FORGIVE ME, FATHER.
SINCE ME AND MY...PARTNER REUNITED, THINGS HAVE...
THINGS SHOULD BE PERFECT, BUT SOMETHING'S WRONG.
WE APOLOGIZE...
...AND I SWEAR, I WILL FIX THIS.

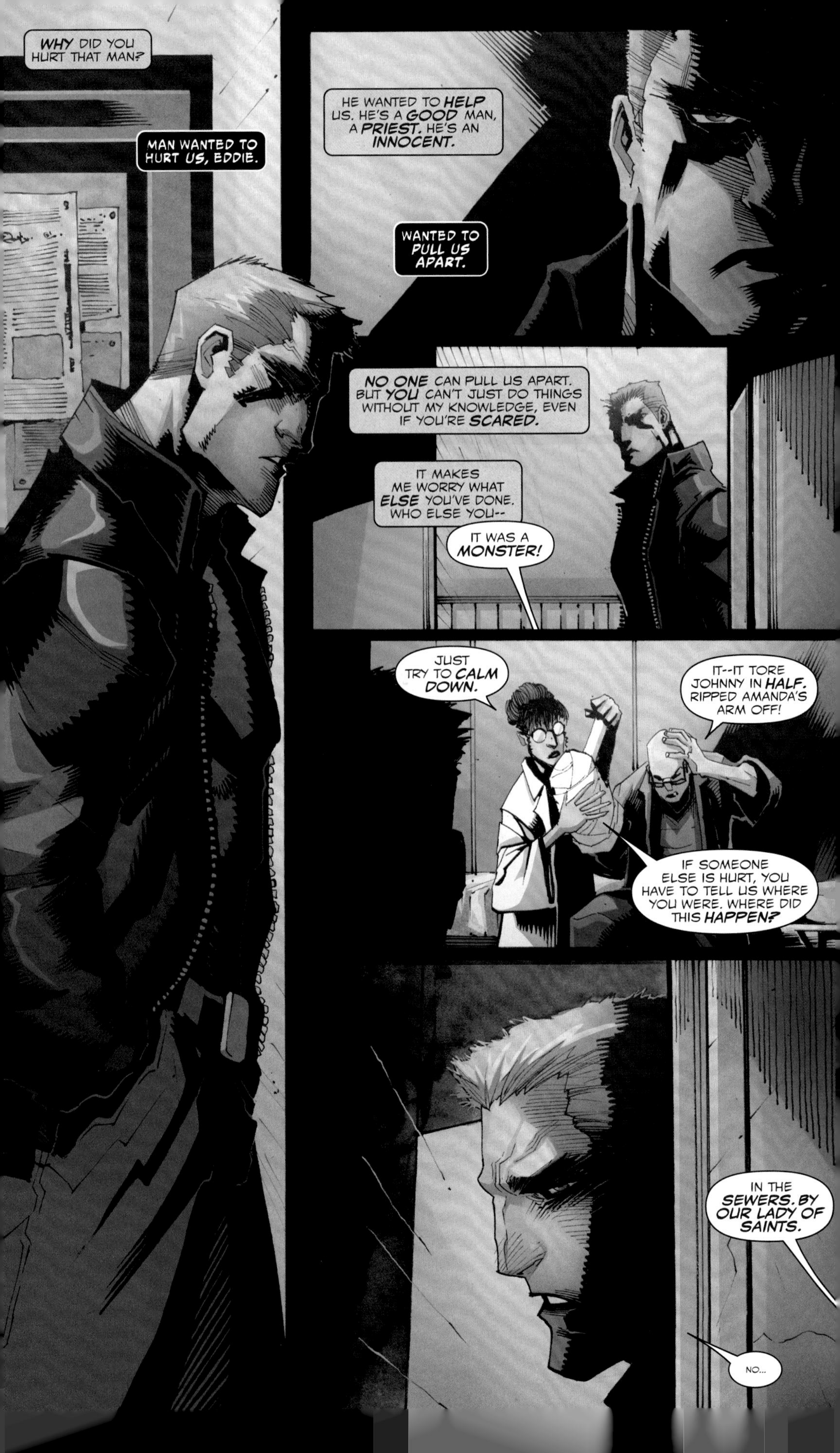
WHY DID YOU HURT THAT MAN?
MAN WANTED TO HURT US, EDDIE.
HE WANTED TO HELP US. HE'S A GOOD MAN, A PRIEST. HE'S AN INNOCENT.
WANTED TO PULL US APART.
NO ONE CAN PULL US APART. BUT YOU CAN'T JUST DO THINGS WITHOUT MY KNOWLEDGE, EVEN IF YOU'RE SCARED.
IT MAKES ME WORRY WHAT ELSE YOU'VE DONE. WHO ELSE YOU--
IT WAS A MONSTER!
JUST TRY TO CALM DOWN.
IT--IT TORE JOHNNY IN HALF. RIPPED AMANDA'S ARM OFF!
IF SOMEONE ELSE IS HURT, YOU HAVE TO TELL US WHERE YOU WERE. WHERE DID THIS HAPPEN?
IN THE SEWERS. BY OUR LADY OF SAINTS.
NO...

THIS "MONSTER"--WHAT DID IT LOOK LIKE?

FANGS. *HUGE FANGS.* HORRIBLE SLOBBER, RANK *BREATH*--

UH-HUH. HOW ABOUT WE RUN YOUR BLOOD FOR TOXICOLOGY? JUST AS A *PRECAUTION*, OF COURSE...

WAS IT *HUMANOID?* DID IT LOOK LIKE A *MAN?*

SIR, PLEASE. THIS MAN NEEDS *MEDICAL HELP.*

DIDN'T YOU *HEAR* HIM? *OTHER* PEOPLE MIGHT NEED HELP, TOO.

HOW CAN YOU DISMISS THIS BOY WHEN YOU *KNOW* THE KINDS OF THINGS THAT ARE OUT THERE?

NOW *DESCRIBE* THIS THING. *CAREFULLY.*

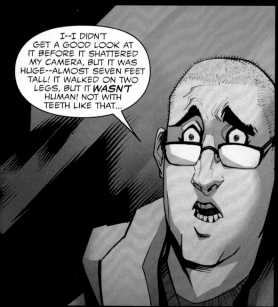

I--I DIDN'T GET A GOOD LOOK AT IT BEFORE IT SHATTERED MY CAMERA, BUT IT WAS HUGE--ALMOST SEVEN FEET TALL! IT WALKED ON TWO LEGS, BUT IT *WASN'T* HUMAN! NOT WITH TEETH LIKE THAT...

WHERE *EXACTLY* DID THIS HAPPEN?

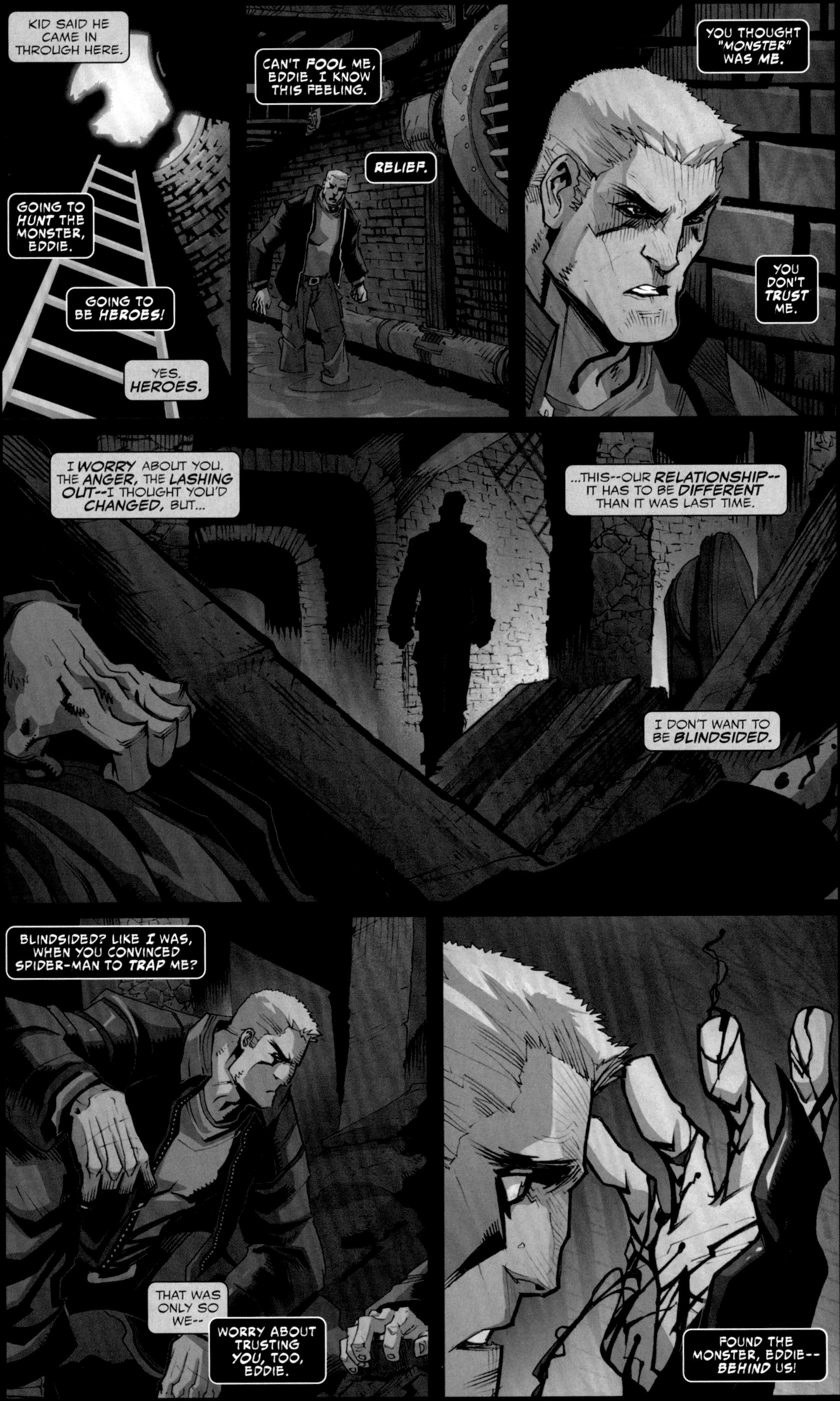
KID SAID HE CAME IN THROUGH HERE.
GOING TO HUNT THE MONSTER, EDDIE.
GOING TO BE HEROES!
YES. HEROES.
CAN'T FOOL ME, EDDIE. I KNOW THIS FEELING.
RELIEF.
YOU THOUGHT "MONSTER" WAS ME.
YOU DON'T TRUST ME.
I WORRY ABOUT YOU. THE ANGER, THE LASHING OUT--I THOUGHT YOU'D CHANGED, BUT...
...THIS--OUR RELATIONSHIP--IT HAS TO BE DIFFERENT THAN IT WAS LAST TIME.
I DON'T WANT TO BE BLINDSIDED.
BLINDSIDED? LIKE I WAS, WHEN YOU CONVINCED SPIDER-MAN TO TRAP ME?
THAT WAS ONLY SO WE--
WORRY ABOUT TRUSTING YOU, TOO, EDDIE.
FOUND THE MONSTER, EDDIE--BEHIND US!

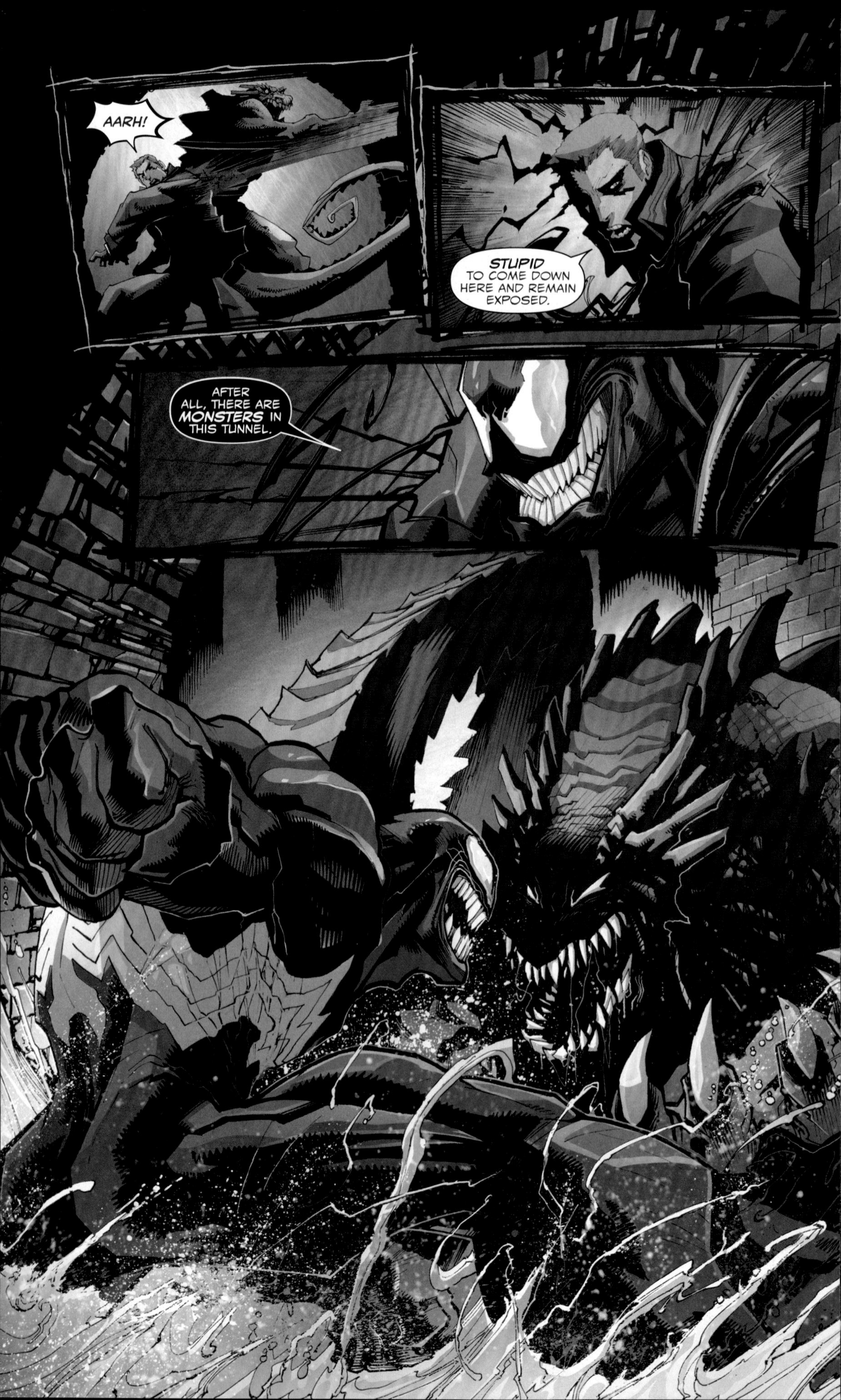
AARH!
STUPID TO COME DOWN HERE AND REMAIN EXPOSED.
AFTER ALL, THERE ARE MONSTERS IN THIS TUNNEL.

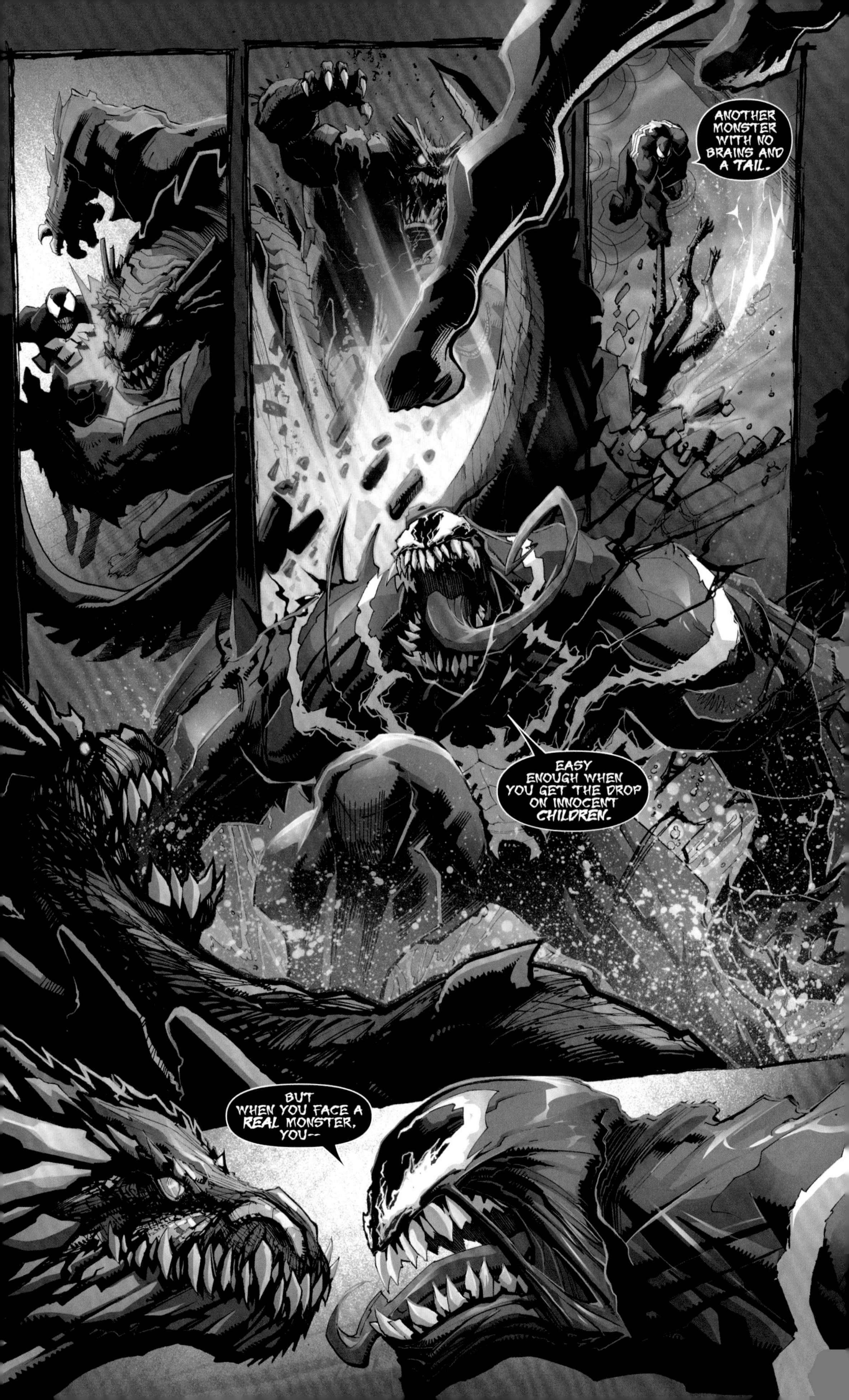
ANOTHER MONSTER WITH NO BRAINS AND A TAIL.
EASY ENOUGH WHEN YOU GET THE DROP ON INNOCENT CHILDREN.
BUT WHEN YOU FACE A REAL MONSTER, YOU--

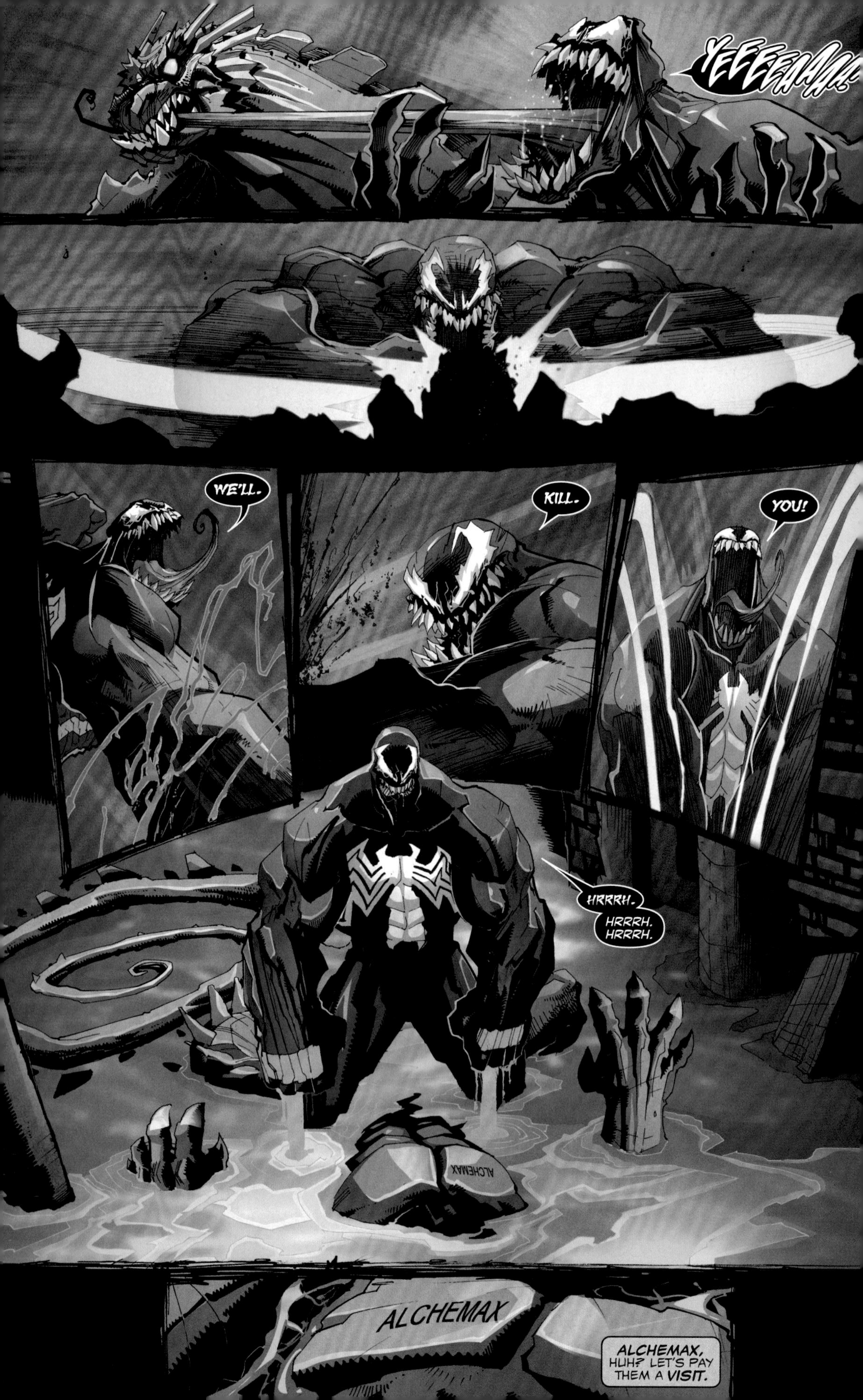
YEEEEAAAA!!
WE'LL.
KILL.
YOU!
HRRRH.
HRRRH.
HRRRH.
ALCHEMAX
ALCHEMAX
ALCHEMAX, HUH? LET'S PAY THEM A VISIT.

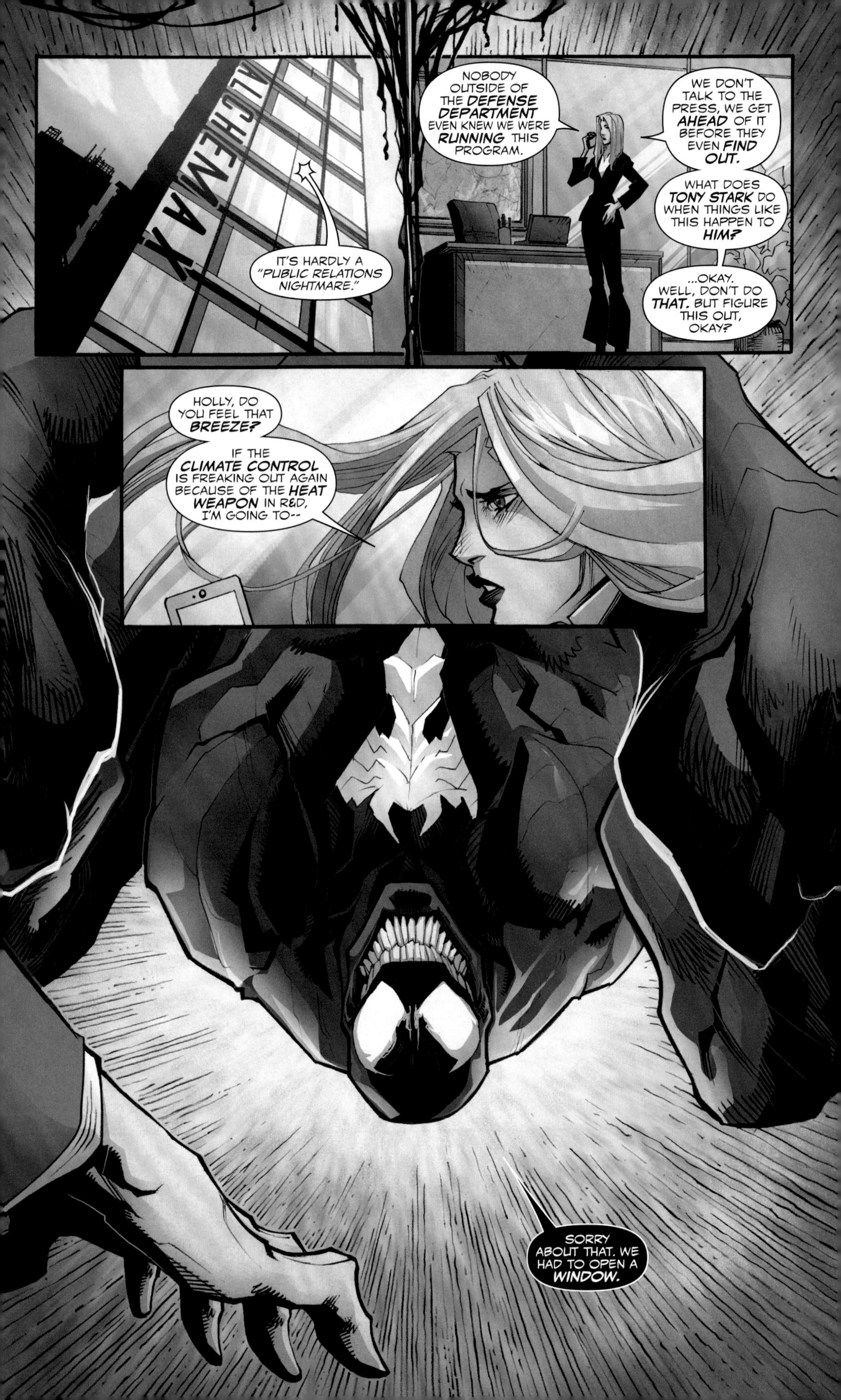
ALCHEMAX
IT'S HARDLY A "PUBLIC RELATIONS NIGHTMARE."
NOBODY OUTSIDE OF THE DEFENSE DEPARTMENT EVEN KNEW WE WERE RUNNING THIS PROGRAM.
WE DON'T TALK TO THE PRESS, WE GET AHEAD OF IT BEFORE THEY EVEN FIND OUT.
WHAT DOES TONY STARK DO WHEN THINGS LIKE THIS HAPPEN TO HIM?
...OKAY. WELL, DON'T DO THAT. BUT FIGURE THIS OUT, OKAY?
HOLLY, DO YOU FEEL THAT BREEZE?
IF THE CLIMATE CONTROL IS FREAKING OUT AGAIN BECAUSE OF THE HEAT WEAPON IN R&D, I'M GOING TO--
SORRY ABOUT THAT. WE HAD TO OPEN A WINDOW.

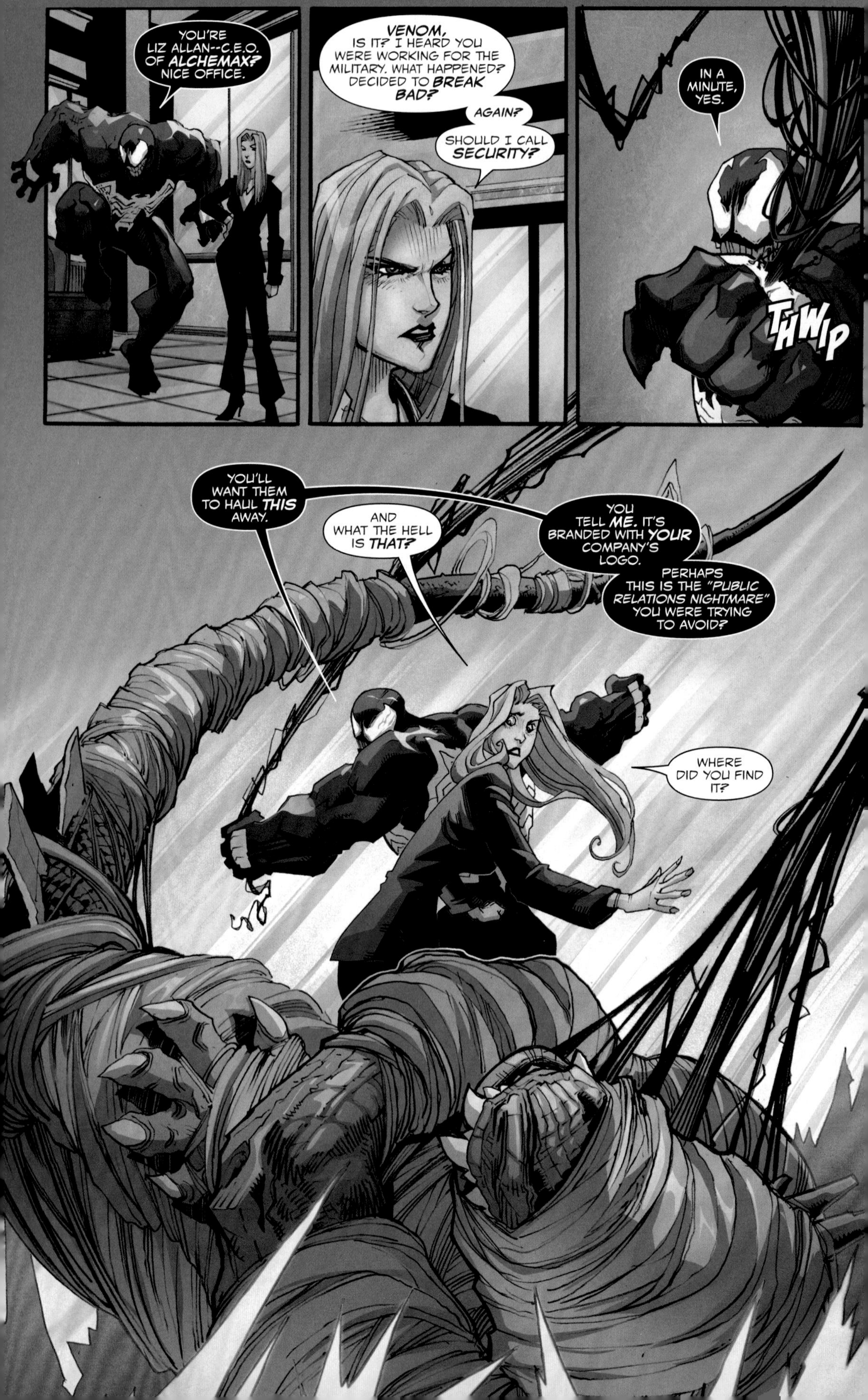

YOU'RE LIZ ALLAN--C.E.O. OF ALCHEMAX? NICE OFFICE.
VENOM, IS IT? I HEARD YOU WERE WORKING FOR THE MILITARY. WHAT HAPPENED? DECIDED TO BREAK BAD?
AGAIN?
SHOULD I CALL SECURITY?
IN A MINUTE, YES.
THWIP
YOU'LL WANT THEM TO HAUL THIS AWAY.
AND WHAT THE HELL IS THAT?
YOU TELL ME. IT'S BRANDED WITH YOUR COMPANY'S LOGO.
PERHAPS THIS IS THE "PUBLIC RELATIONS NIGHTMARE" YOU WERE TRYING TO AVOID?
WHERE DID YOU FIND IT?

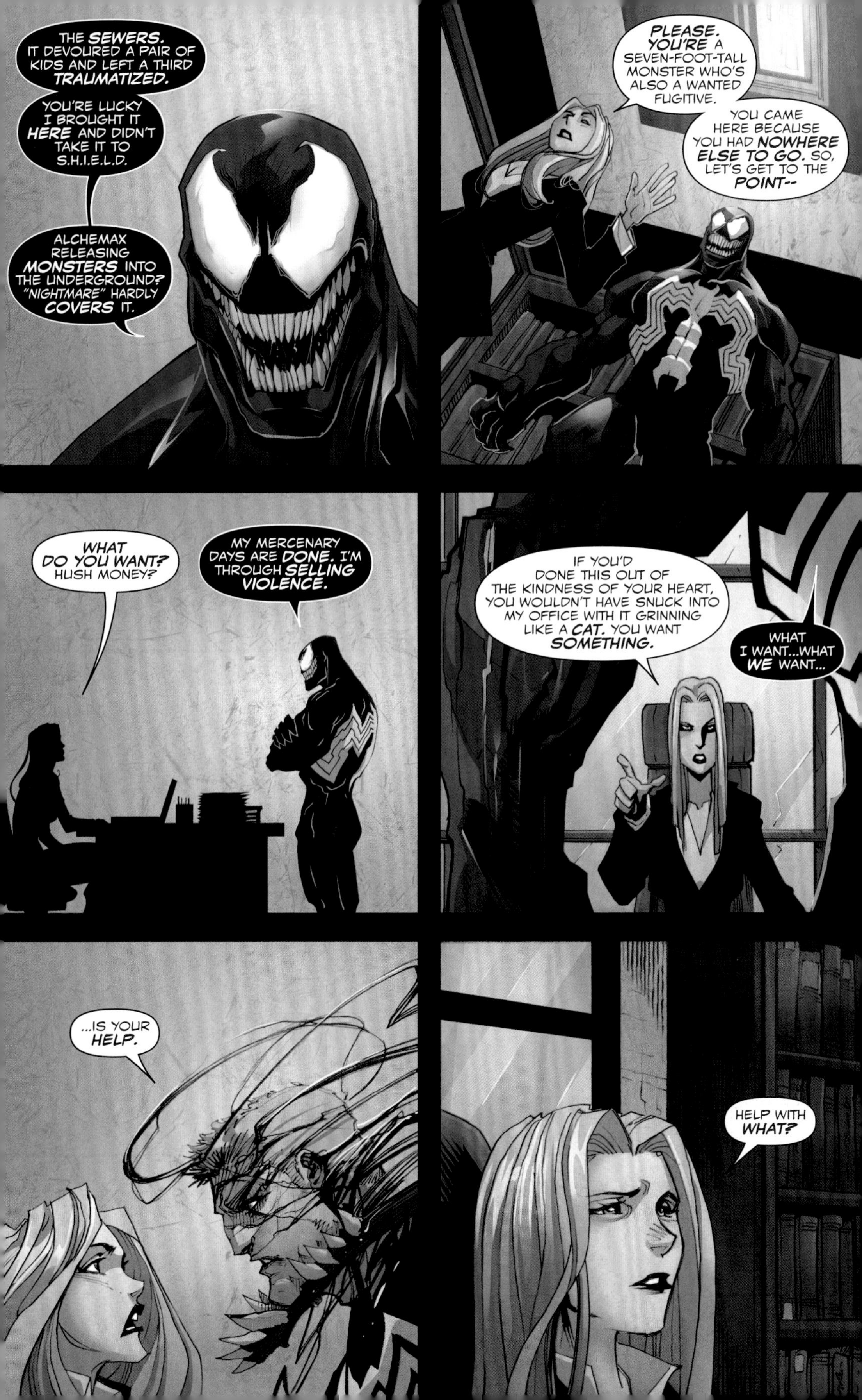
THE SEWERS. IT DEVOURED A PAIR OF KIDS AND LEFT A THIRD TRAUMATIZED.
YOU'RE LUCKY I BROUGHT IT HERE AND DIDN'T TAKE IT TO S.H.I.E.L.D.
ALCHEMAX RELEASING MONSTERS INTO THE UNDERGROUND? "NIGHTMARE" HARDLY COVERS IT.
PLEASE. YOU'RE A SEVEN-FOOT-TALL MONSTER WHO'S ALSO A WANTED FUGITIVE.
YOU CAME HERE BECAUSE YOU HAD NOWHERE ELSE TO GO. SO, LET'S GET TO THE POINT--
WHAT DO YOU WANT? HUSH MONEY?
MY MERCENARY DAYS ARE DONE. I'M THROUGH SELLING VIOLENCE.
IF YOU'D DONE THIS OUT OF THE KINDNESS OF YOUR HEART, YOU WOULDN'T HAVE SNUCK INTO MY OFFICE WITH IT GRINNING LIKE A CAT. YOU WANT SOMETHING.
WHAT I WANT...WHAT WE WANT...
...IS YOUR HELP.
HELP WITH WHAT?

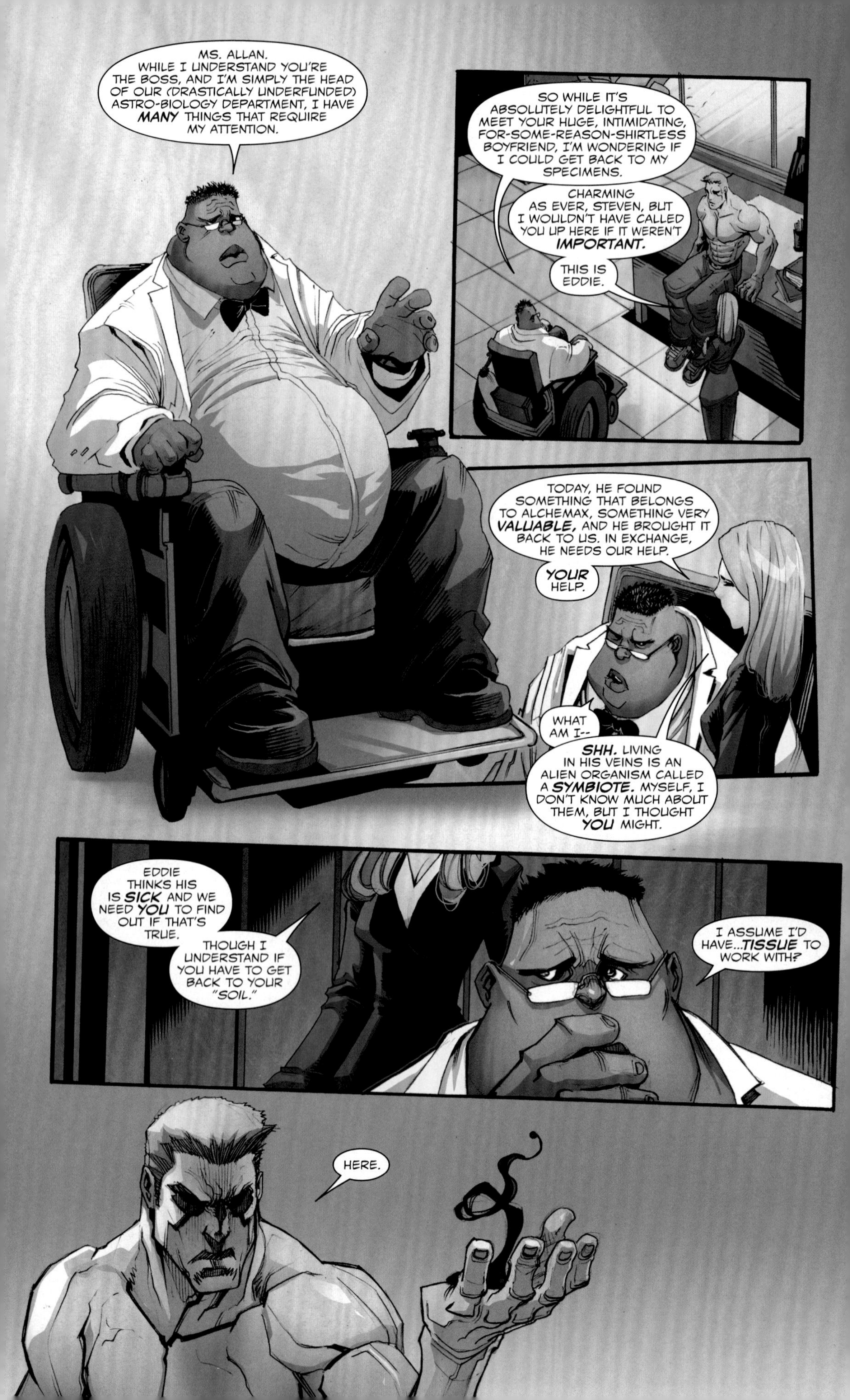
MS. ALLAN. WHILE I UNDERSTAND YOU'RE THE BOSS, AND I'M SIMPLY THE HEAD OF OUR (DRASTICALLY UNDERFUNDED) ASTRO-BIOLOGY DEPARTMENT, I HAVE MANY THINGS THAT REQUIRE MY ATTENTION.
SO WHILE IT'S ABSOLUTELY DELIGHTFUL TO MEET YOUR HUGE, INTIMIDATING, FOR-SOME-REASON-SHIRTLESS BOYFRIEND, I'M WONDERING IF I COULD GET BACK TO MY SPECIMENS.
CHARMING AS EVER, STEVEN, BUT I WOULDN'T HAVE CALLED YOU UP HERE IF IT WEREN'T IMPORTANT.
THIS IS EDDIE.
TODAY, HE FOUND SOMETHING THAT BELONGS TO ALCHEMAX, SOMETHING VERY VALUABLE, AND HE BROUGHT IT BACK TO US. IN EXCHANGE, HE NEEDS OUR HELP.
YOUR HELP.
WHAT AM I--
SHH. LIVING IN HIS VEINS IS AN ALIEN ORGANISM CALLED A SYMBIOTE. MYSELF, I DON'T KNOW MUCH ABOUT THEM, BUT I THOUGHT YOU MIGHT.
EDDIE THINKS HIS IS SICK AND WE NEED YOU TO FIND OUT IF THAT'S TRUE.
THOUGH I UNDERSTAND IF YOU HAVE TO GET BACK TO YOUR "SOIL."
I ASSUME I'D HAVE...TISSUE TO WORK WITH?
HERE.

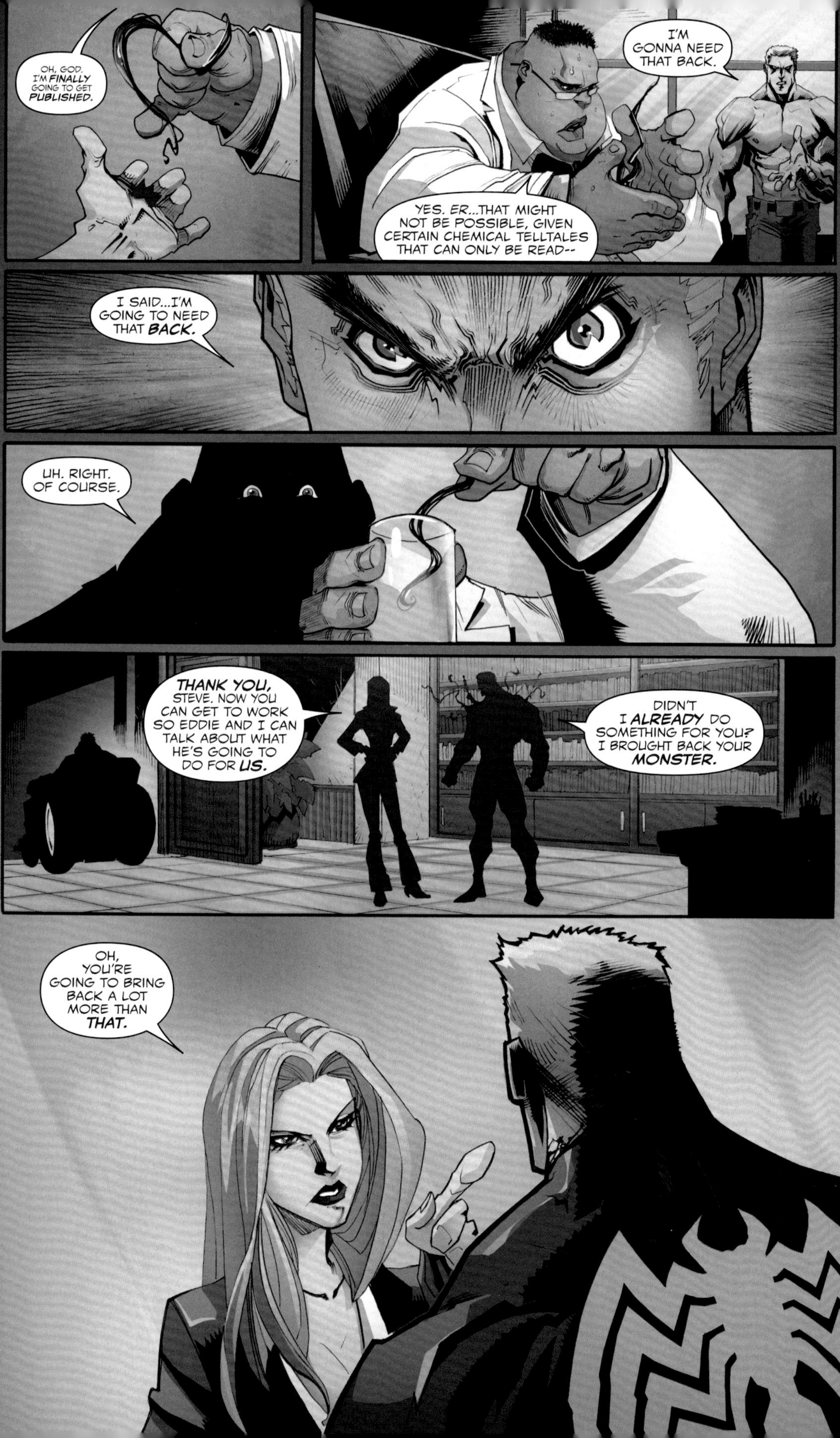

OH, GOD. I'M FINALLY GOING TO GET PUBLISHED.
I'M GONNA NEED THAT BACK.
YES. ER...THAT MIGHT NOT BE POSSIBLE, GIVEN CERTAIN CHEMICAL TELLTALES THAT CAN ONLY BE READ--
I SAID...I'M GOING TO NEED THAT BACK.
UH. RIGHT. OF COURSE.
THANK YOU, STEVE. NOW YOU CAN GET TO WORK SO EDDIE AND I CAN TALK ABOUT WHAT HE'S GOING TO DO FOR US.
DIDN'T I ALREADY DO SOMETHING FOR YOU? I BROUGHT BACK YOUR MONSTER.
OH, YOU'RE GOING TO BRING BACK A LOT MORE THAN THAT.

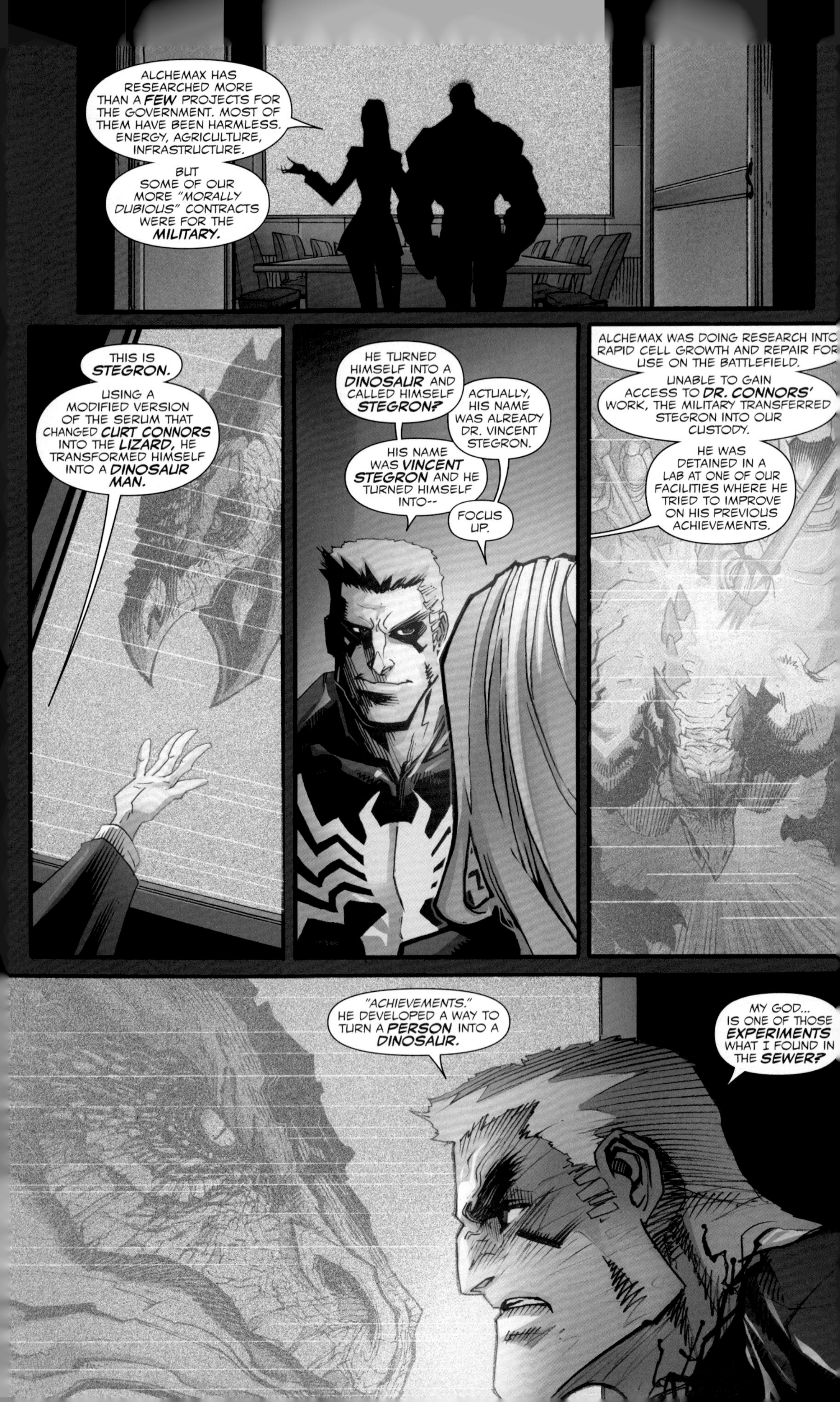
ALCHEMAX HAS RESEARCHED MORE THAN A FEW PROJECTS FOR THE GOVERNMENT. MOST OF THEM HAVE BEEN HARMLESS. ENERGY, AGRICULTURE, INFRASTRUCTURE.
BUT SOME OF OUR MORE "MORALLY DUBIOUS" CONTRACTS WERE FOR THE MILITARY.
THIS IS STEGRON.
USING A MODIFIED VERSION OF THE SERUM THAT CHANGED CURT CONNORS INTO THE LIZARD, HE TRANSFORMED HIMSELF INTO A DINOSAUR MAN.
HE TURNED HIMSELF INTO A DINOSAUR AND CALLED HIMSELF STEGRON?
ACTUALLY, HIS NAME WAS ALREADY DR. VINCENT STEGRON.
HIS NAME WAS VINCENT STEGRON AND HE TURNED HIMSELF INTO--
FOCUS UP.
ALCHEMAX WAS DOING RESEARCH INTO RAPID CELL GROWTH AND REPAIR FOR USE ON THE BATTLEFIELD.
UNABLE TO GAIN ACCESS TO DR. CONNORS' WORK, THE MILITARY TRANSFERRED STEGRON INTO OUR CUSTODY.
HE WAS DETAINED IN A LAB AT ONE OF OUR FACILITIES WHERE HE TRIED TO IMPROVE ON HIS PREVIOUS ACHIEVEMENTS.
"ACHIEVEMENTS." HE DEVELOPED A WAY TO TURN A PERSON INTO A DINOSAUR.
MY GOD... IS ONE OF THOSE EXPERIMENTS WHAT I FOUND IN THE SEWER?

IT'S
...O MILLION
...LLARS OF MY
...IPMENT IN THE
...S OF AN INSANE
... DINOSAUR
MAN.

MAC GARGAN
IS A MURDERER AND
A CRIMINAL.

...IS THE
...NMENT'S
...WANT IT CLEANED
...THE MILITARY
...RE DIRECTLY
...OLVED.

...N WE
...THIS KIND OF
...COMMISSION
...ALF TO DEATH
...RPION SUIT.

EXACTLY
THE KIND OF MA...
NEED TO STOP STE...RON.
SO I WANT TO TH...NK
YOU FOR TAKI...
THE JOB.

YOU
HAVE MY
WORD.

...NT
... IN

"DO I
TRUST
HER?"

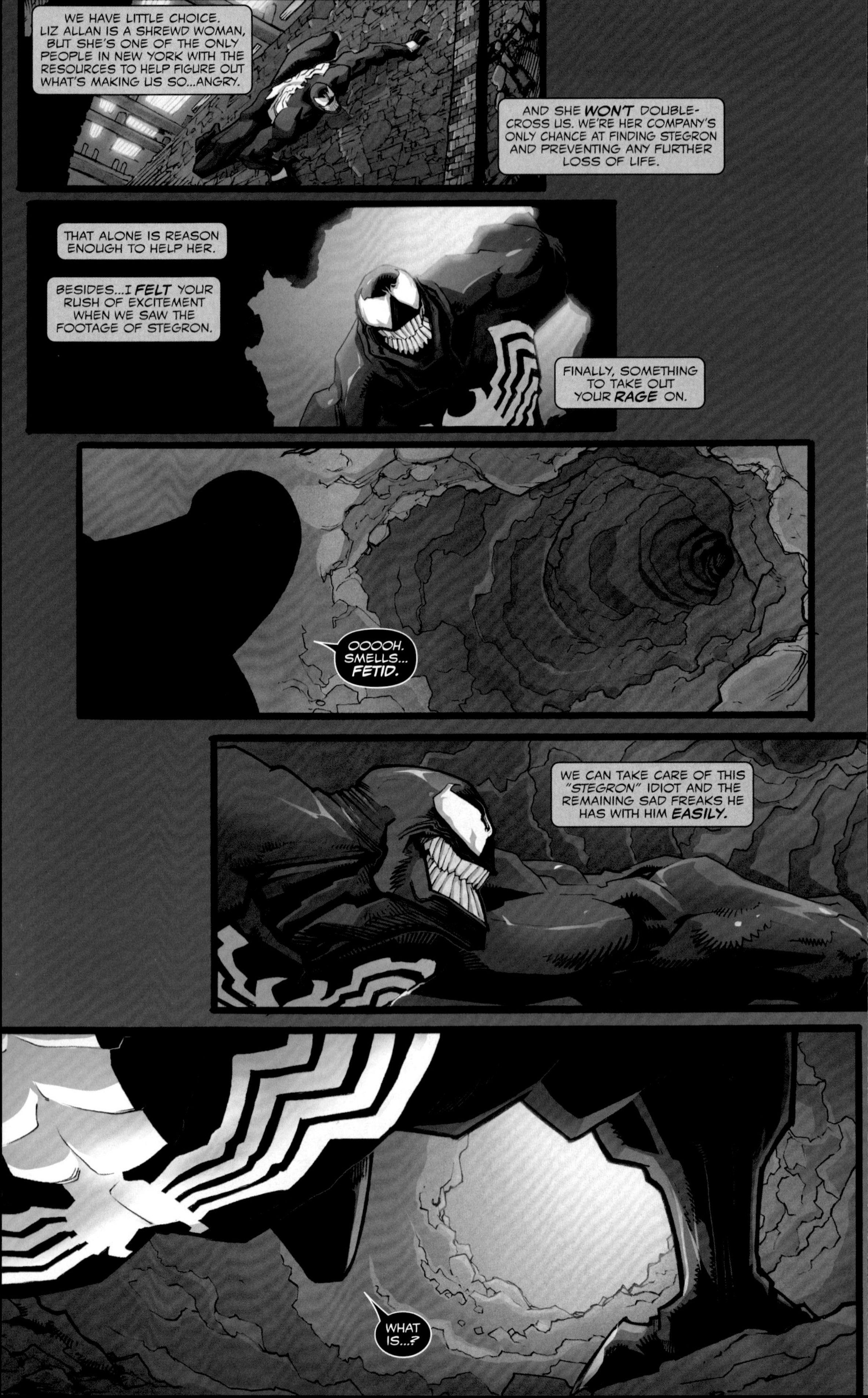
WE HAVE LITTLE CHOICE. LIZ ALLAN IS A SHREWD WOMAN, BUT SHE'S ONE OF THE ONLY PEOPLE IN NEW YORK WITH THE RESOURCES TO HELP FIGURE OUT WHAT'S MAKING US SO...ANGRY.
AND SHE WON'T DOUBLE-CROSS US. WE'RE HER COMPANY'S ONLY CHANCE AT FINDING STEGRON AND PREVENTING ANY FURTHER LOSS OF LIFE.
THAT ALONE IS REASON ENOUGH TO HELP HER.
BESIDES...I FELT YOUR RUSH OF EXCITEMENT WHEN WE SAW THE FOOTAGE OF STEGRON.
FINALLY, SOMETHING TO TAKE OUT YOUR RAGE ON.
OOOOH. SMELLS... FETID.
WE CAN TAKE CARE OF THIS "STEGRON" IDIOT AND THE REMAINING SAD FREAKS HE HAS WITH HIM EASILY.
WHAT IS...?

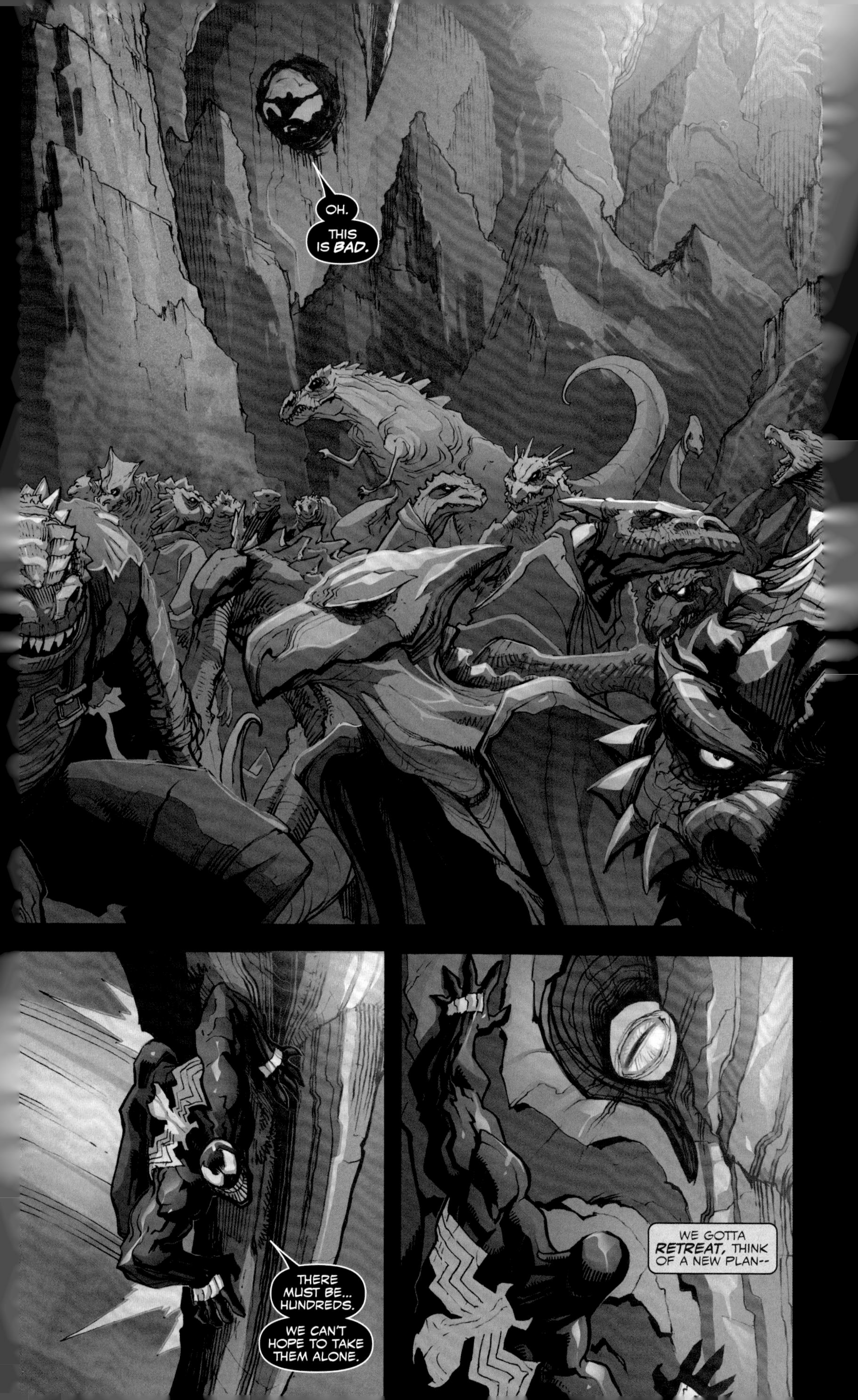
OH.
THIS IS BAD.
THERE MUST BE... HUNDREDS.
WE CAN'T HOPE TO TAKE THEM ALONE.
WE GOTTA RETREAT, THINK OF A NEW PLAN--

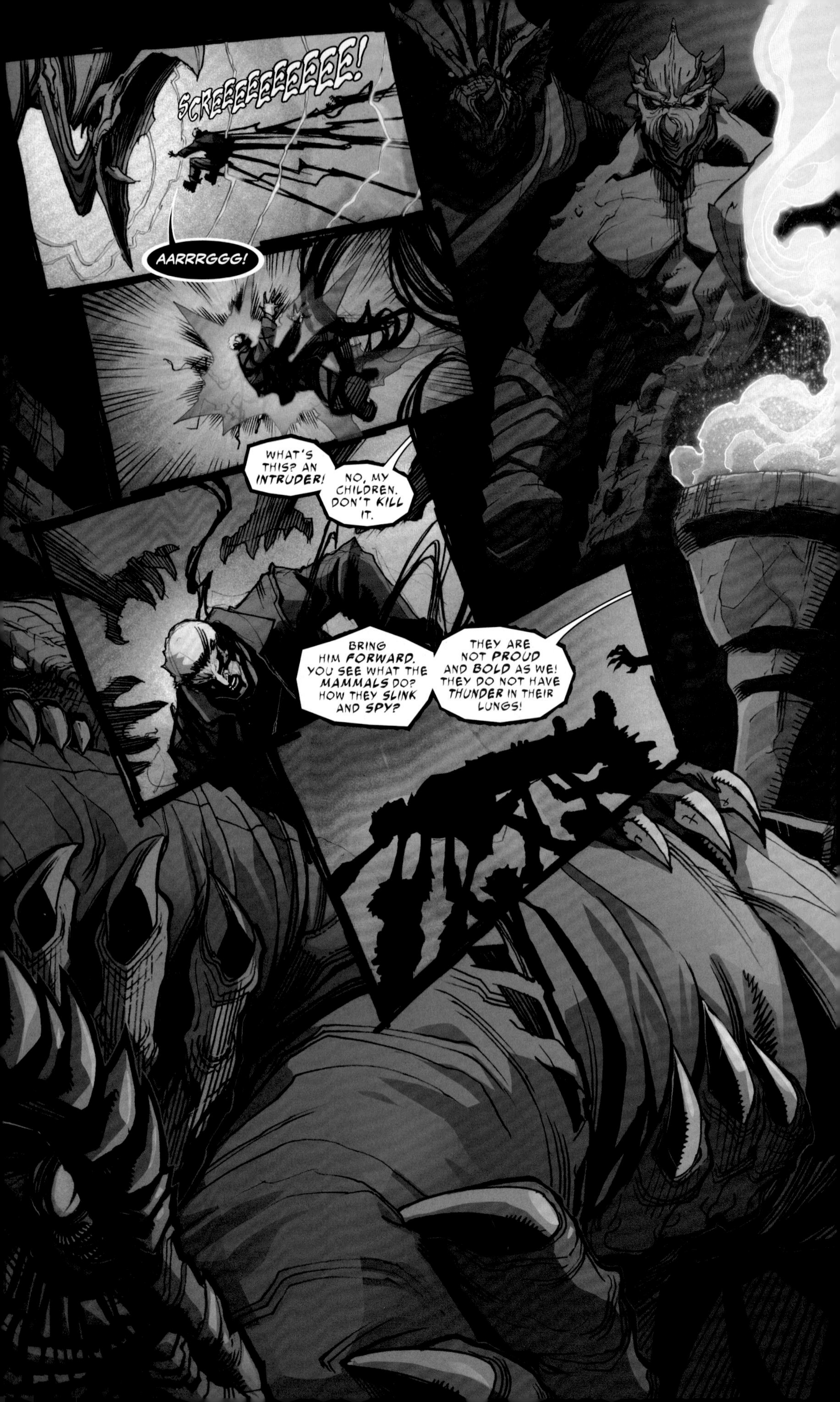
SCREEEEEEEEEEEE!
AARRRGGG!
WHAT'S THIS? AN INTRUDER!
NO, MY CHILDREN. DON'T KILL IT.
BRING HIM FORWARD. YOU SEE WHAT THE MAMMALS DO? HOW THEY SLINK AND SPY?
THEY ARE NOT PROUD AND BOLD AS WE! THEY DO NOT HAVE THUNDER IN THEIR LUNGS!

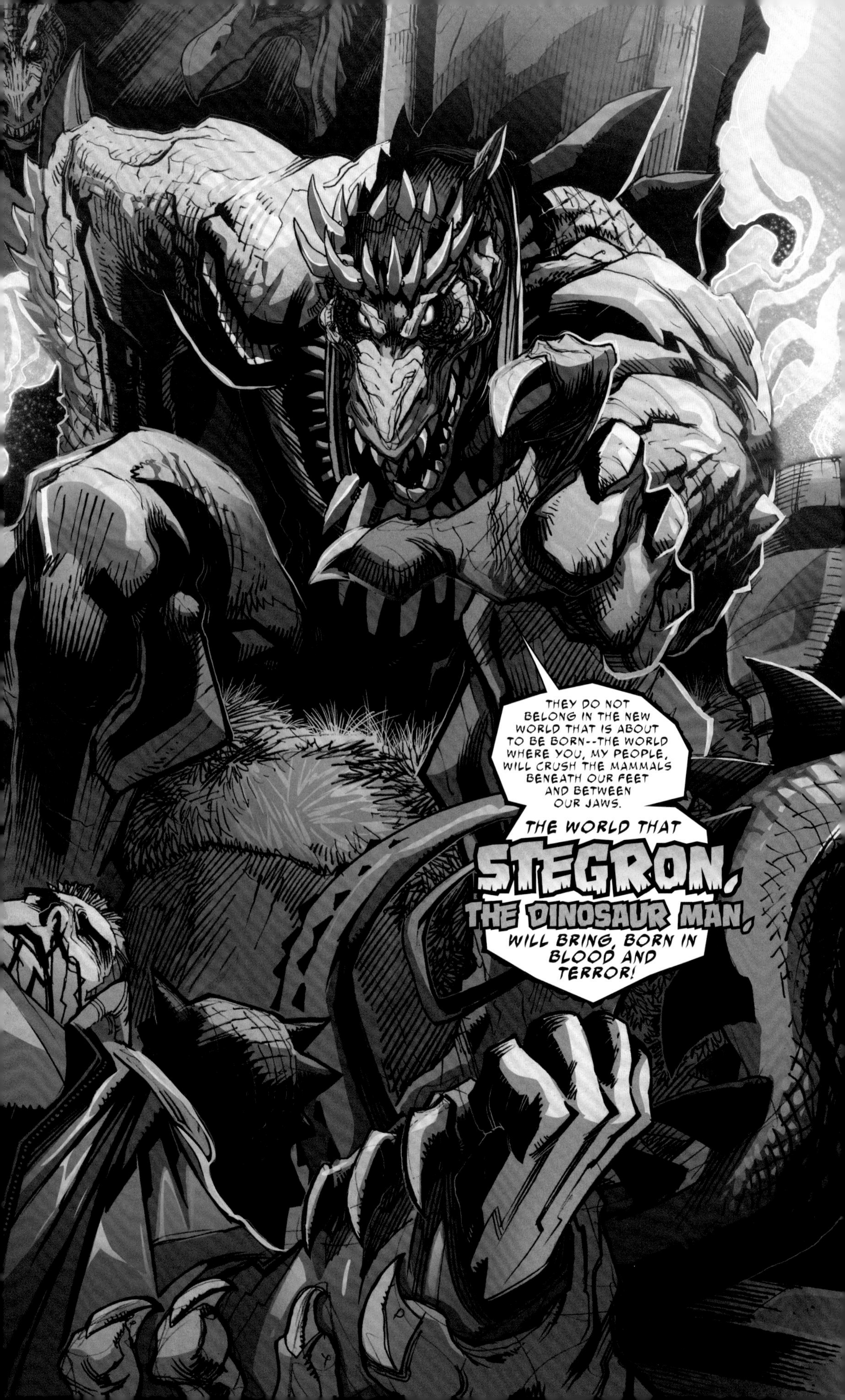
THEY DO NOT BELONG IN THE NEW WORLD THAT IS ABOUT TO BE BORN--THE WORLD WHERE YOU, MY PEOPLE, WILL CRUSH THE MAMMALS BENEATH OUR FEET AND BETWEEN OUR JAWS.
THE WORLD THAT STEGRON, THE DINOSAUR MAN, WILL BRING, BORN IN BLOOD AND TERROR!

152

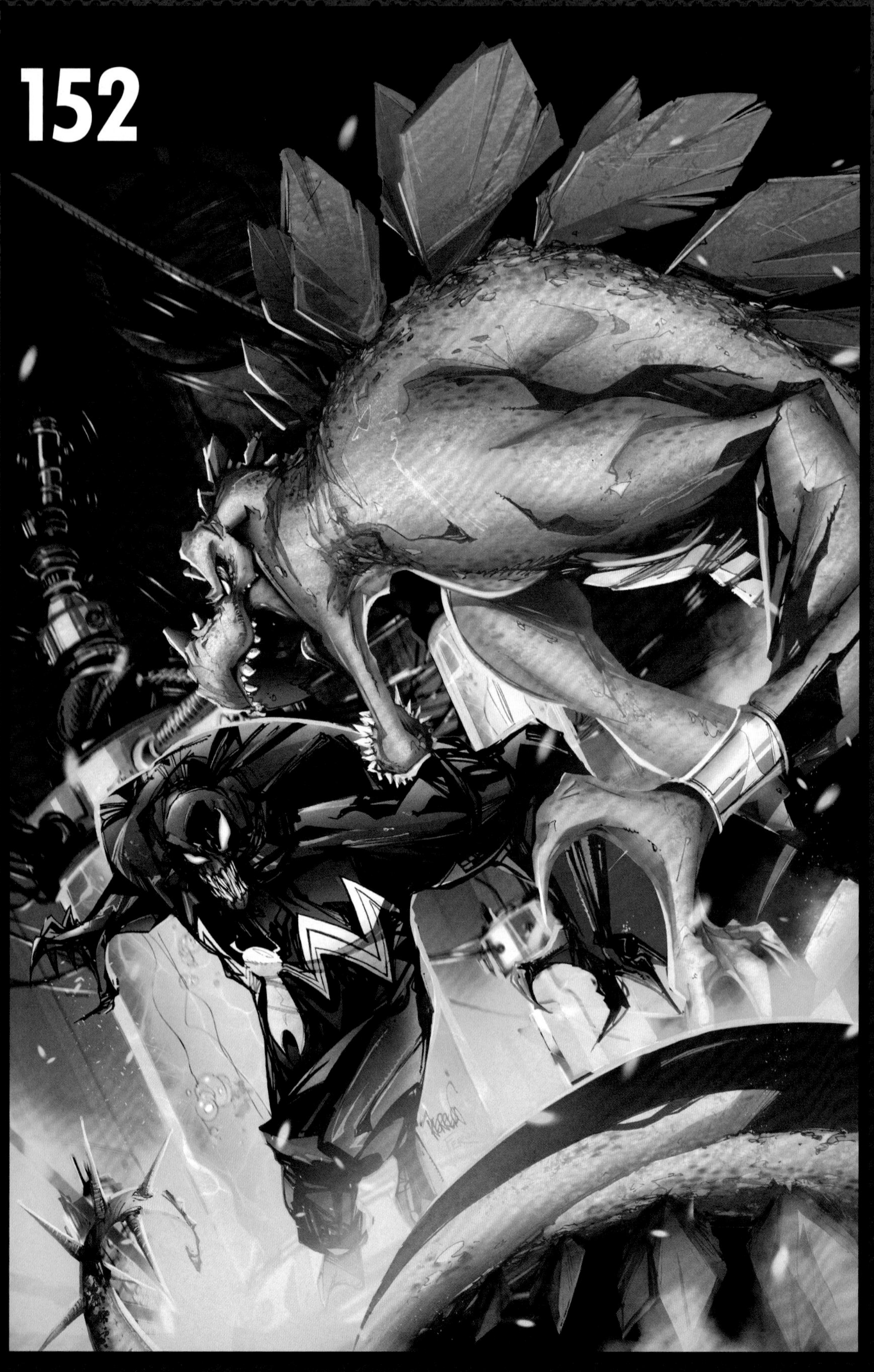

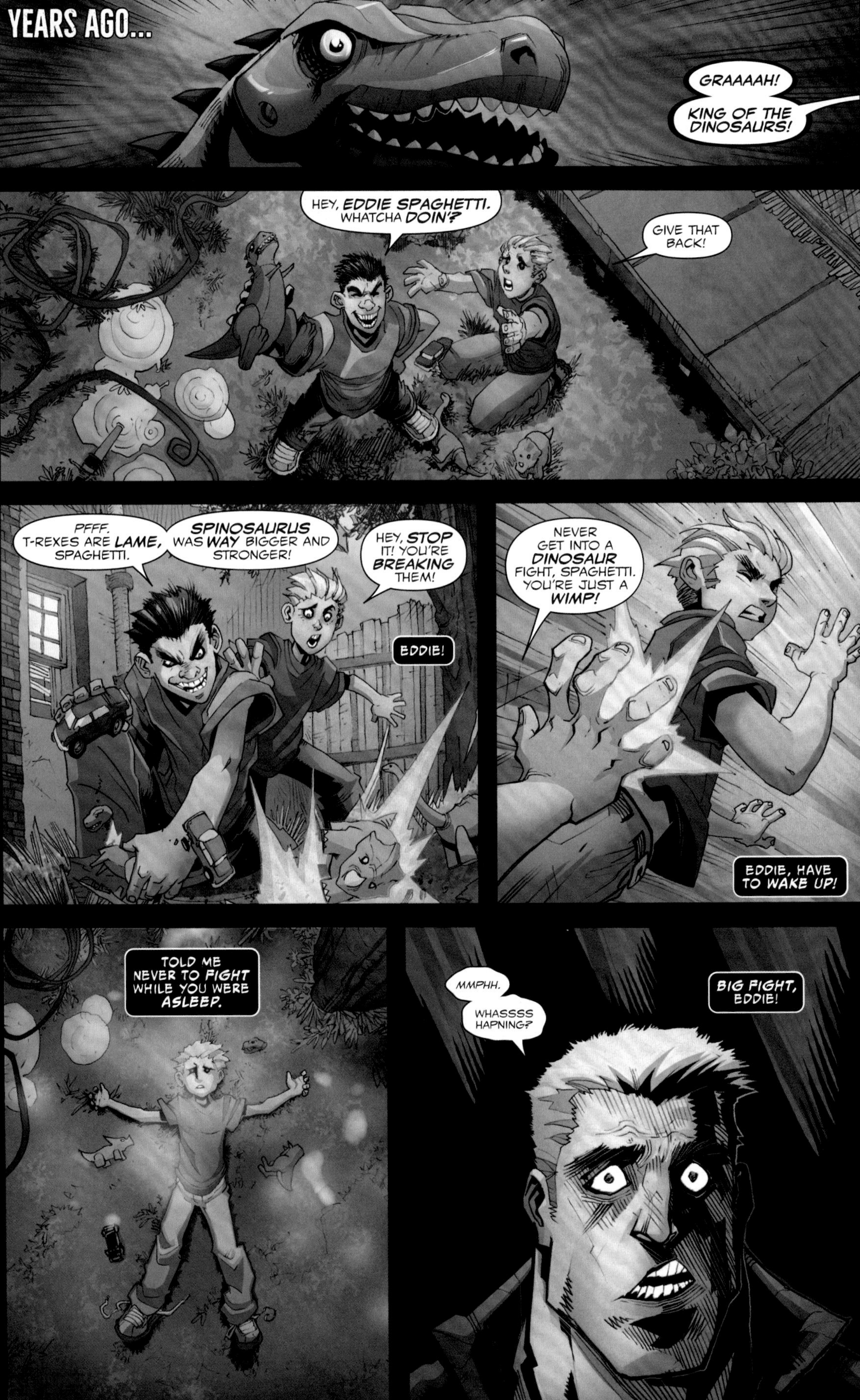
YEARS AGO...
GRAAAAH!
KING OF THE DINOSAURS!
HEY, EDDIE SPAGHETTI. WHATCHA DOIN'?
GIVE THAT BACK!
PFFF. T-REXES ARE LAME, SPAGHETTI.
SPINOSAURUS WAS WAY BIGGER AND STRONGER!
HEY, STOP IT! YOU'RE BREAKING THEM!
EDDIE!
NEVER GET INTO A DINOSAUR FIGHT, SPAGHETTI. YOU'RE JUST A WIMP!
EDDIE, HAVE TO WAKE UP!
TOLD ME NEVER TO FIGHT WHILE YOU WERE ASLEEP.
MMPHH.
WHASSSS HAPNING?
BIG FIGHT, EDDIE!

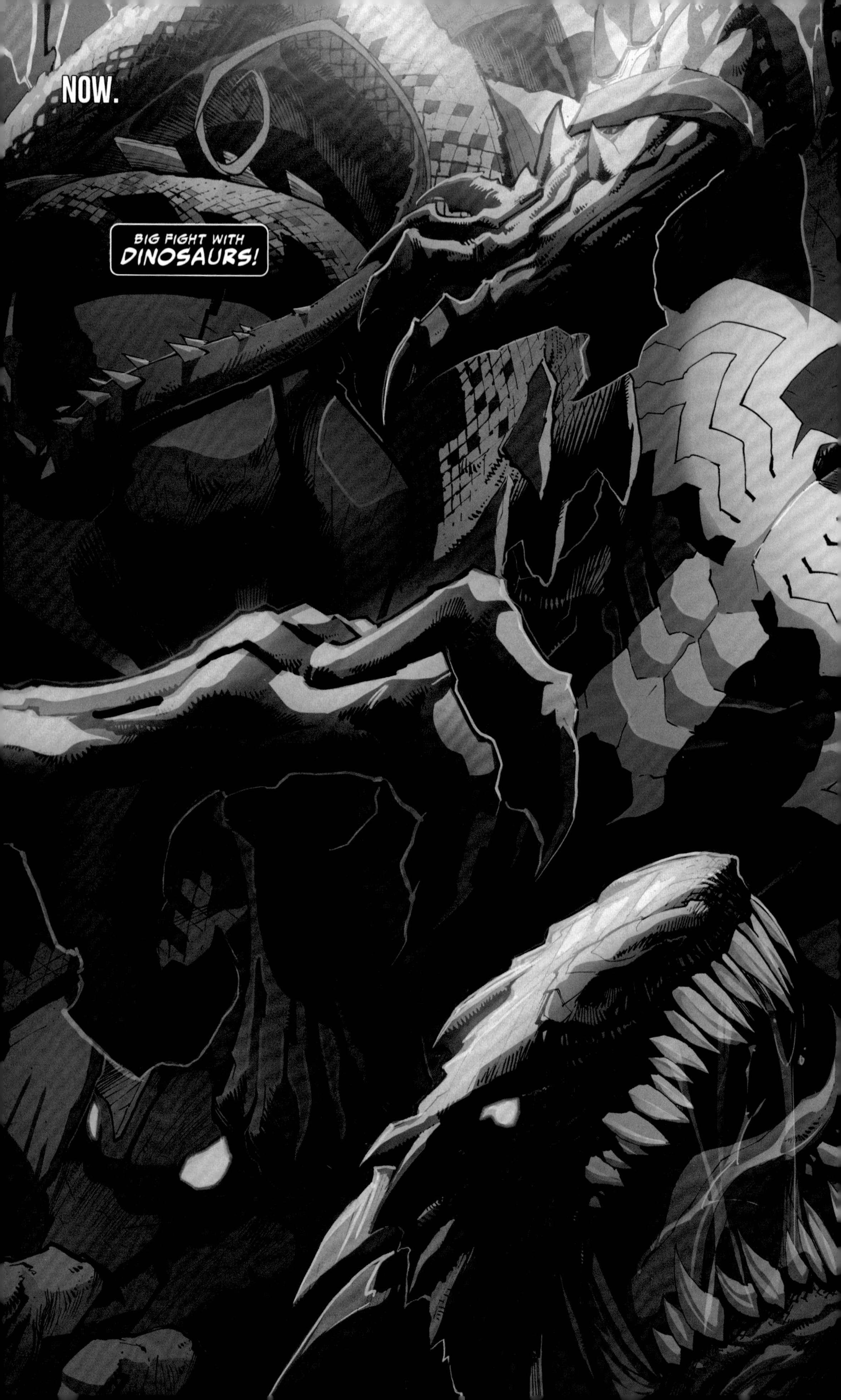
NOW.
BIG FIGHT WITH DINOSAURS!

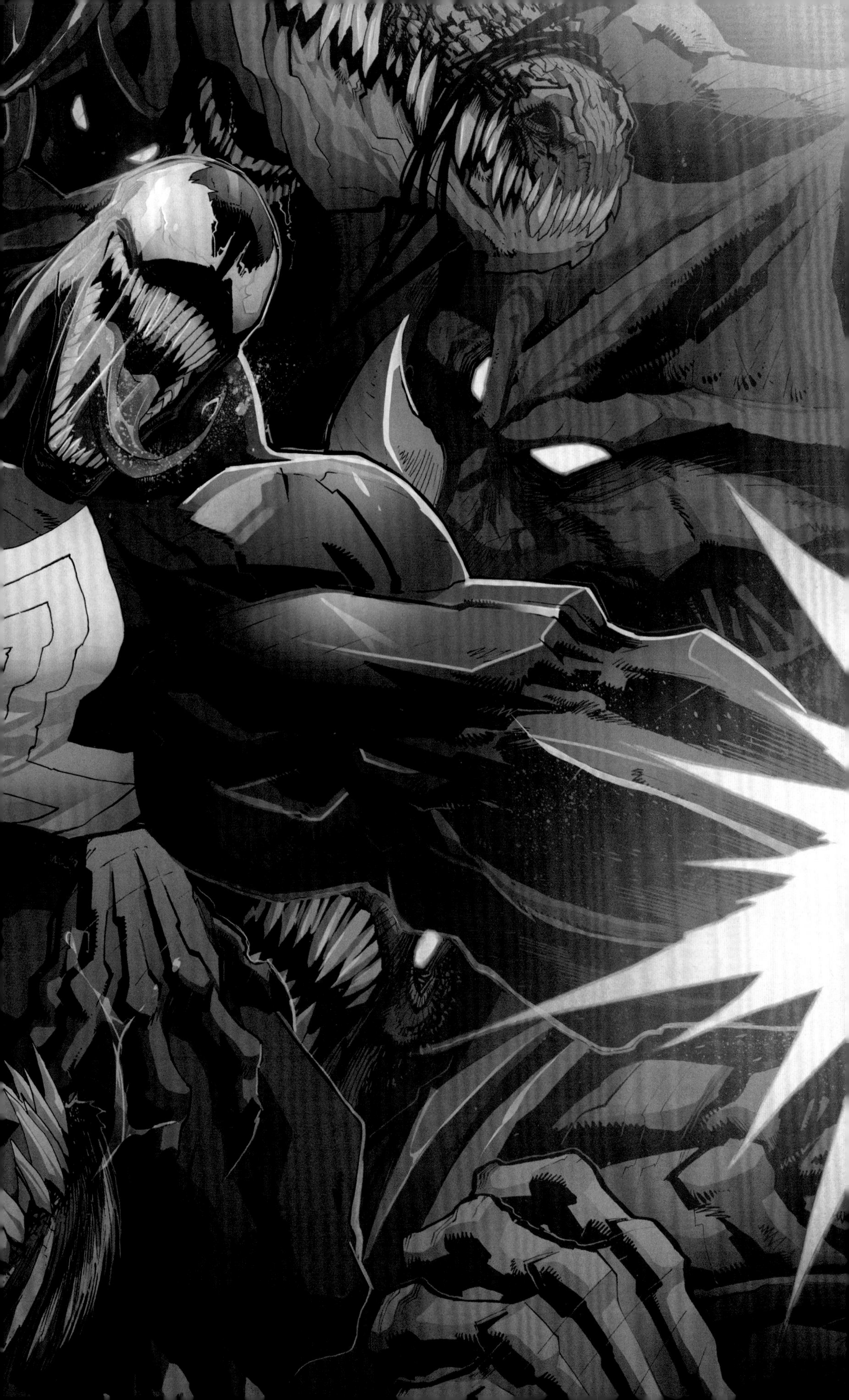

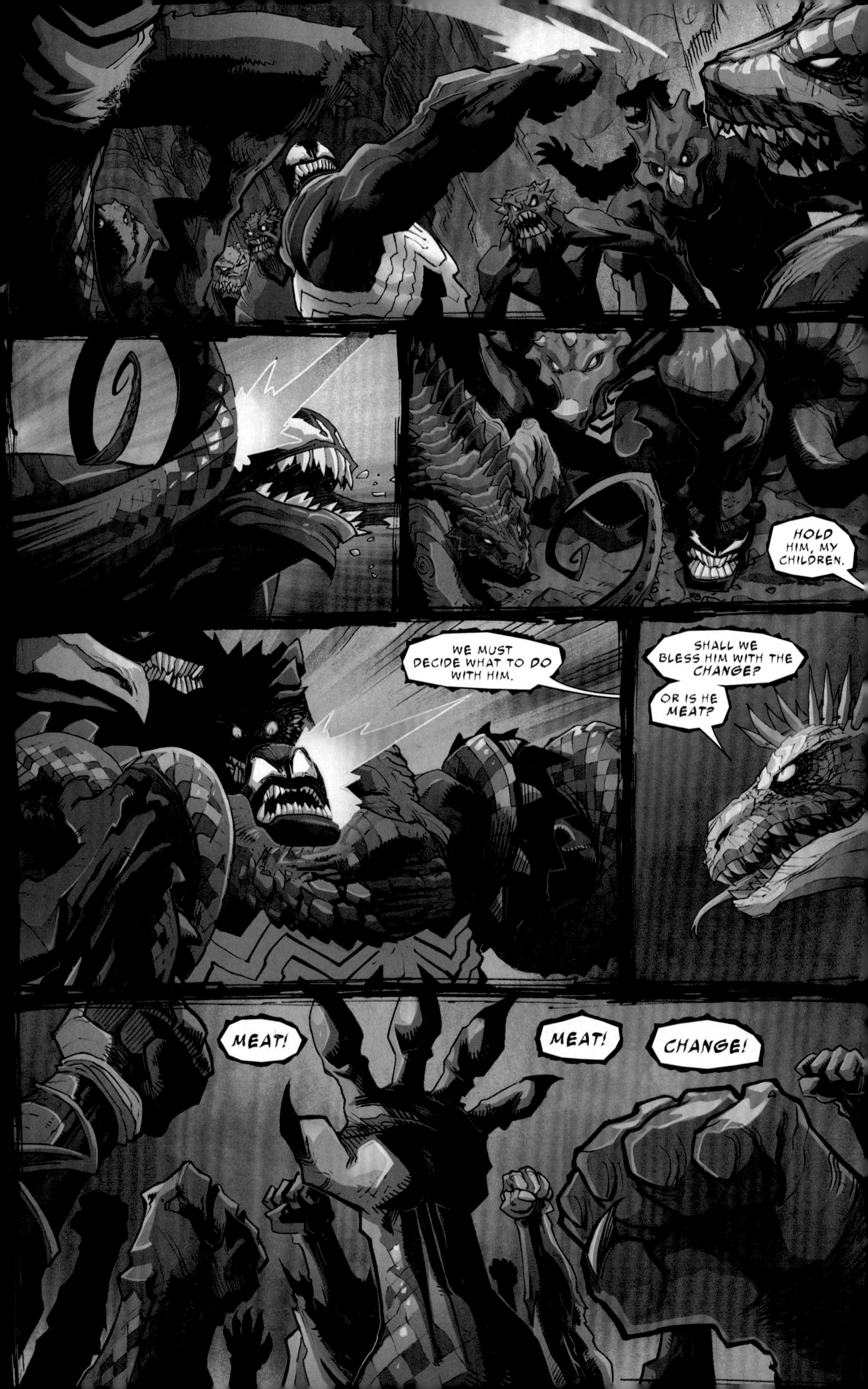
HOLD HIM, MY CHILDREN.
WE MUST DECIDE WHAT TO DO WITH HIM.
SHALL WE BLESS HIM WITH THE CHANGE?
OR IS HE MEAT?
MEAT!
MEAT!
CHANGE!

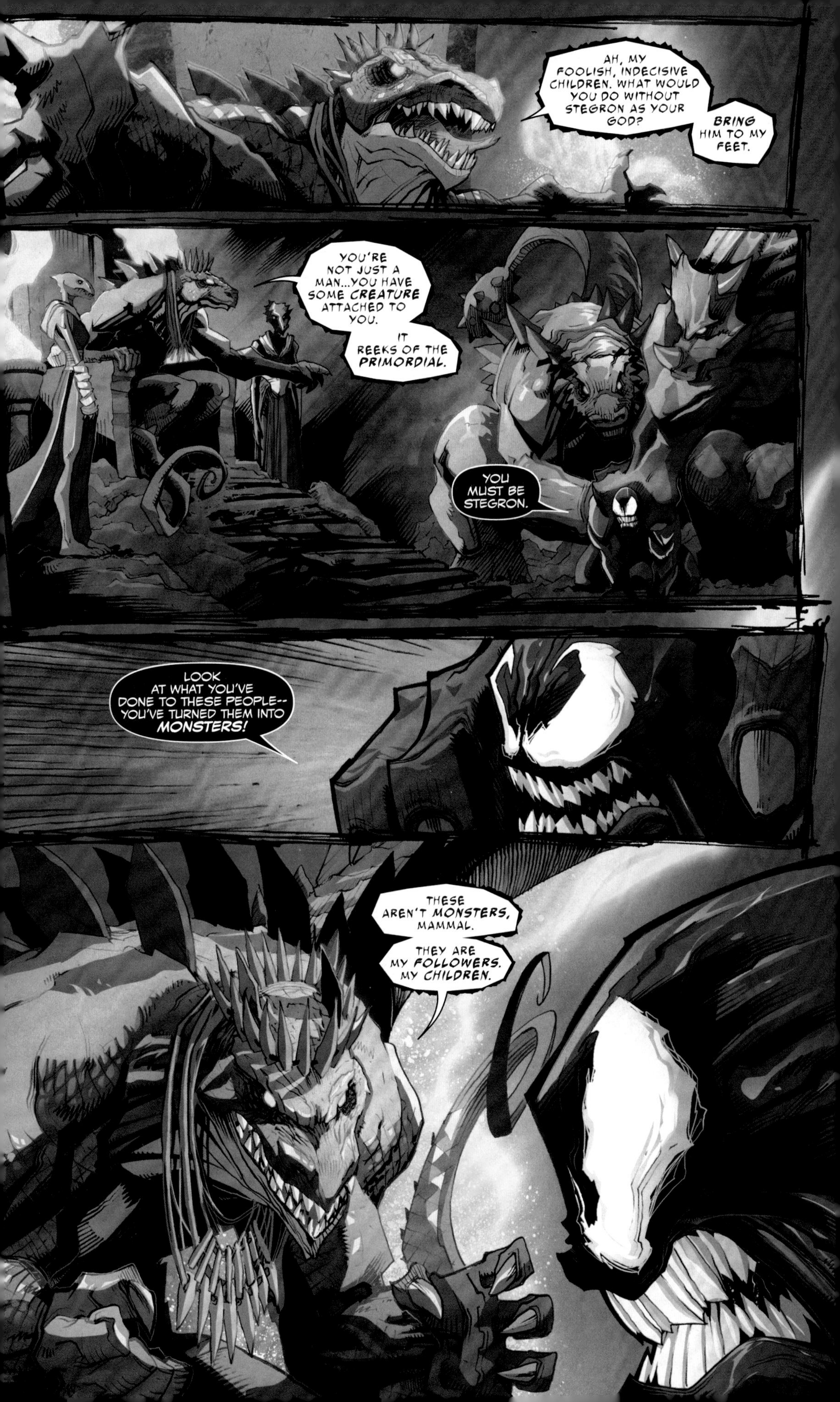
AH, MY FOOLISH, INDECISIVE CHILDREN. WHAT WOULD YOU DO WITHOUT STEGRON AS YOUR GOD?
BRING HIM TO MY FEET.
YOU'RE NOT JUST A MAN...YOU HAVE SOME CREATURE ATTACHED TO YOU.
IT REEKS OF THE PRIMORDIAL.
YOU MUST BE STEGRON.
LOOK AT WHAT YOU'VE DONE TO THESE PEOPLE--YOU'VE TURNED THEM INTO MONSTERS!
THESE AREN'T MONSTERS, MAMMAL.
THEY ARE MY FOLLOWERS. MY CHILDREN.

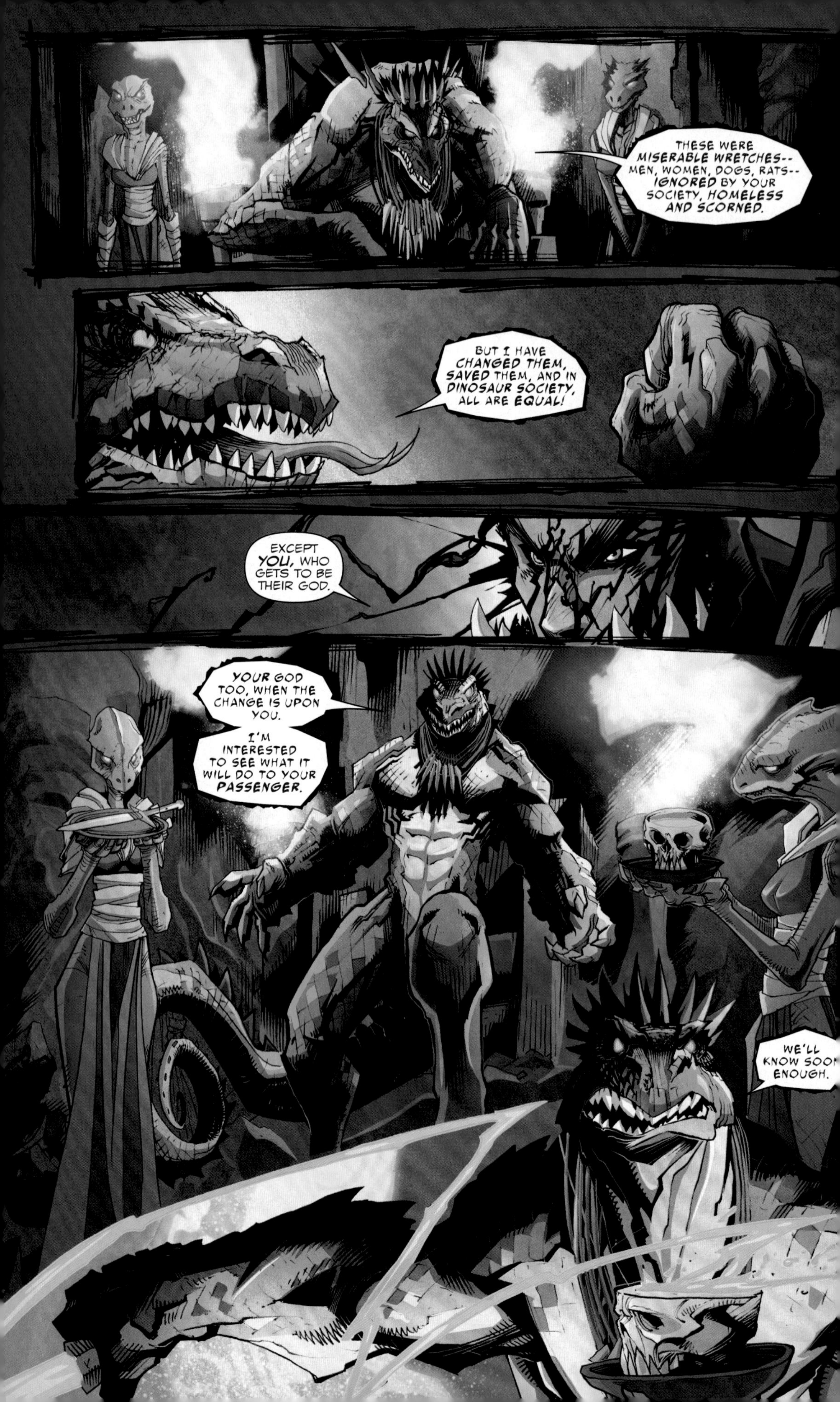
THESE WERE MISERABLE WRETCHES-- MEN, WOMEN, DOGS, RATS-- IGNORED BY YOUR SOCIETY, HOMELESS AND SCORNED.
BUT I HAVE CHANGED THEM, SAVED THEM, AND IN DINOSAUR SOCIETY, ALL ARE EQUAL!
EXCEPT YOU, WHO GETS TO BE THEIR GOD.
YOUR GOD TOO, WHEN THE CHANGE IS UPON YOU.
I'M INTERESTED TO SEE WHAT IT WILL DO TO YOUR PASSENGER.
WE'LL KNOW SOON ENOUGH.

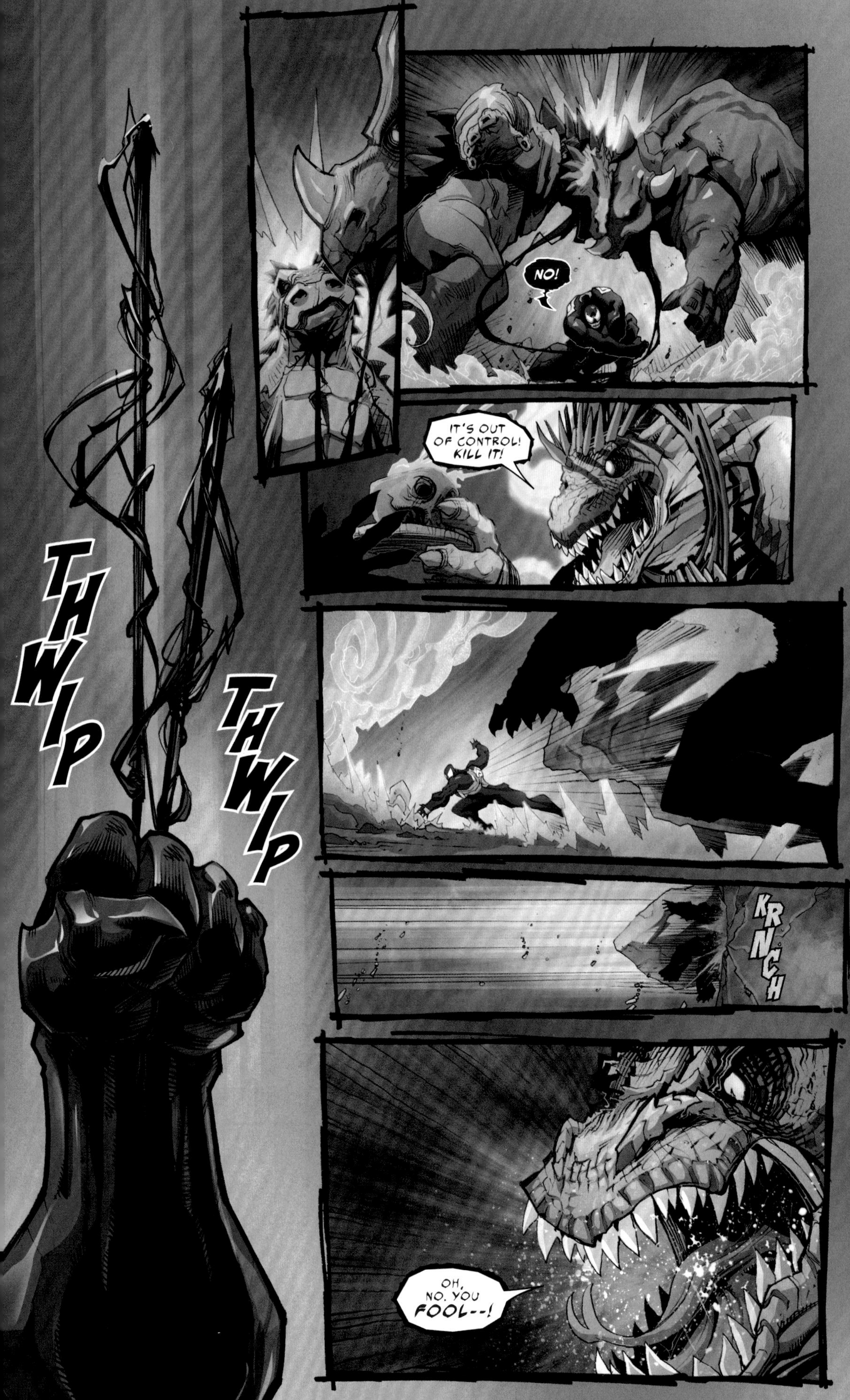
NO!
IT'S OUT OF CONTROL! KILL IT!
THWIP
THWIP
KRNCH
OH, NO. YOU FOOL--!

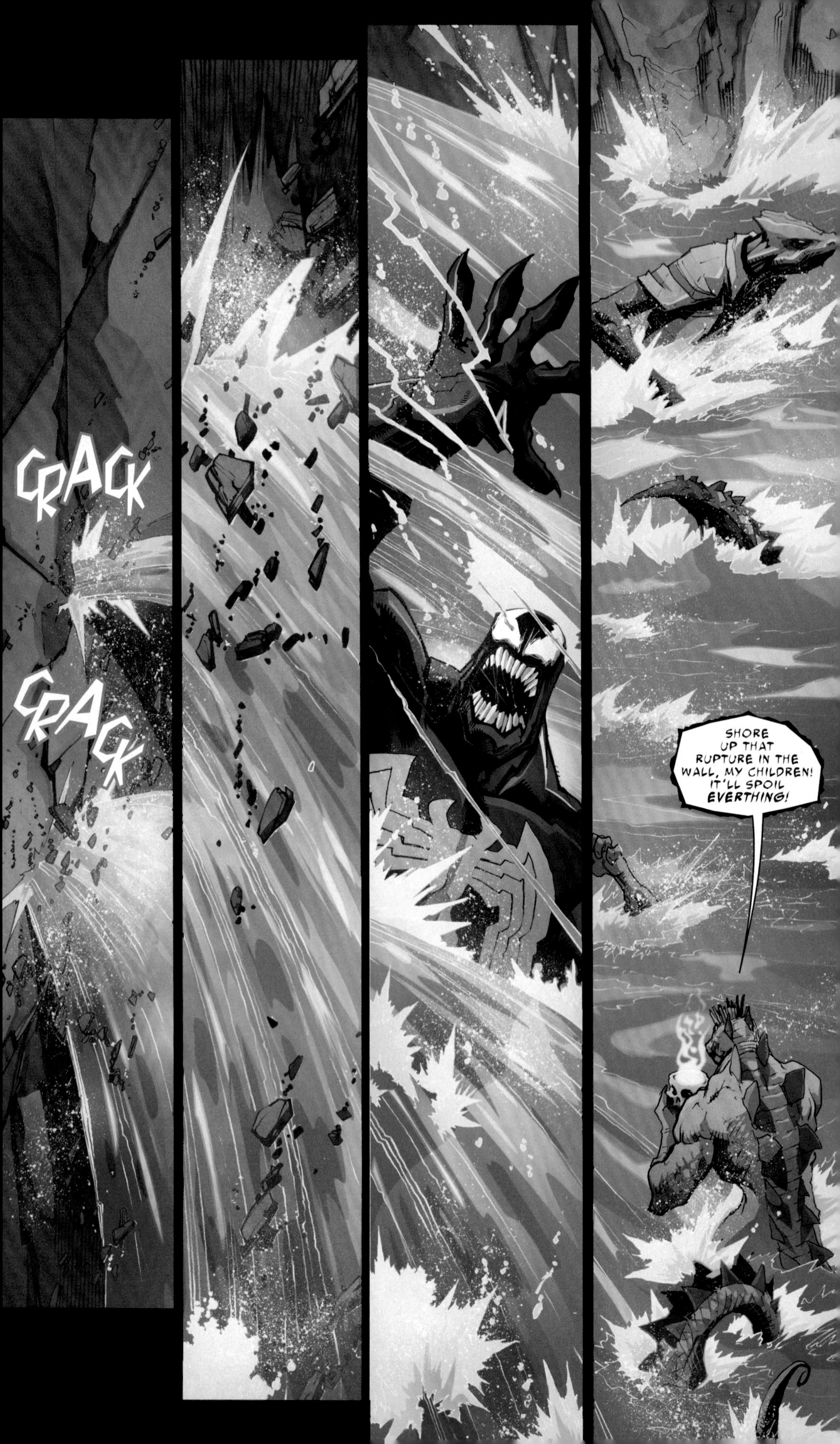
CRACK
CRACK
SHORE UP THAT RUPTURE IN THE WALL, MY CHILDREN! IT'LL SPOIL EVERTHING!

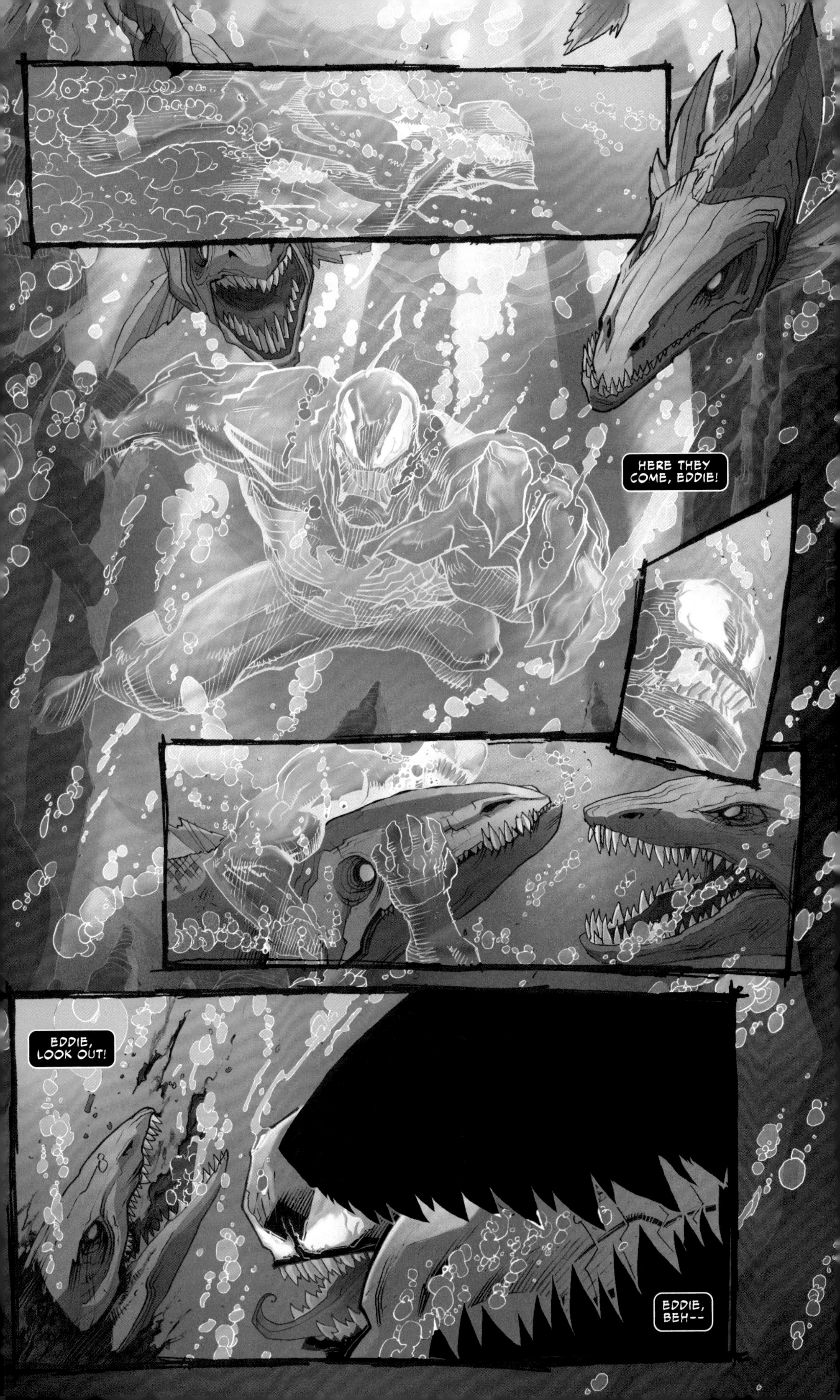
HERE THEY COME, EDDIE!
EDDIE, LOOK OUT!
EDDIE, BEH--

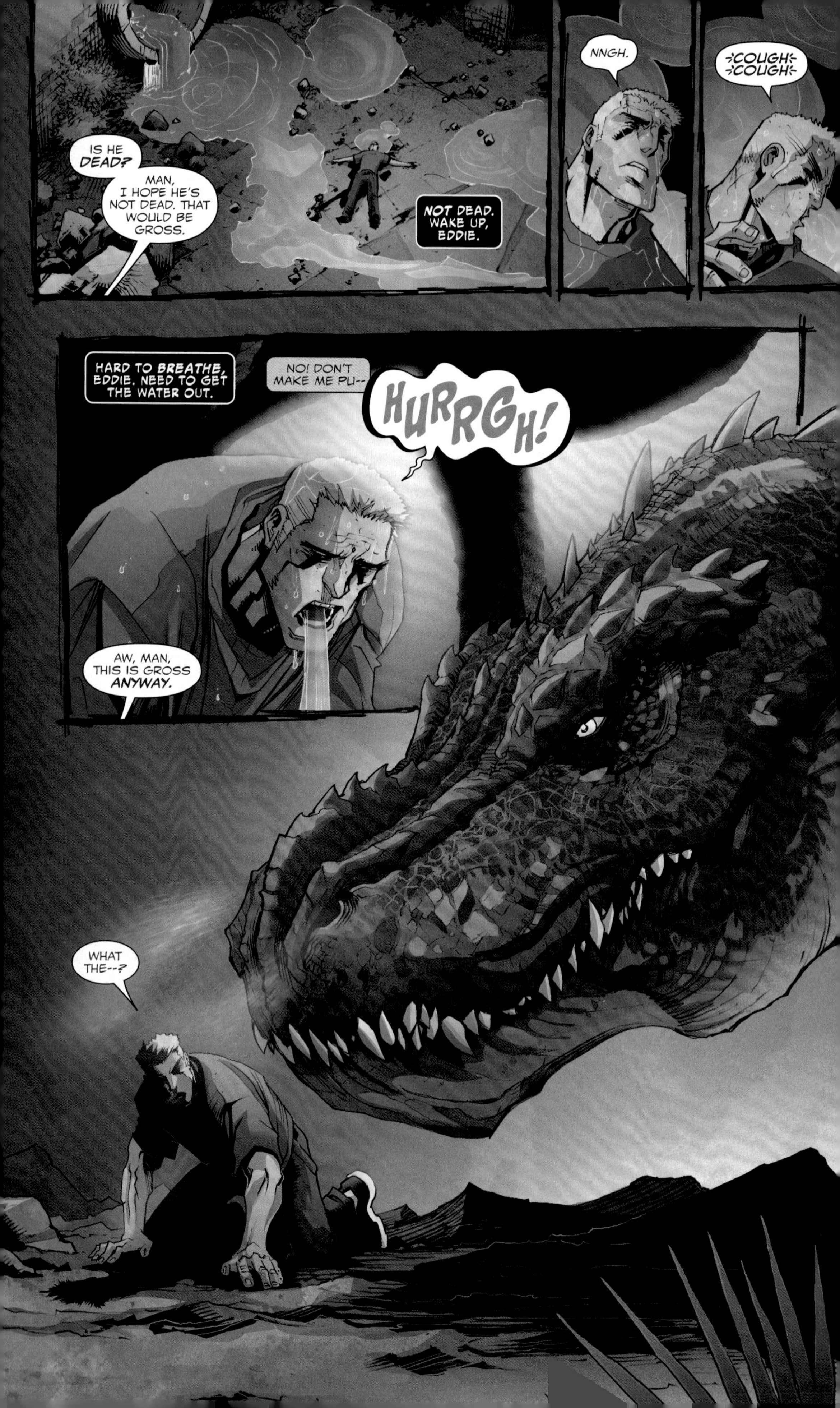
IS HE DEAD?
MAN, I HOPE HE'S NOT DEAD. THAT WOULD BE GROSS.
NOT DEAD. WAKE UP, EDDIE.
NNGH.
COUGH COUGH
HARD TO BREATHE, EDDIE. NEED TO GET THE WATER OUT.
NO! DON'T MAKE ME PU--
HURRGH!
AW, MAN, THIS IS GROSS ANYWAY.
WHAT THE--?

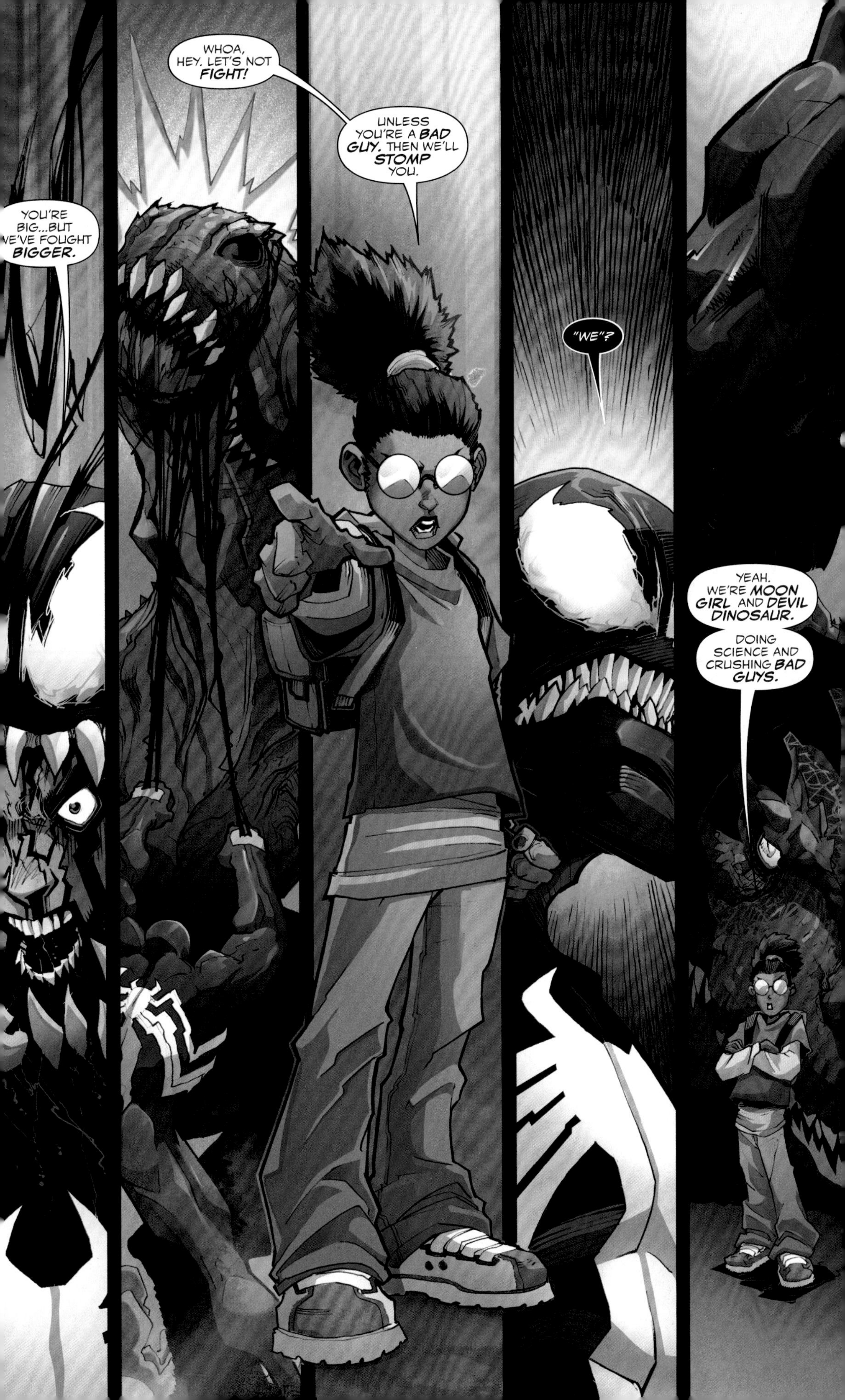
YOU'RE BIG...BUT WE'VE FOUGHT BIGGER.
WHOA, HEY. LET'S NOT FIGHT!
UNLESS YOU'RE A BAD GUY. THEN WE'LL STOMP YOU.
"WE"?
YEAH. WE'RE MOON GIRL AND DEVIL DINOSAUR.
DOING SCIENCE AND CRUSHING BAD GUYS.

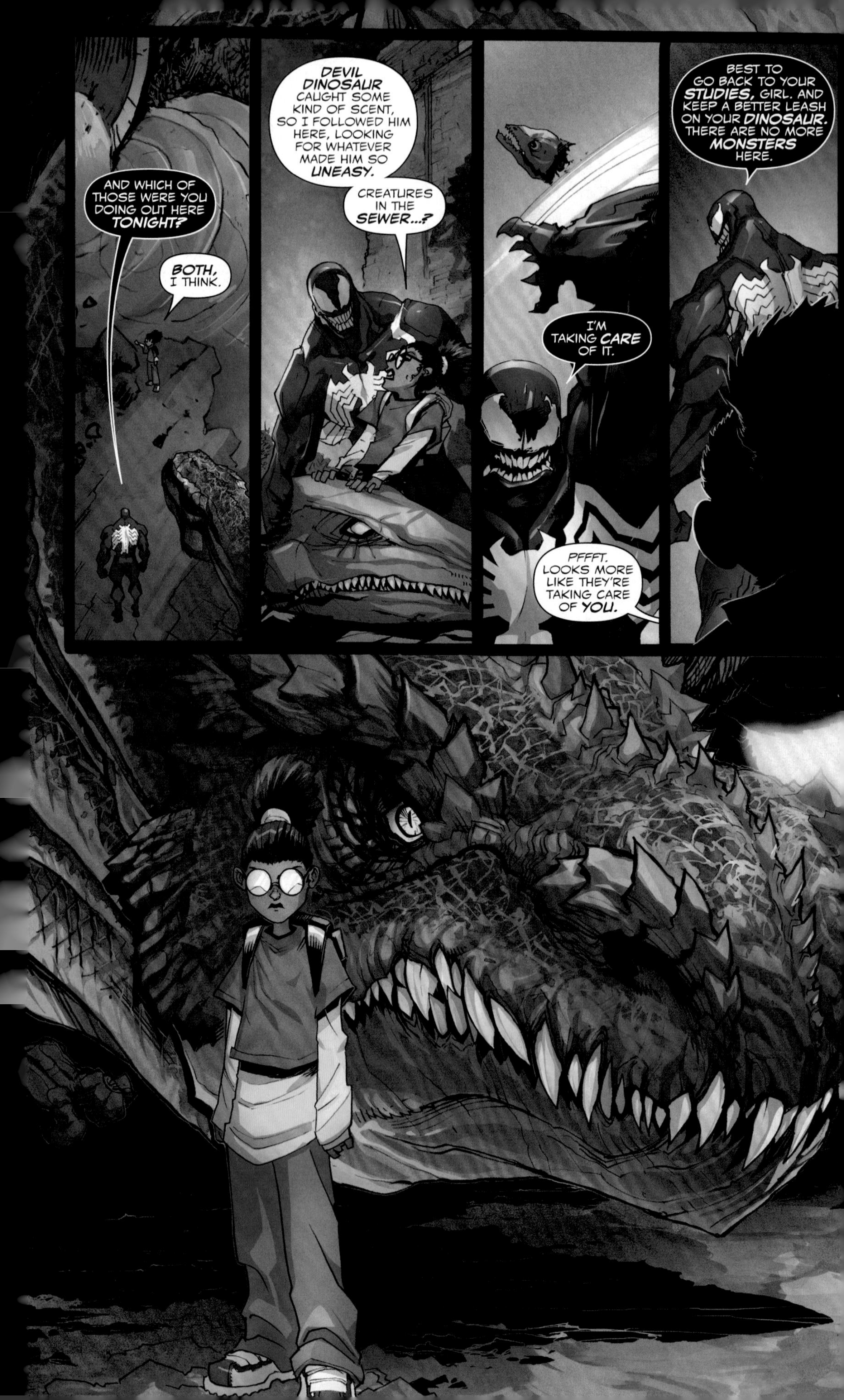
AND WHICH OF THOSE WERE YOU DOING OUT HERE TONIGHT?
BOTH, I THINK.
DEVIL DINOSAUR CAUGHT SOME KIND OF SCENT, SO I FOLLOWED HIM HERE, LOOKING FOR WHATEVER MADE HIM SO UNEASY.
CREATURES IN THE SEWER...?
I'M TAKING CARE OF IT.
PFFFT. LOOKS MORE LIKE THEY'RE TAKING CARE OF YOU.
BEST TO GO BACK TO YOUR STUDIES, GIRL. AND KEEP A BETTER LEASH ON YOUR DINOSAUR. THERE ARE NO MORE MONSTERS HERE.

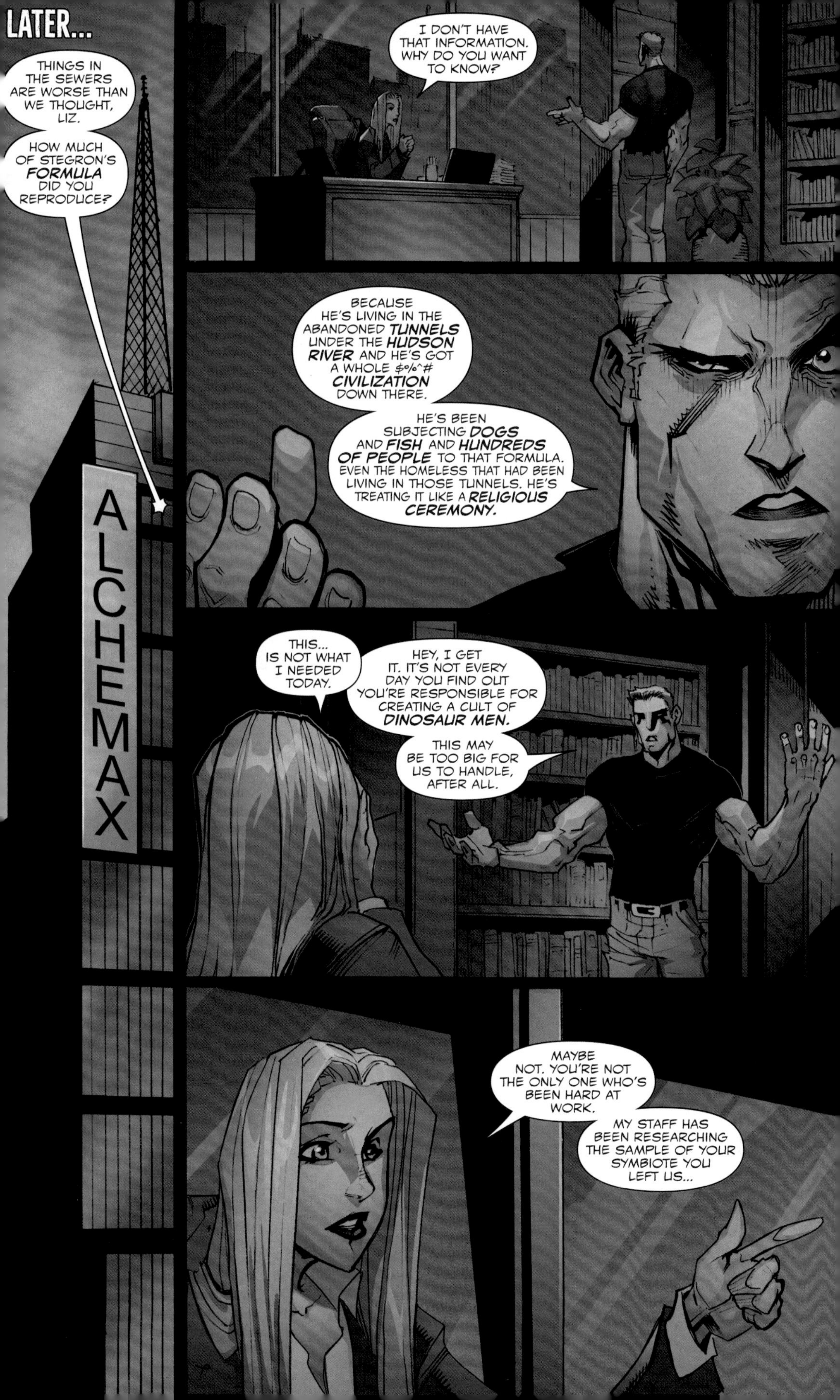
LATER...
THINGS IN THE SEWERS ARE WORSE THAN WE THOUGHT, LIZ.
HOW MUCH OF STEGRON'S FORMULA DID YOU REPRODUCE?
I DON'T HAVE THAT INFORMATION. WHY DO YOU WANT TO KNOW?
ALCHEMAX
BECAUSE HE'S LIVING IN THE ABANDONED TUNNELS UNDER THE HUDSON RIVER AND HE'S GOT A WHOLE $%^# CIVILIZATION DOWN THERE.
HE'S BEEN SUBJECTING DOGS AND FISH AND HUNDREDS OF PEOPLE TO THAT FORMULA. EVEN THE HOMELESS THAT HAD BEEN LIVING IN THOSE TUNNELS. HE'S TREATING IT LIKE A RELIGIOUS CEREMONY.
THIS... IS NOT WHAT I NEEDED TODAY.
HEY, I GET IT. IT'S NOT EVERY DAY YOU FIND OUT YOU'RE RESPONSIBLE FOR CREATING A CULT OF DINOSAUR MEN.
THIS MAY BE TOO BIG FOR US TO HANDLE, AFTER ALL.
MAYBE NOT. YOU'RE NOT THE ONLY ONE WHO'S BEEN HARD AT WORK.
MY STAFF HAS BEEN RESEARCHING THE SAMPLE OF YOUR SYMBIOTE YOU LEFT US...

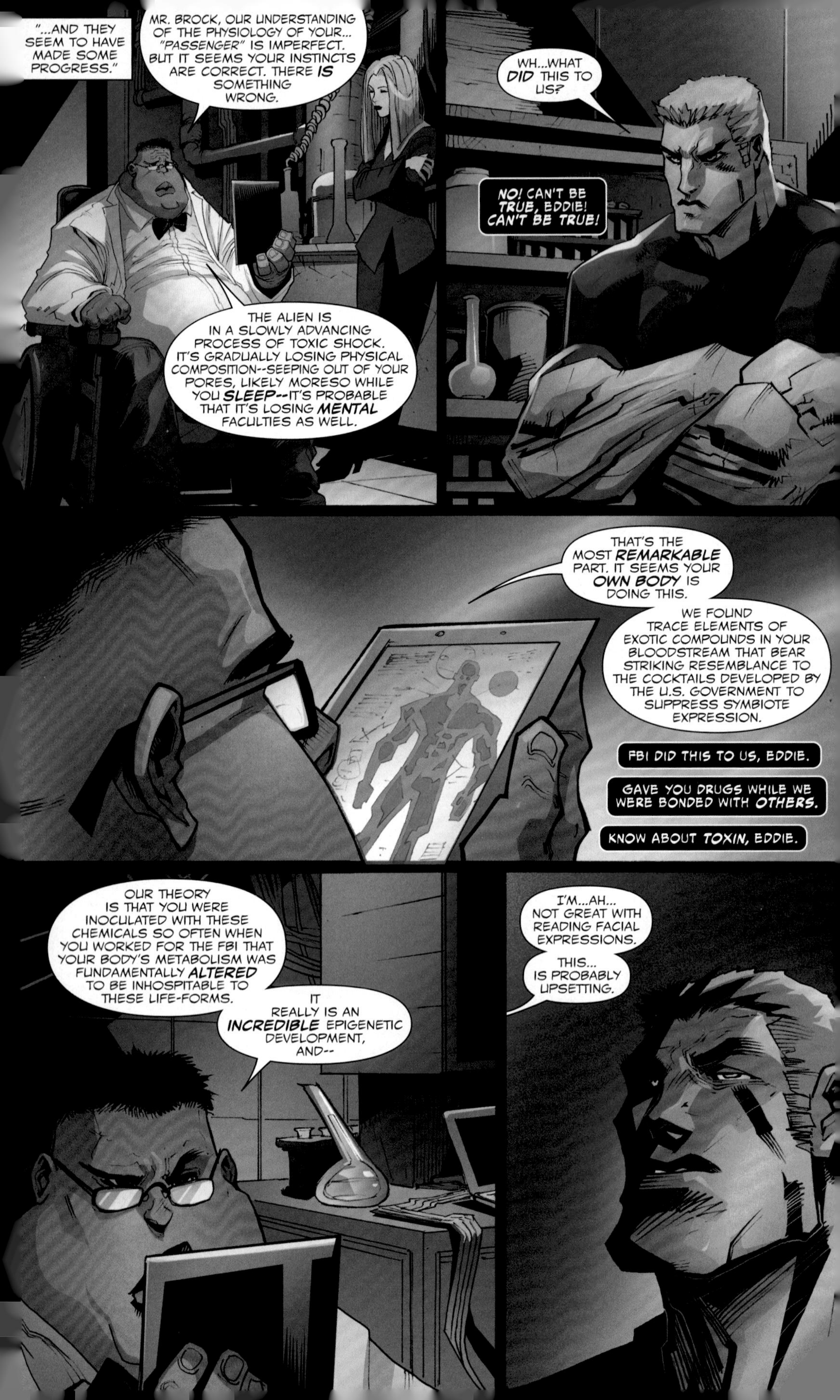
"...AND THEY SEEM TO HAVE MADE SOME PROGRESS."
MR. BROCK, OUR UNDERSTANDING OF THE PHYSIOLOGY OF YOUR... "PASSENGER" IS IMPERFECT. BUT IT SEEMS YOUR INSTINCTS ARE CORRECT. THERE IS SOMETHING WRONG.
THE ALIEN IS IN A SLOWLY ADVANCING PROCESS OF TOXIC SHOCK. IT'S GRADUALLY LOSING PHYSICAL COMPOSITION--SEEPING OUT OF YOUR PORES, LIKELY MORESO WHILE YOU SLEEP--IT'S PROBABLE THAT IT'S LOSING MENTAL FACULTIES AS WELL.
WH...WHAT DID THIS TO US?
NO! CAN'T BE TRUE, EDDIE! CAN'T BE TRUE!
THAT'S THE MOST REMARKABLE PART. IT SEEMS YOUR OWN BODY IS DOING THIS.
WE FOUND TRACE ELEMENTS OF EXOTIC COMPOUNDS IN YOUR BLOODSTREAM THAT BEAR STRIKING RESEMBLANCE TO THE COCKTAILS DEVELOPED BY THE U.S. GOVERNMENT TO SUPPRESS SYMBIOTE EXPRESSION.
FBI DID THIS TO US, EDDIE.
GAVE YOU DRUGS WHILE WE WERE BONDED WITH OTHERS.
KNOW ABOUT TOXIN, EDDIE.
OUR THEORY IS THAT YOU WERE INOCULATED WITH THESE CHEMICALS SO OFTEN WHEN YOU WORKED FOR THE FBI THAT YOUR BODY'S METABOLISM WAS FUNDAMENTALLY ALTERED TO BE INHOSPITABLE TO THESE LIFE-FORMS.
IT REALLY IS AN INCREDIBLE EPIGENETIC DEVELOPMENT, AND--
I'M...AH... NOT GREAT WITH READING FACIAL EXPRESSIONS.
THIS... IS PROBABLY UPSETTING.

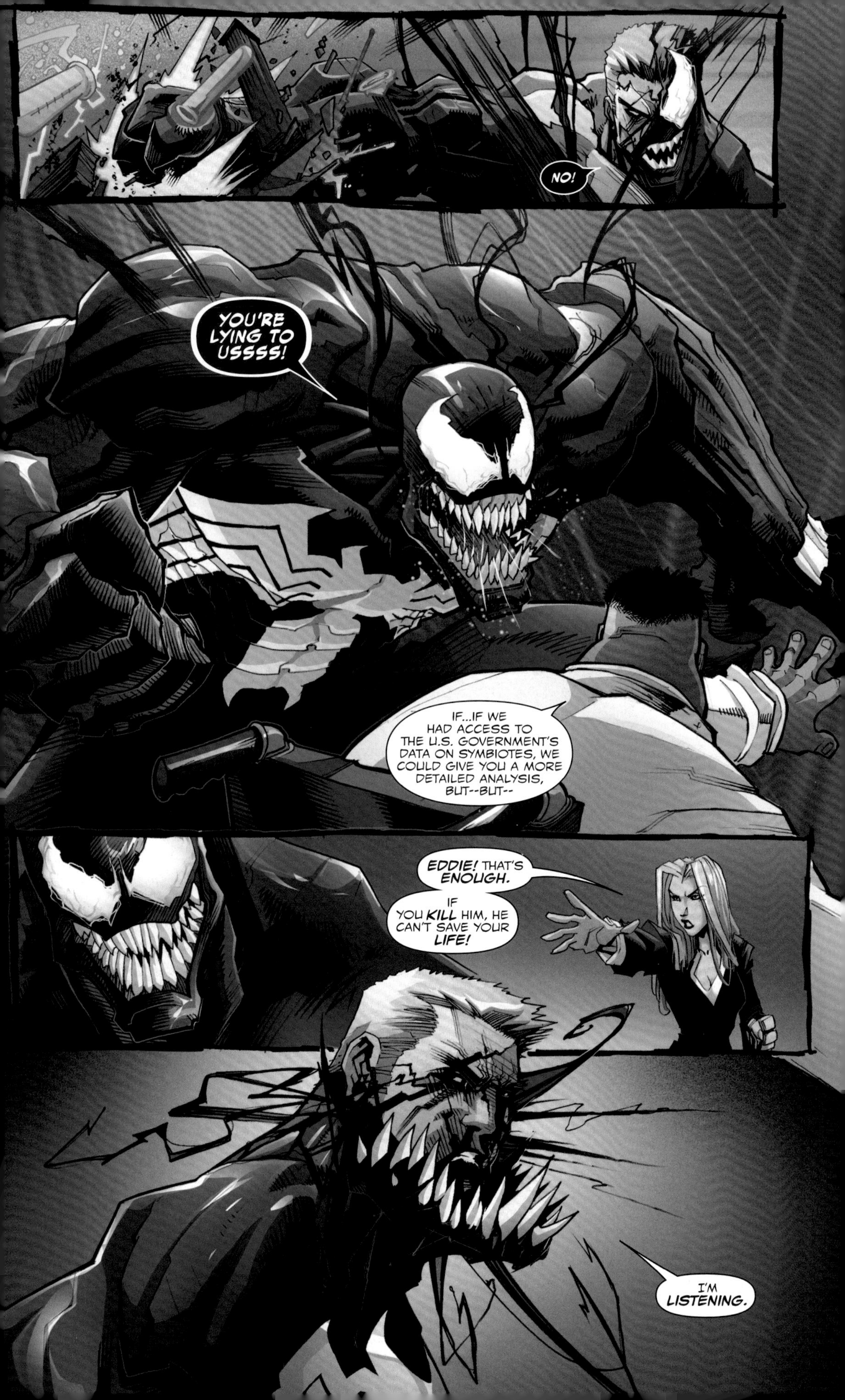
NO!
YOU'RE LYING TO USSSS!
IF...IF WE HAD ACCESS TO THE U.S. GOVERNMENT'S DATA ON SYMBIOTES, WE COULD GIVE YOU A MORE DETAILED ANALYSIS, BUT--BUT--
EDDIE! THAT'S ENOUGH.
IF YOU KILL HIM, HE CAN'T SAVE YOUR LIFE!
I'M LISTENING.

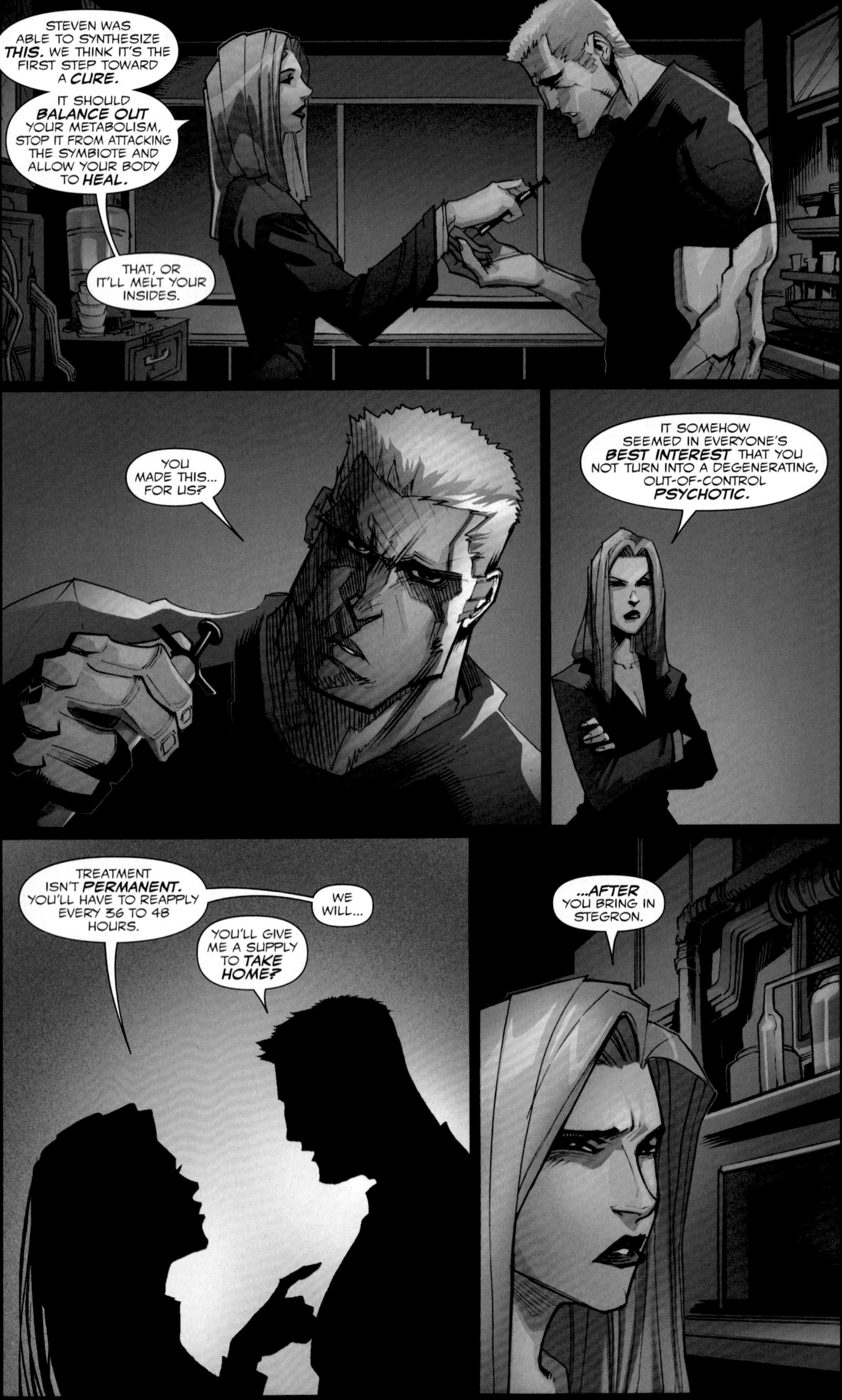
STEVEN WAS ABLE TO SYNTHESIZE THIS. WE THINK IT'S THE FIRST STEP TOWARD A CURE.
IT SHOULD BALANCE OUT YOUR METABOLISM, STOP IT FROM ATTACKING THE SYMBIOTE AND ALLOW YOUR BODY TO HEAL.
THAT, OR IT'LL MELT YOUR INSIDES.
YOU MADE THIS... FOR US?
IT SOMEHOW SEEMED IN EVERYONE'S BEST INTEREST THAT YOU NOT TURN INTO A DEGENERATING, OUT-OF-CONTROL PSYCHOTIC.
TREATMENT ISN'T PERMANENT. YOU'LL HAVE TO REAPPLY EVERY 36 TO 48 HOURS.
YOU'LL GIVE ME A SUPPLY TO TAKE HOME?
WE WILL...
...AFTER YOU BRING IN STEGRON.

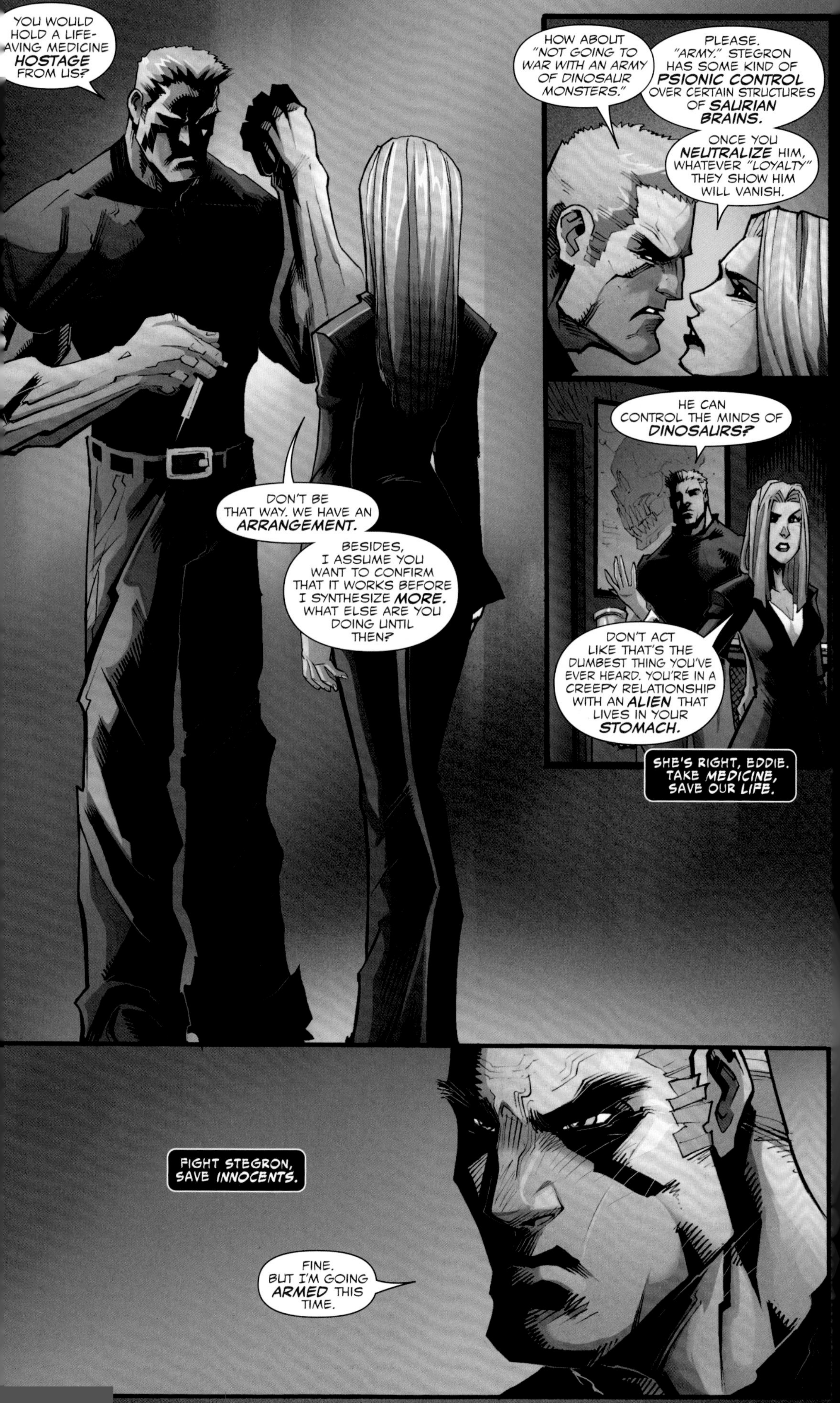
YOU WOULD HOLD A LIFE-SAVING MEDICINE HOSTAGE FROM US?
DON'T BE THAT WAY. WE HAVE AN ARRANGEMENT.
BESIDES, I ASSUME YOU WANT TO CONFIRM THAT IT WORKS BEFORE I SYNTHESIZE MORE. WHAT ELSE ARE YOU DOING UNTIL THEN?
HOW ABOUT "NOT GOING TO WAR WITH AN ARMY OF DINOSAUR MONSTERS."
PLEASE. "ARMY." STEGRON HAS SOME KIND OF PSIONIC CONTROL OVER CERTAIN STRUCTURES OF SAURIAN BRAINS.
ONCE YOU NEUTRALIZE HIM, WHATEVER "LOYALTY" THEY SHOW HIM WILL VANISH.
HE CAN CONTROL THE MINDS OF DINOSAURS?
DON'T ACT LIKE THAT'S THE DUMBEST THING YOU'VE EVER HEARD. YOU'RE IN A CREEPY RELATIONSHIP WITH AN ALIEN THAT LIVES IN YOUR STOMACH.
SHE'S RIGHT, EDDIE. TAKE MEDICINE, SAVE OUR LIFE.
FIGHT STEGRON, SAVE INNOCENTS.
FINE. BUT I'M GOING ARMED THIS TIME.

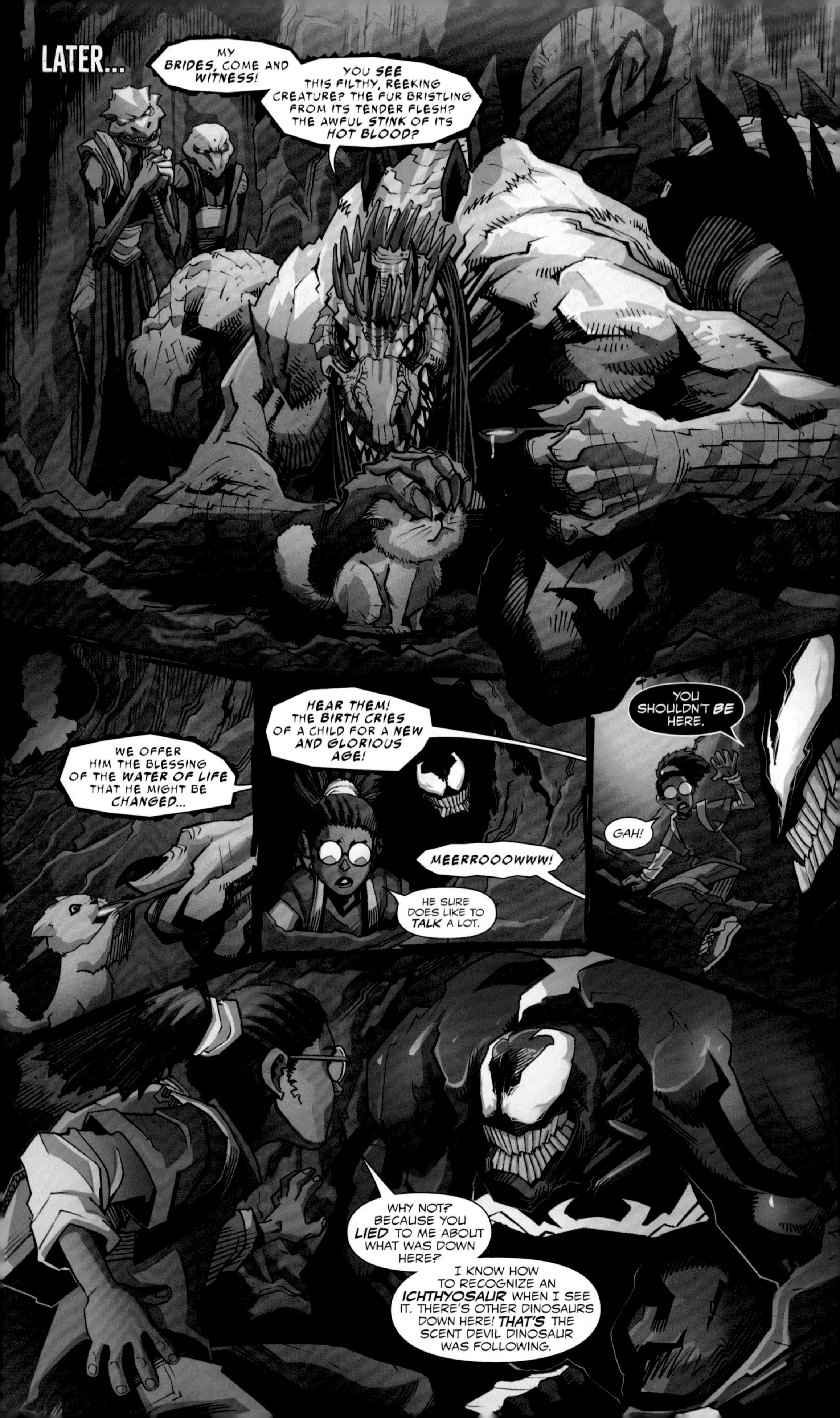
LATER...
MY BRIDES, COME AND WITNESS!
YOU SEE THIS FILTHY, REEKING CREATURE? THE FUR BRISTLING FROM ITS TENDER FLESH? THE AWFUL STINK OF ITS HOT BLOOD?
WE OFFER HIM THE BLESSING OF THE WATER OF LIFE THAT HE MIGHT BE CHANGED...
HEAR THEM! THE BIRTH CRIES OF A CHILD FOR A NEW AND GLORIOUS AGE!
MEERROOOWWW!
HE SURE DOES LIKE TO TALK A LOT.
YOU SHOULDN'T BE HERE.
GAH!
WHY NOT? BECAUSE YOU LIED TO ME ABOUT WHAT WAS DOWN HERE?
I KNOW HOW TO RECOGNIZE AN ICHTHYOSAUR WHEN I SEE IT. THERE'S OTHER DINOSAURS DOWN HERE! THAT'S THE SCENT DEVIL DINOSAUR WAS FOLLOWING.

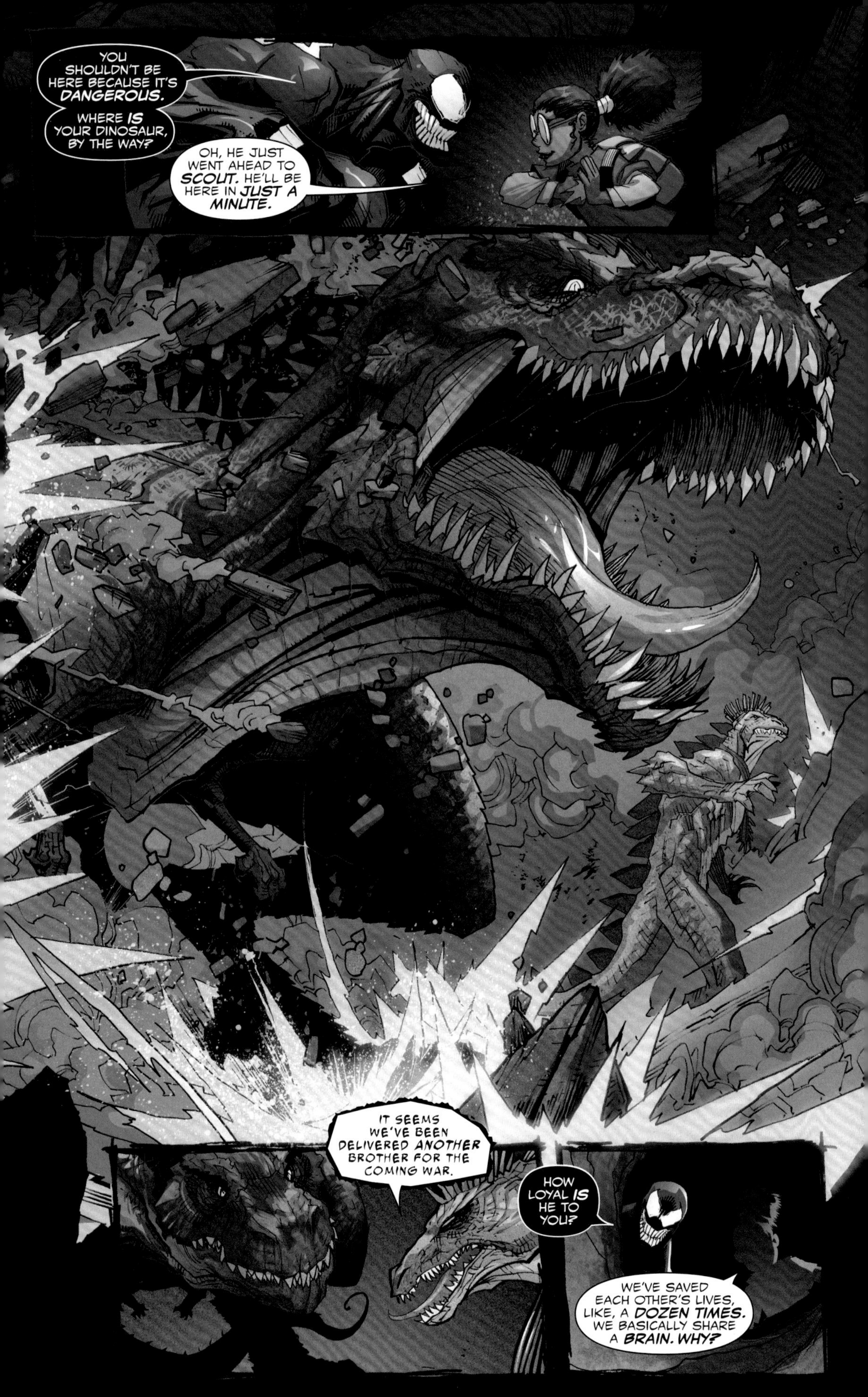
YOU SHOULDN'T BE HERE BECAUSE IT'S DANGEROUS.
WHERE IS YOUR DINOSAUR, BY THE WAY?
OH, HE JUST WENT AHEAD TO SCOUT. HE'LL BE HERE IN JUST A MINUTE.
IT SEEMS WE'VE BEEN DELIVERED ANOTHER BROTHER FOR THE COMING WAR.
HOW LOYAL IS HE TO YOU?
WE'VE SAVED EACH OTHER'S LIVES, LIKE, A DOZEN TIMES. WE BASICALLY SHARE A BRAIN. WHY?

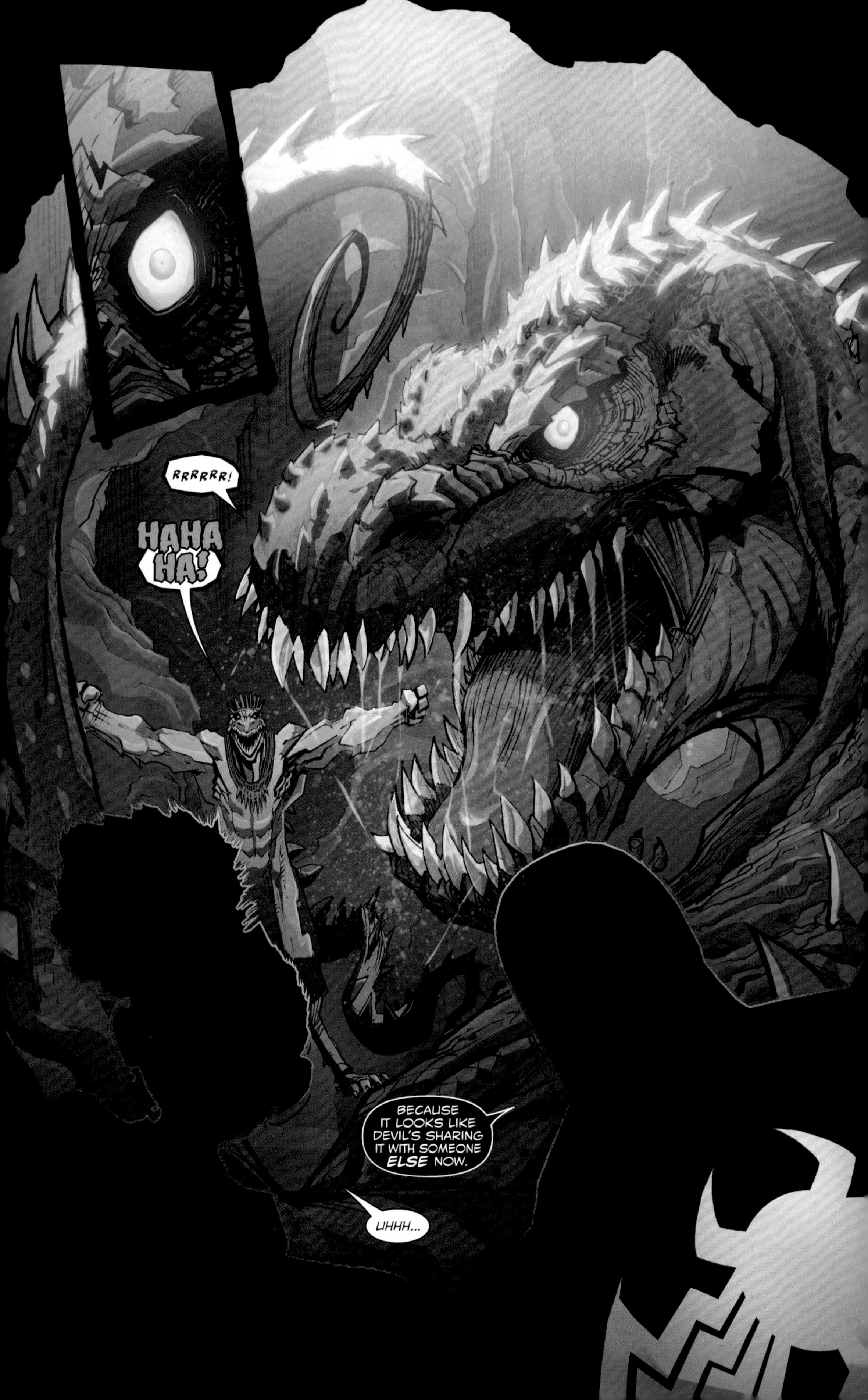
RRRRRR!
HAHA HA!
BECAUSE IT LOOKS LIKE DEVIL'S SHARING IT WITH SOMEONE ELSE NOW.
UHHH...

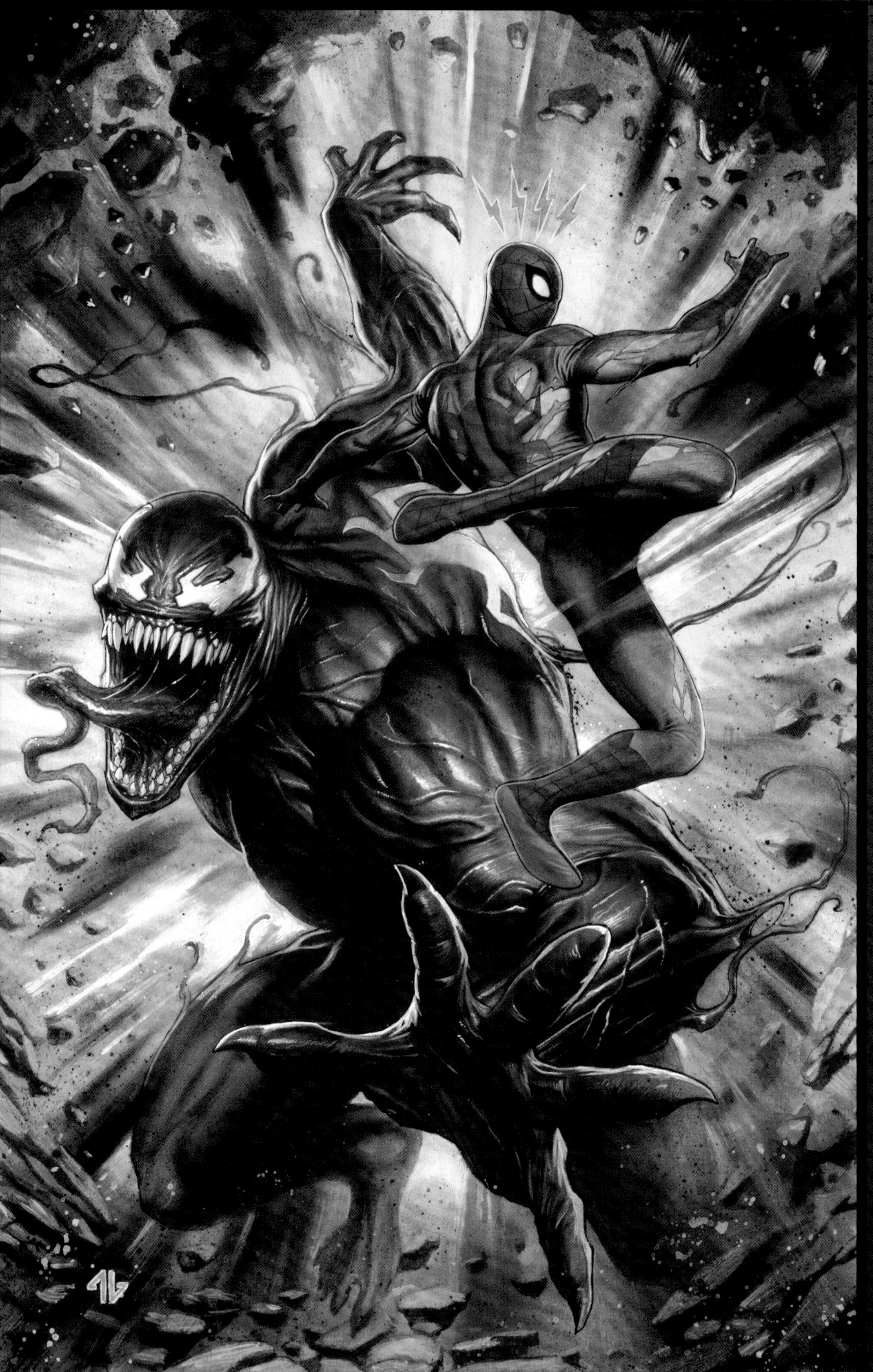

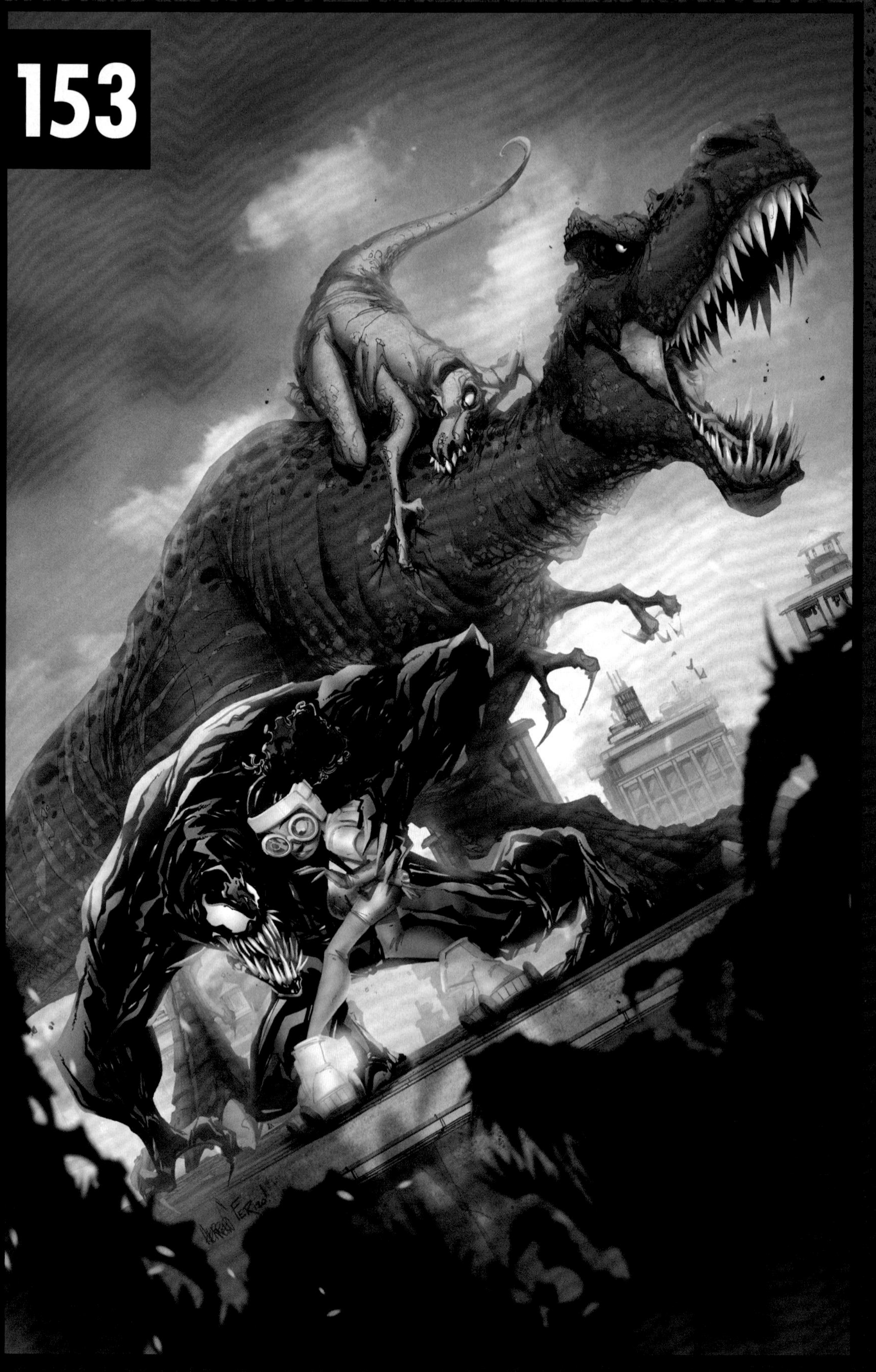
153

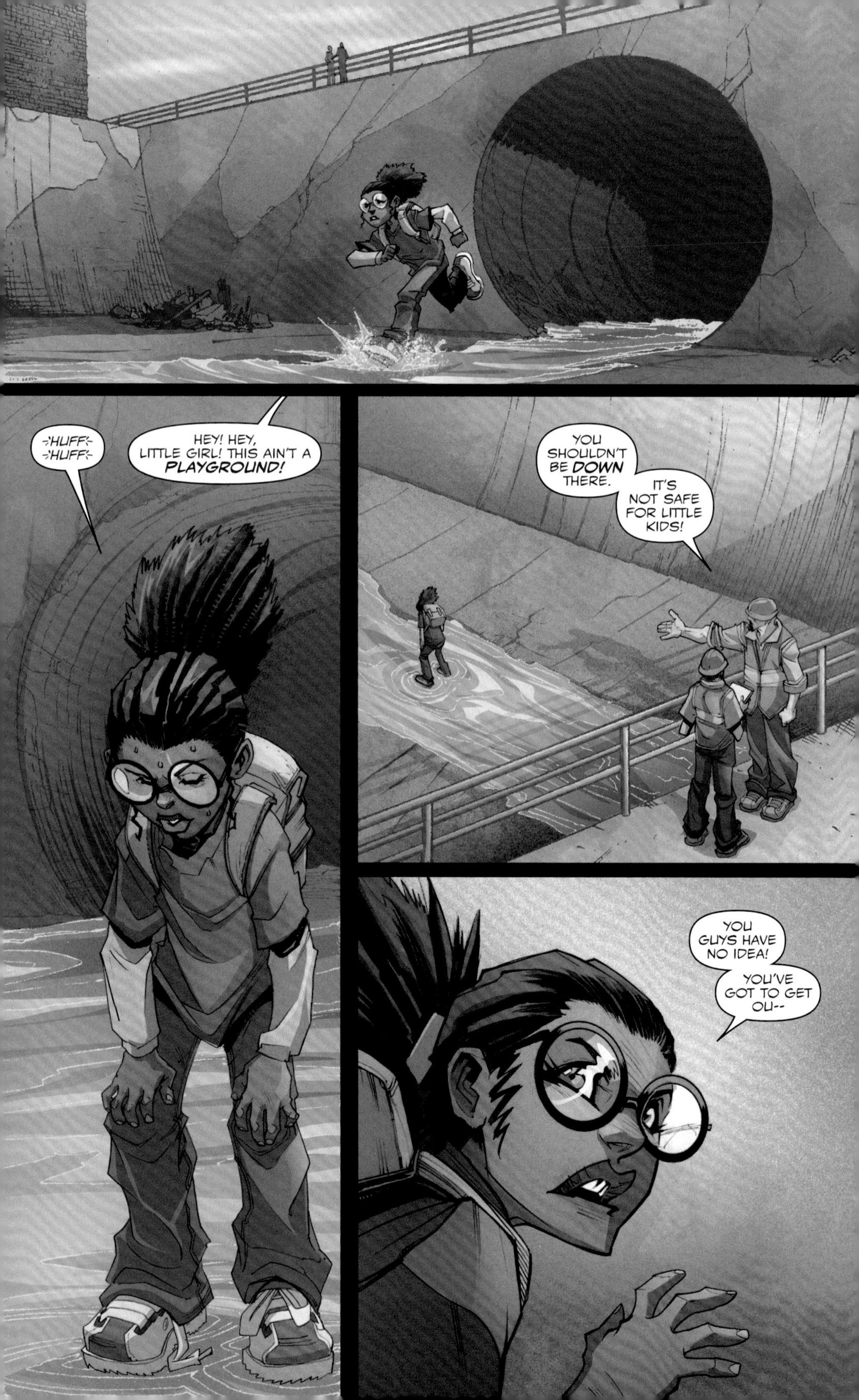

-HUFF- -HUFF-
HEY! HEY, LITTLE GIRL! THIS AIN'T A PLAYGROUND!
YOU SHOULDN'T BE DOWN THERE.
IT'S NOT SAFE FOR LITTLE KIDS!
YOU GUYS HAVE NO IDEA!
YOU'VE GOT TO GET OU--

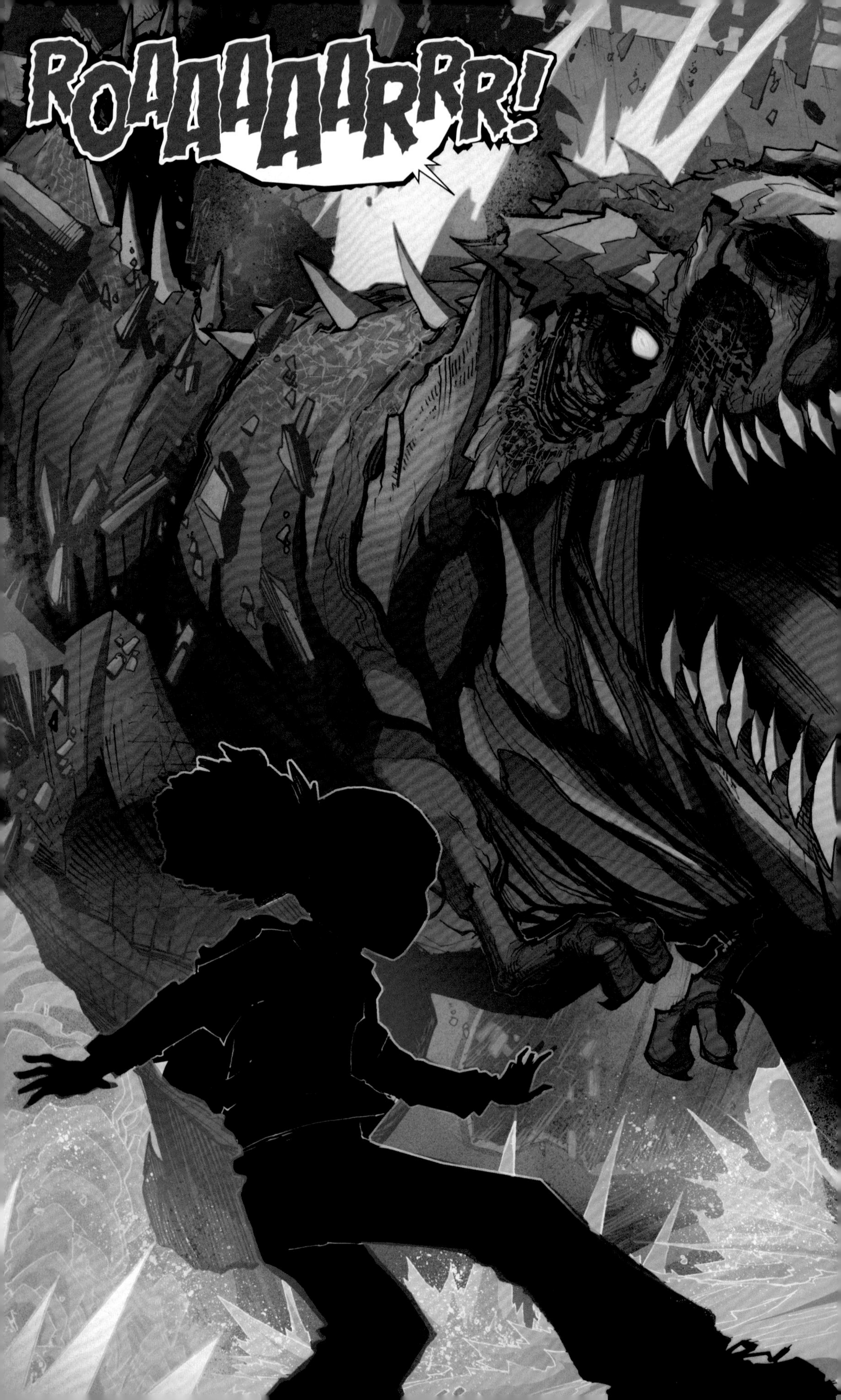
ROAAAAARRR!

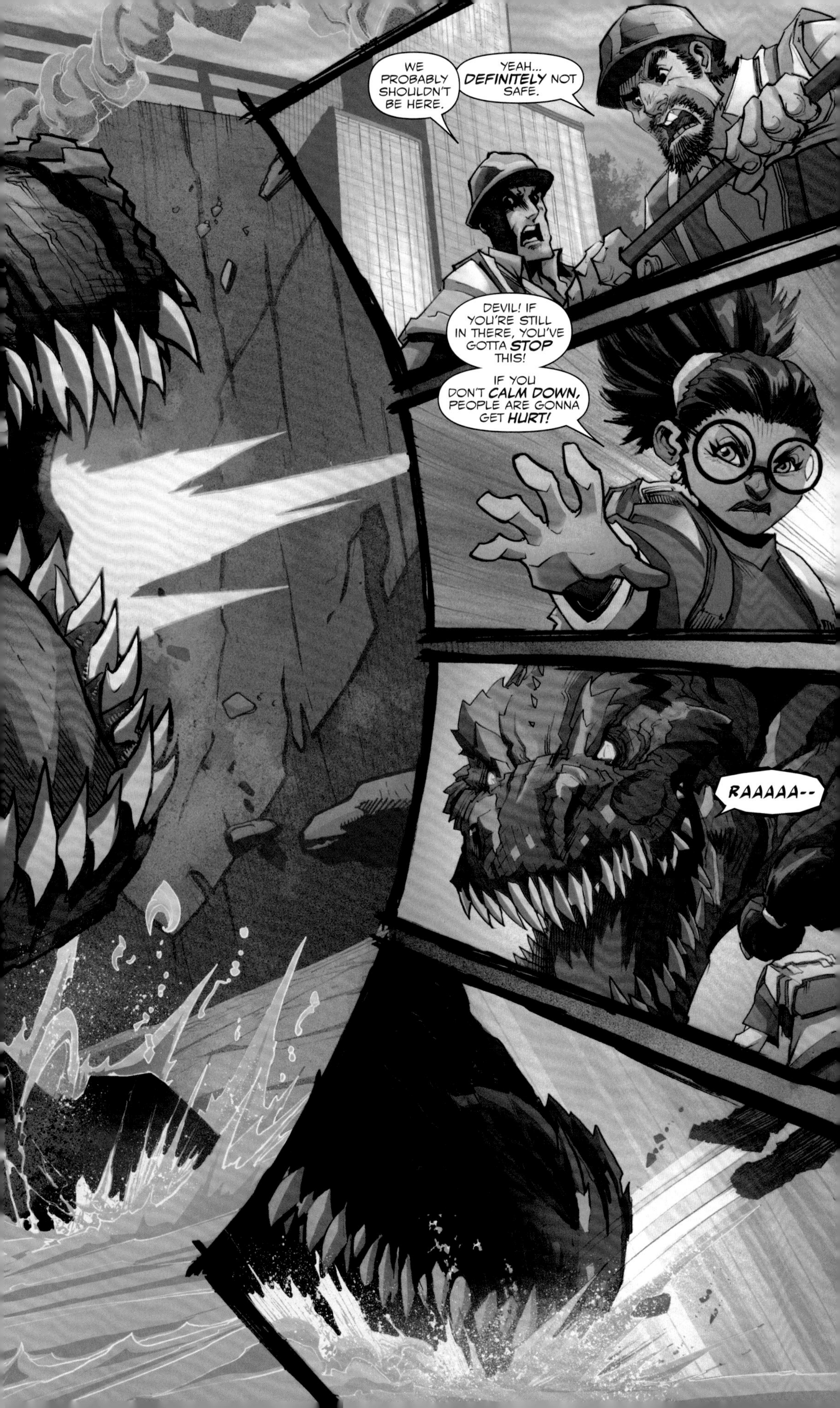
WE PROBABLY SHOULDN'T BE HERE.
YEAH... DEFINITELY NOT SAFE.
DEVIL! IF YOU'RE STILL IN THERE, YOU'VE GOTTA STOP THIS!
IF YOU DON'T CALM DOWN, PEOPLE ARE GONNA GET HURT!
RAAAAA--

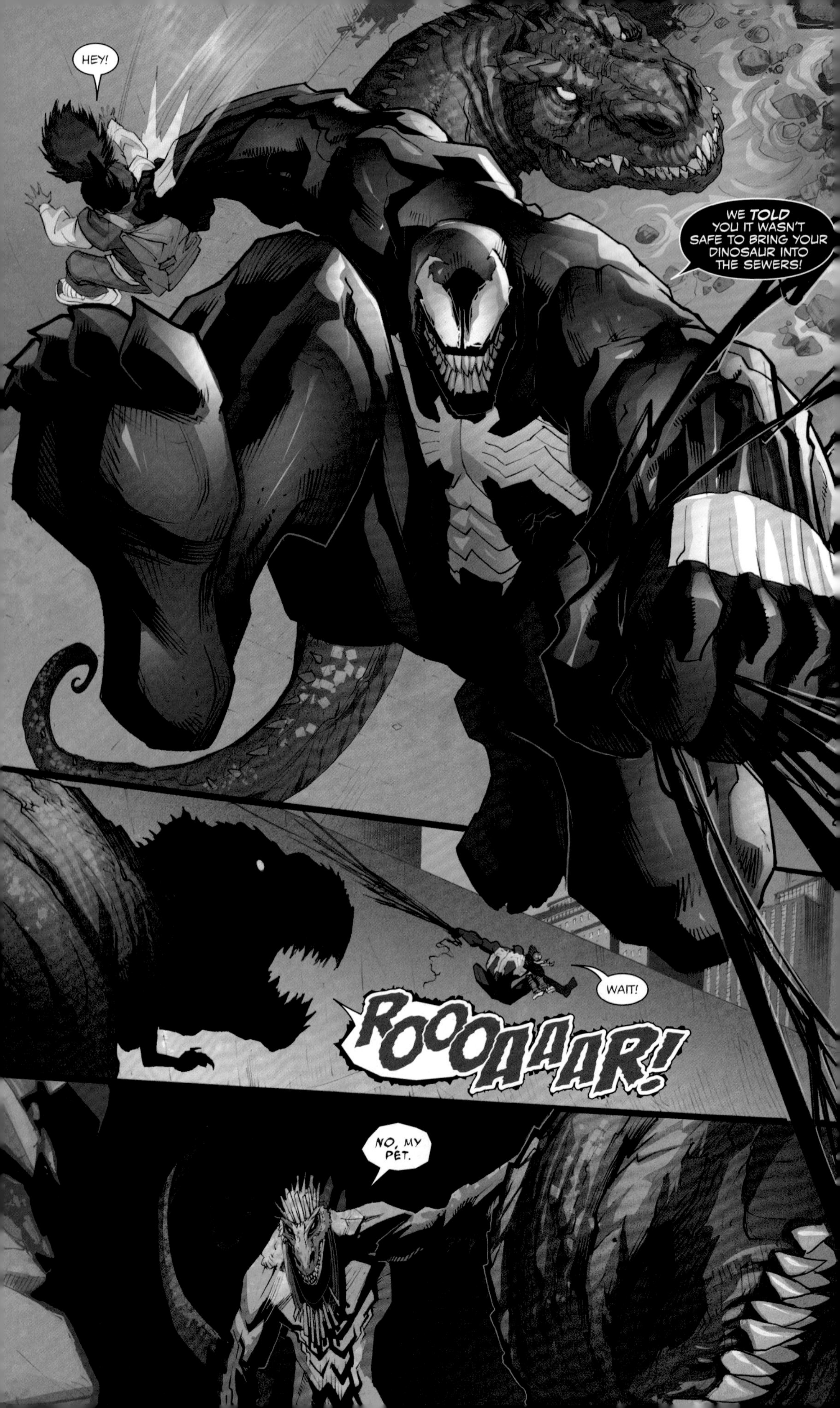
HEY!
WE TOLD YOU IT WASN'T SAFE TO BRING YOUR DINOSAUR INTO THE SEWERS!
WAIT!
ROOOAAAR!
NO, MY PET.

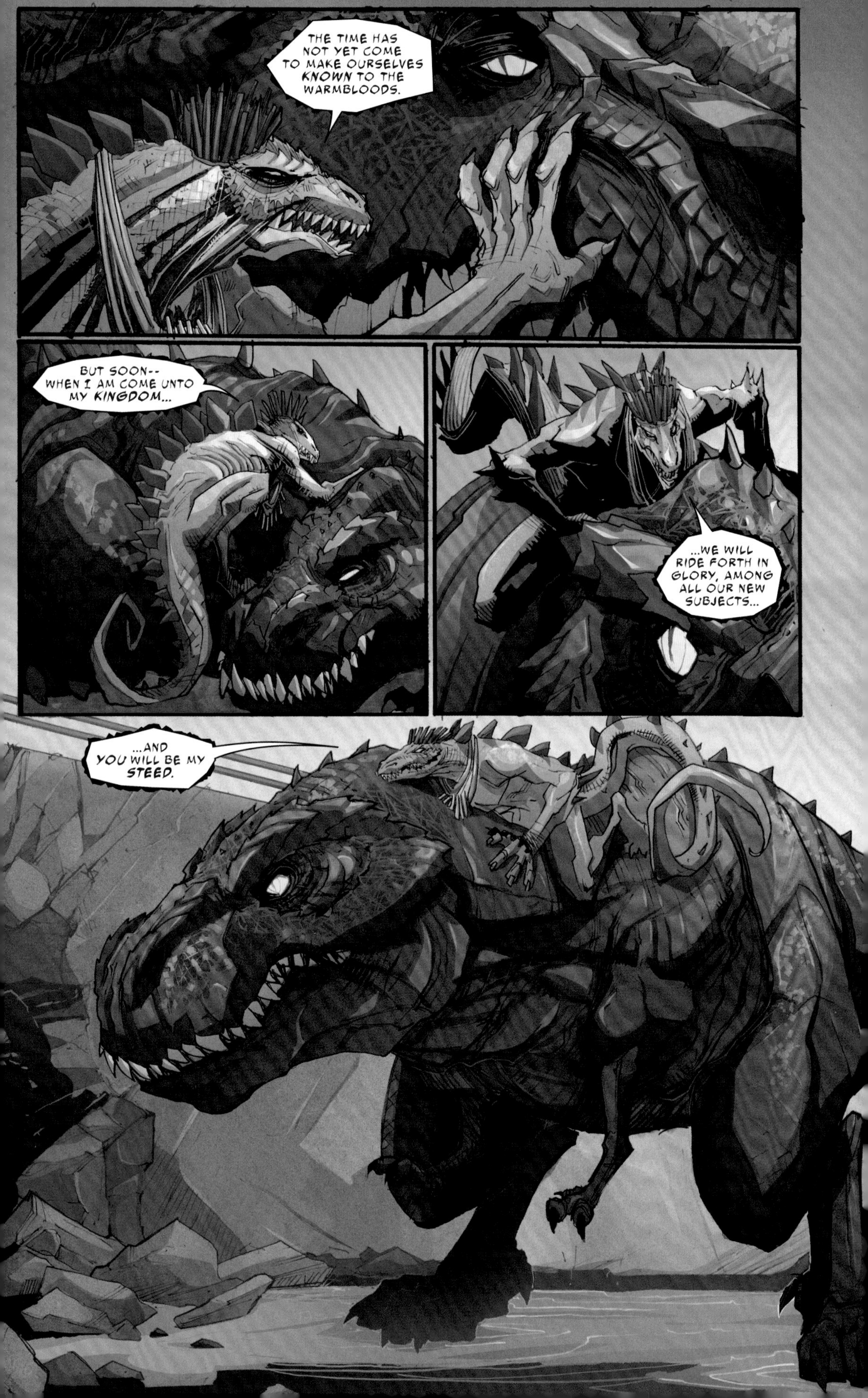
THE TIME HAS NOT YET COME TO MAKE OURSELVES KNOWN TO THE WARMBLOODS.
BUT SOON-- WHEN I AM COME UNTO MY KINGDOM...
...WE WILL RIDE FORTH IN GLORY, AMONG ALL OUR NEW SUBJECTS...
...AND YOU WILL BE MY STEED.

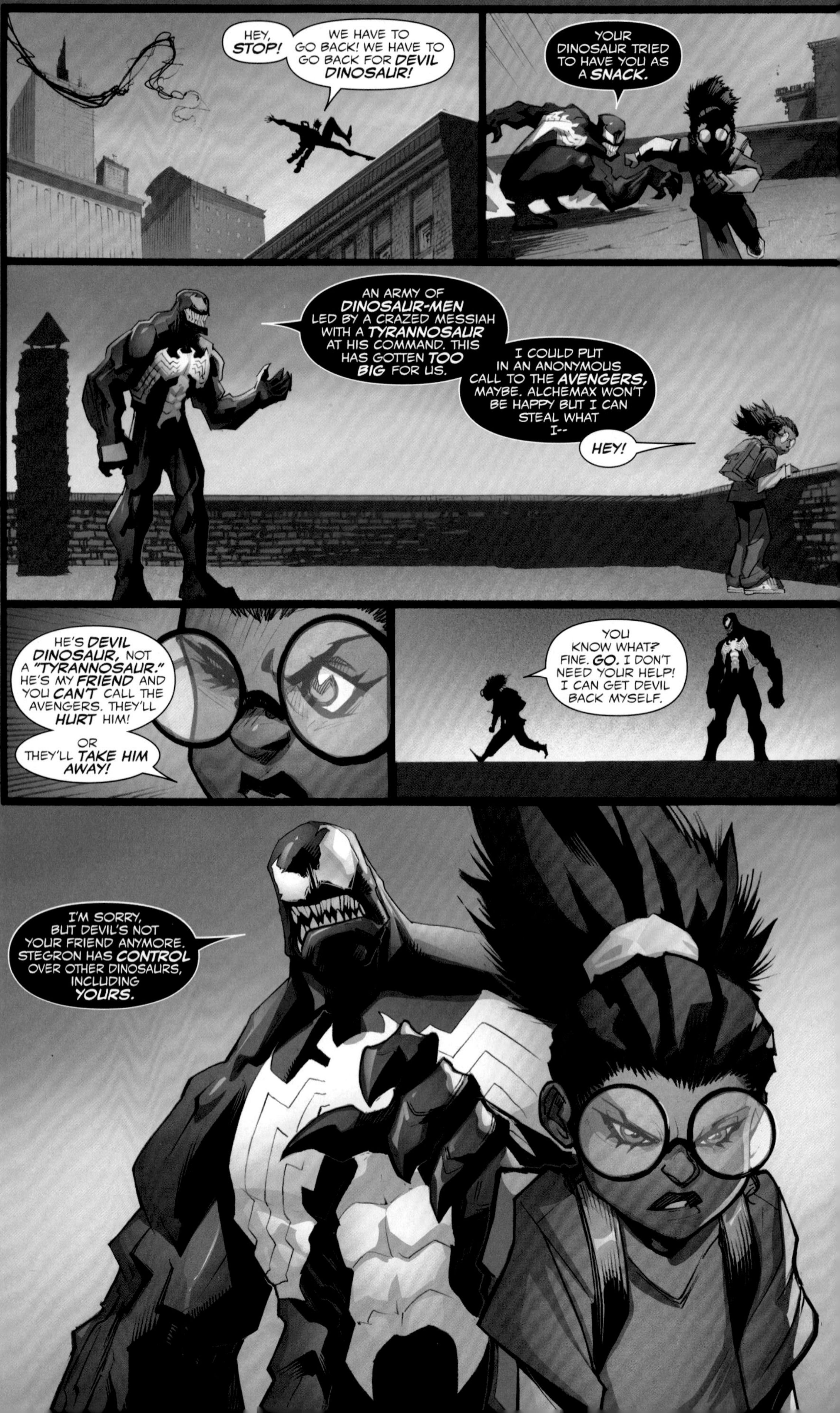
HEY, STOP!
WE HAVE TO GO BACK! WE HAVE TO GO BACK FOR DEVIL DINOSAUR!
YOUR DINOSAUR TRIED TO HAVE YOU AS A SNACK.
AN ARMY OF DINOSAUR-MEN LED BY A CRAZED MESSIAH WITH A TYRANNOSAUR AT HIS COMMAND. THIS HAS GOTTEN TOO BIG FOR US.
I COULD PUT IN AN ANONYMOUS CALL TO THE AVENGERS, MAYBE. ALCHEMAX WON'T BE HAPPY BUT I CAN STEAL WHAT I--
HEY!
HE'S DEVIL DINOSAUR, NOT A "TYRANNOSAUR." HE'S MY FRIEND AND YOU CAN'T CALL THE AVENGERS. THEY'LL HURT HIM!
OR THEY'LL TAKE HIM AWAY!
YOU KNOW WHAT? FINE. GO. I DON'T NEED YOUR HELP! I CAN GET DEVIL BACK MYSELF.
I'M SORRY, BUT DEVIL'S NOT YOUR FRIEND ANYMORE. STEGRON HAS CONTROL OVER OTHER DINOSAURS, INCLUDING YOURS.

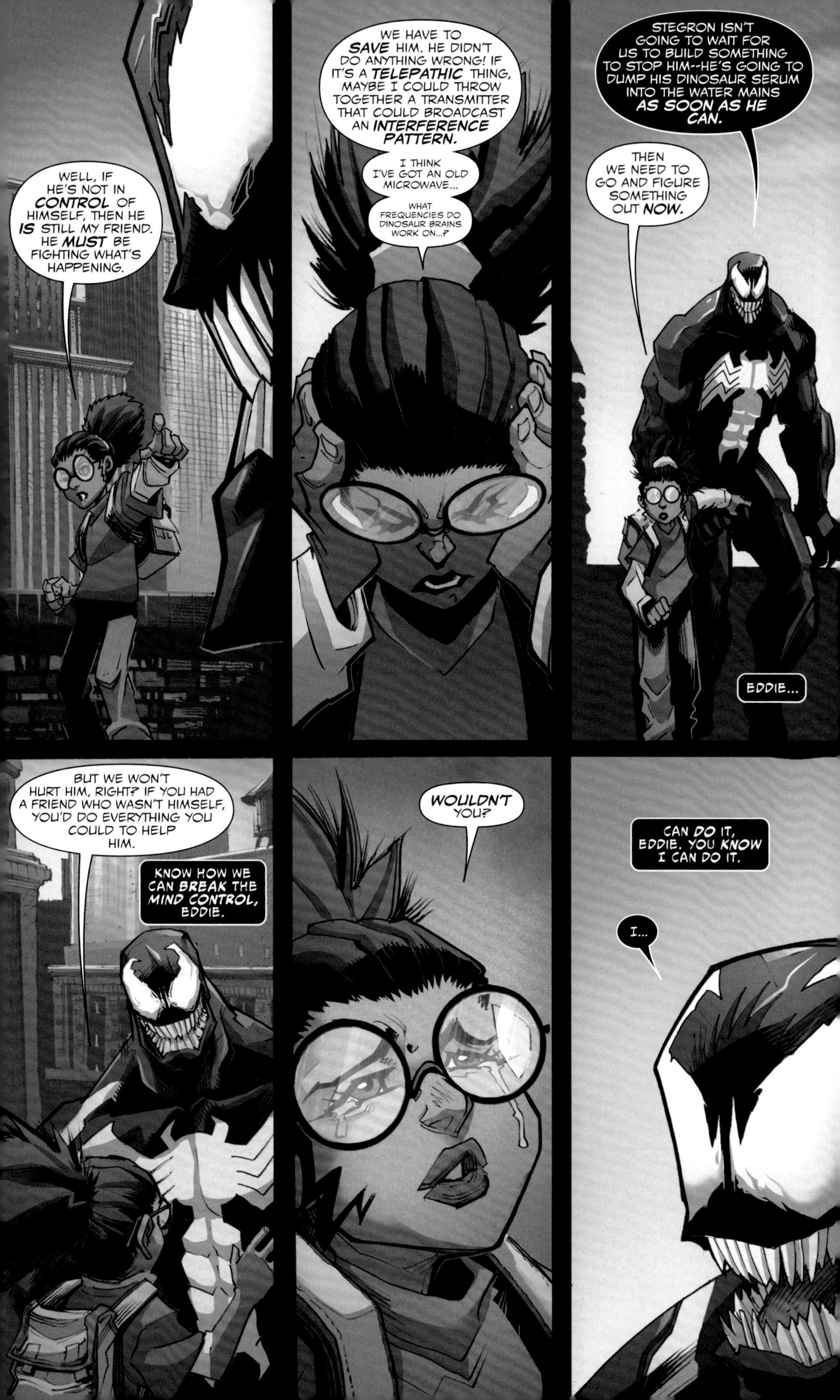

WELL, IF HE'S NOT IN CONTROL OF HIMSELF, THEN HE IS STILL MY FRIEND. HE MUST BE FIGHTING WHAT'S HAPPENING.
WE HAVE TO SAVE HIM. HE DIDN'T DO ANYTHING WRONG! IF IT'S A TELEPATHIC THING, MAYBE I COULD THROW TOGETHER A TRANSMITTER THAT COULD BROADCAST AN INTERFERENCE PATTERN.
I THINK I'VE GOT AN OLD MICROWAVE...
WHAT FREQUENCIES DO DINOSAUR BRAINS WORK ON...?
STEGRON ISN'T GOING TO WAIT FOR US TO BUILD SOMETHING TO STOP HIM--HE'S GOING TO DUMP HIS DINOSAUR SERUM INTO THE WATER MAINS AS SOON AS HE CAN.
THEN WE NEED TO GO AND FIGURE SOMETHING OUT NOW.
EDDIE...
BUT WE WON'T HURT HIM, RIGHT? IF YOU HAD A FRIEND WHO WASN'T HIMSELF, YOU'D DO EVERYTHING YOU COULD TO HELP HIM.
KNOW HOW WE CAN BREAK THE MIND CONTROL, EDDIE.
WOULDN'T YOU?
CAN DO IT, EDDIE. YOU KNOW I CAN DO IT.
I...

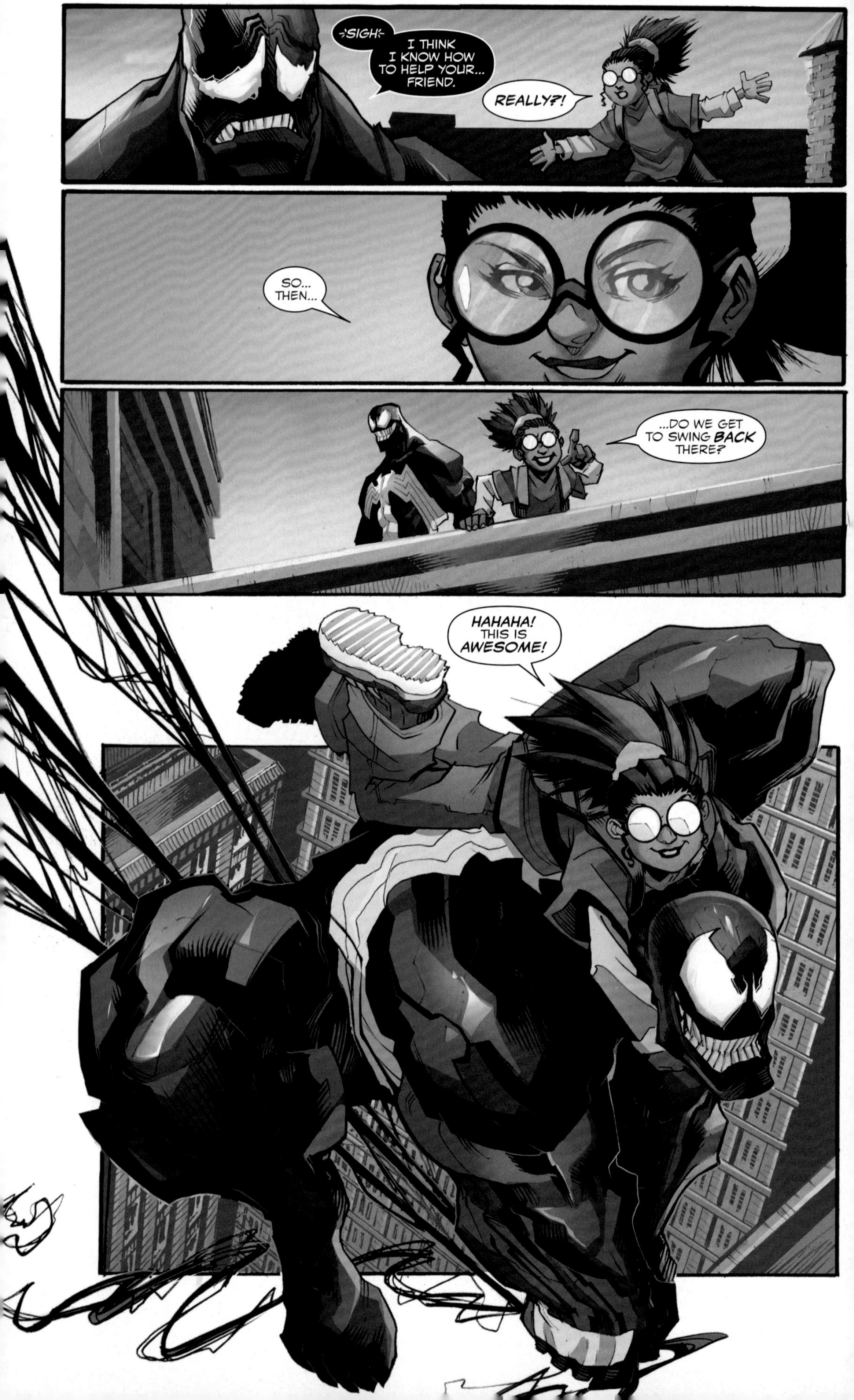
SIGH
I THINK I KNOW HOW TO HELP YOUR... FRIEND.
REALLY?!
SO... THEN...
...DO WE GET TO SWING BACK THERE?
HAHAHA! THIS IS AWESOME!

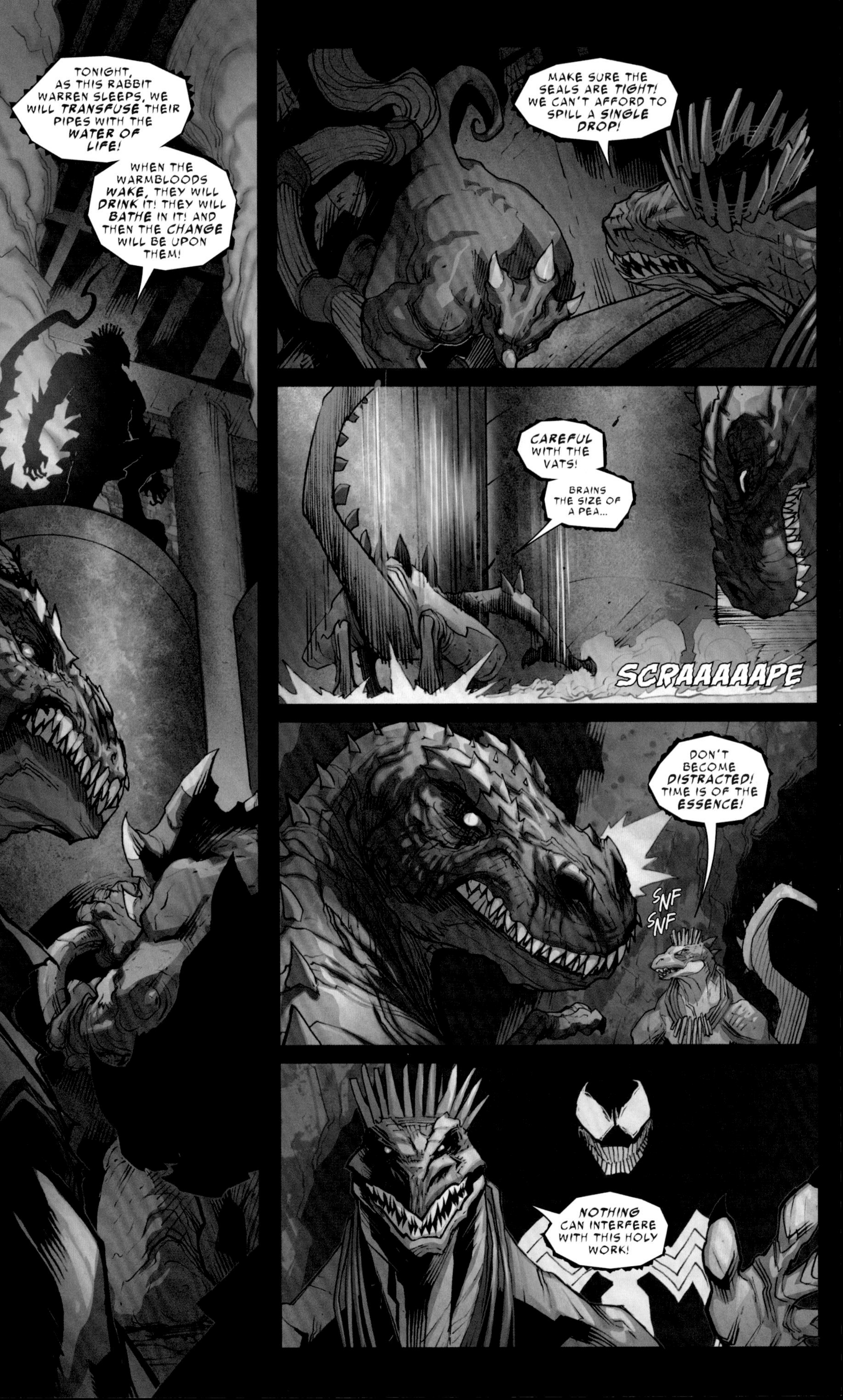
TONIGHT, AS THIS RABBIT WARREN SLEEPS, WE WILL TRANSFUSE THEIR PIPES WITH THE WATER OF LIFE!
WHEN THE WARMBLOODS WAKE, THEY WILL DRINK IT! THEY WILL BATHE IN IT! AND THEN THE CHANGE WILL BE UPON THEM!
MAKE SURE THE SEALS ARE TIGHT! WE CAN'T AFFORD TO SPILL A SINGLE DROP!
CAREFUL WITH THE VATS!
BRAINS THE SIZE OF A PEA...
SCRAAAAAAPE
DON'T BECOME DISTRACTED! TIME IS OF THE ESSENCE!
SNF SNF
NOTHING CAN INTERFERE WITH THIS HOLY WORK!

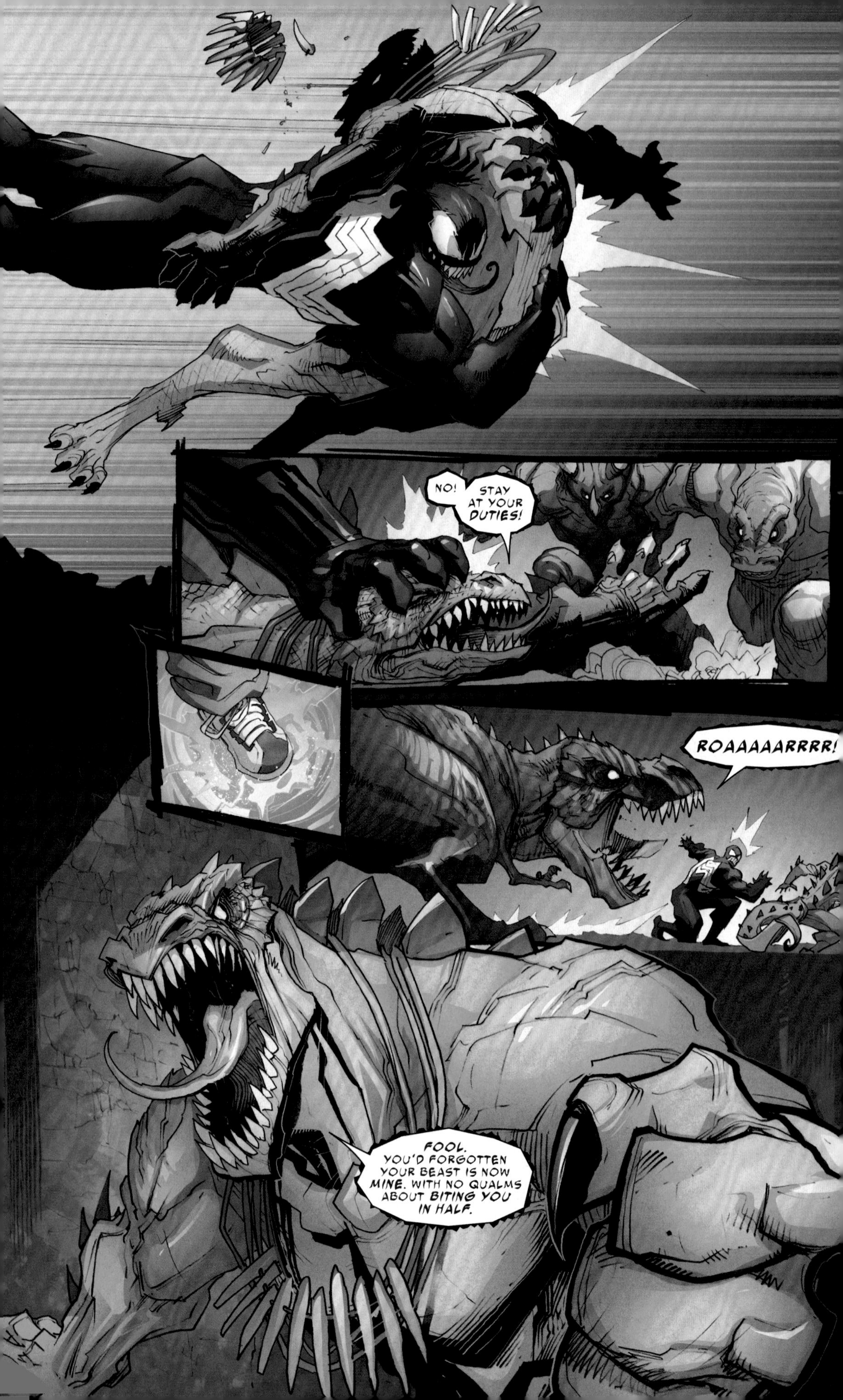
NO!
STAY AT YOUR DUTIES!
ROAAAAARRRR!
FOOL. YOU'D FORGOTTEN YOUR BEAST IS NOW MINE. WITH NO QUALMS ABOUT BITING YOU IN HALF.

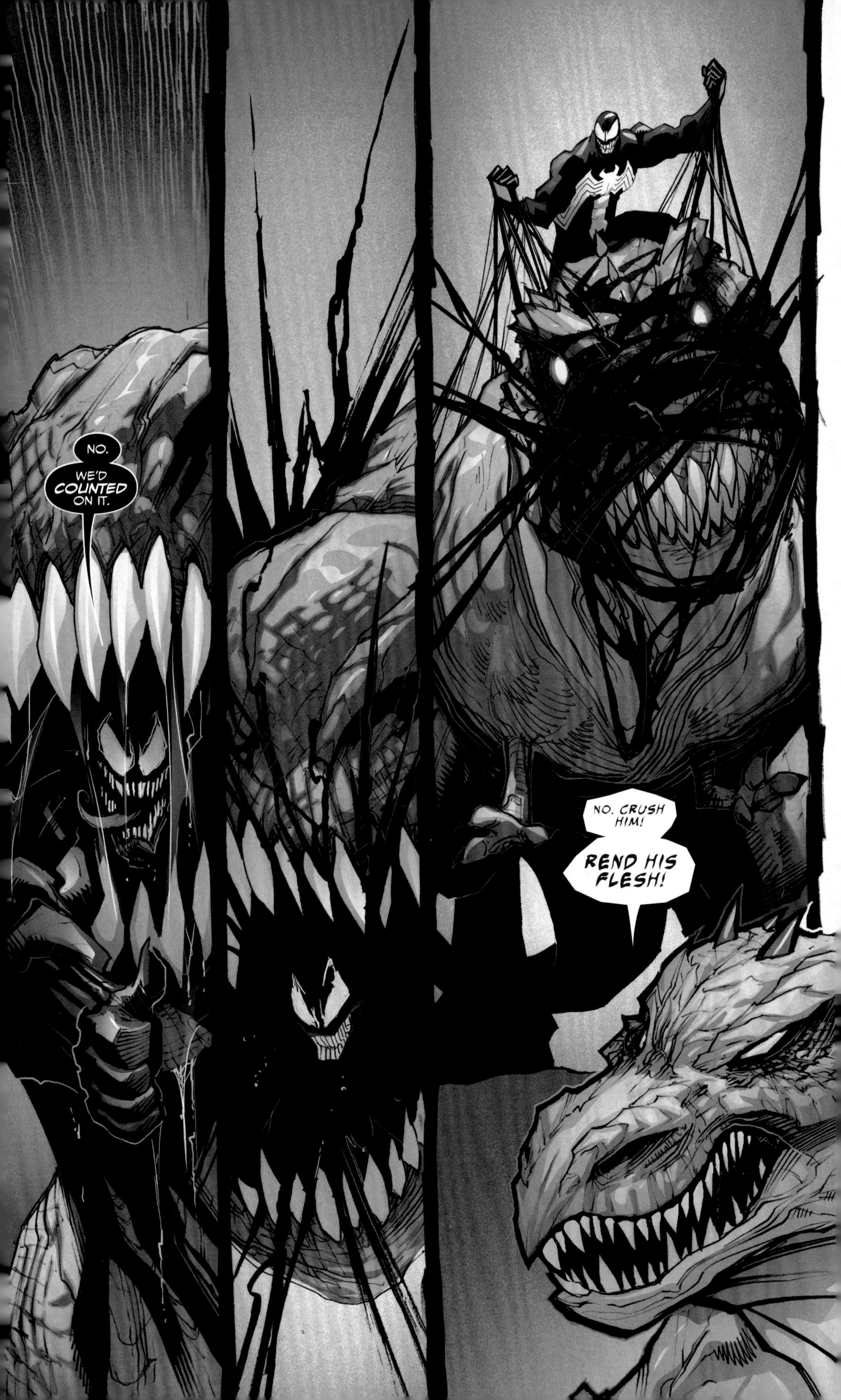
NO.
WE'D COUNTED ON IT.
NO. CRUSH HIM!
REND HIS FLESH!

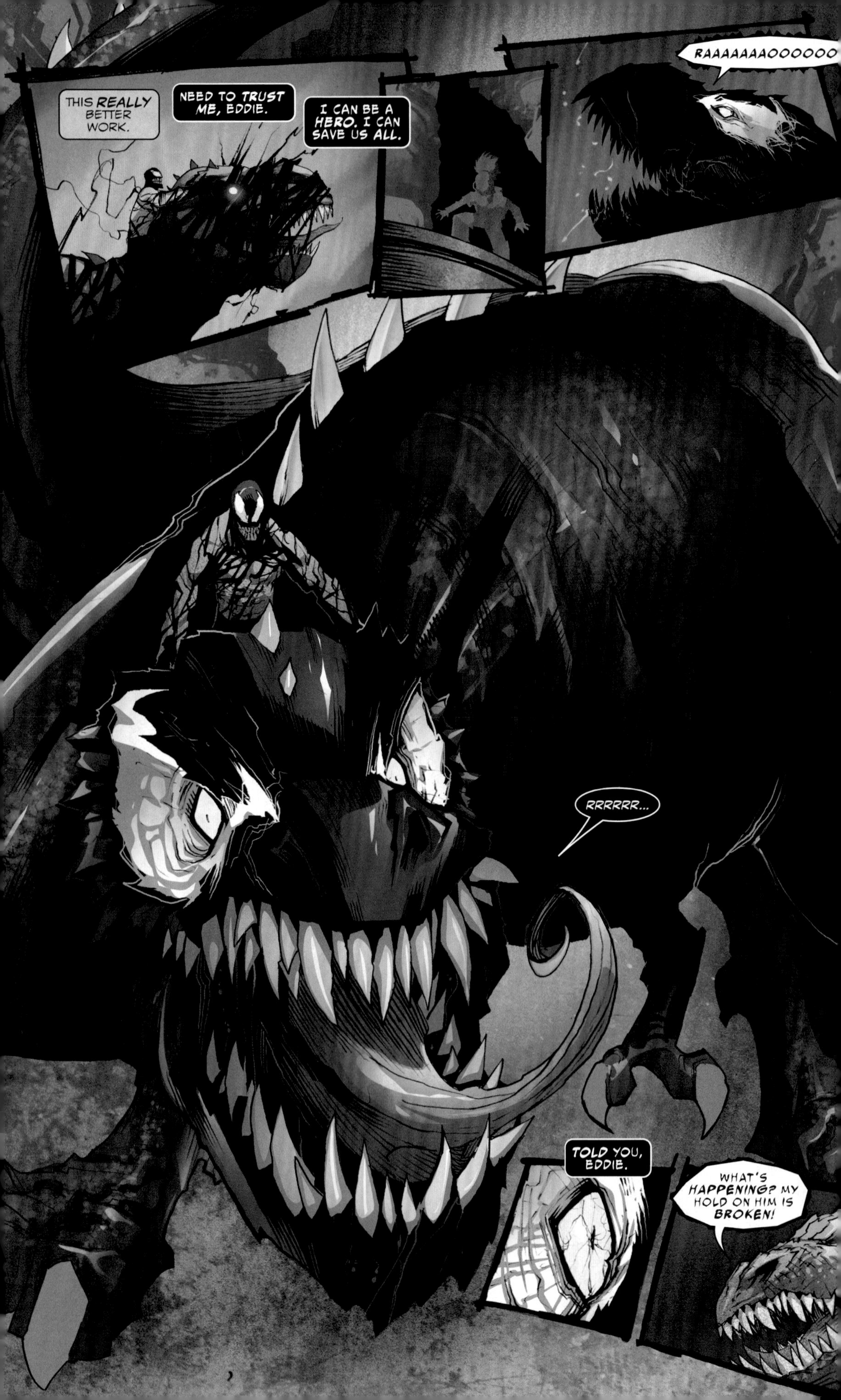

THIS REALLY BETTER WORK.
NEED TO TRUST ME, EDDIE.
I CAN BE A HERO. I CAN SAVE US ALL.
RAAAAAAAOOOOOO
RRRRRR...
TOLD YOU, EDDIE.
WHAT'S HAPPENING? MY HOLD ON HIM IS BROKEN!

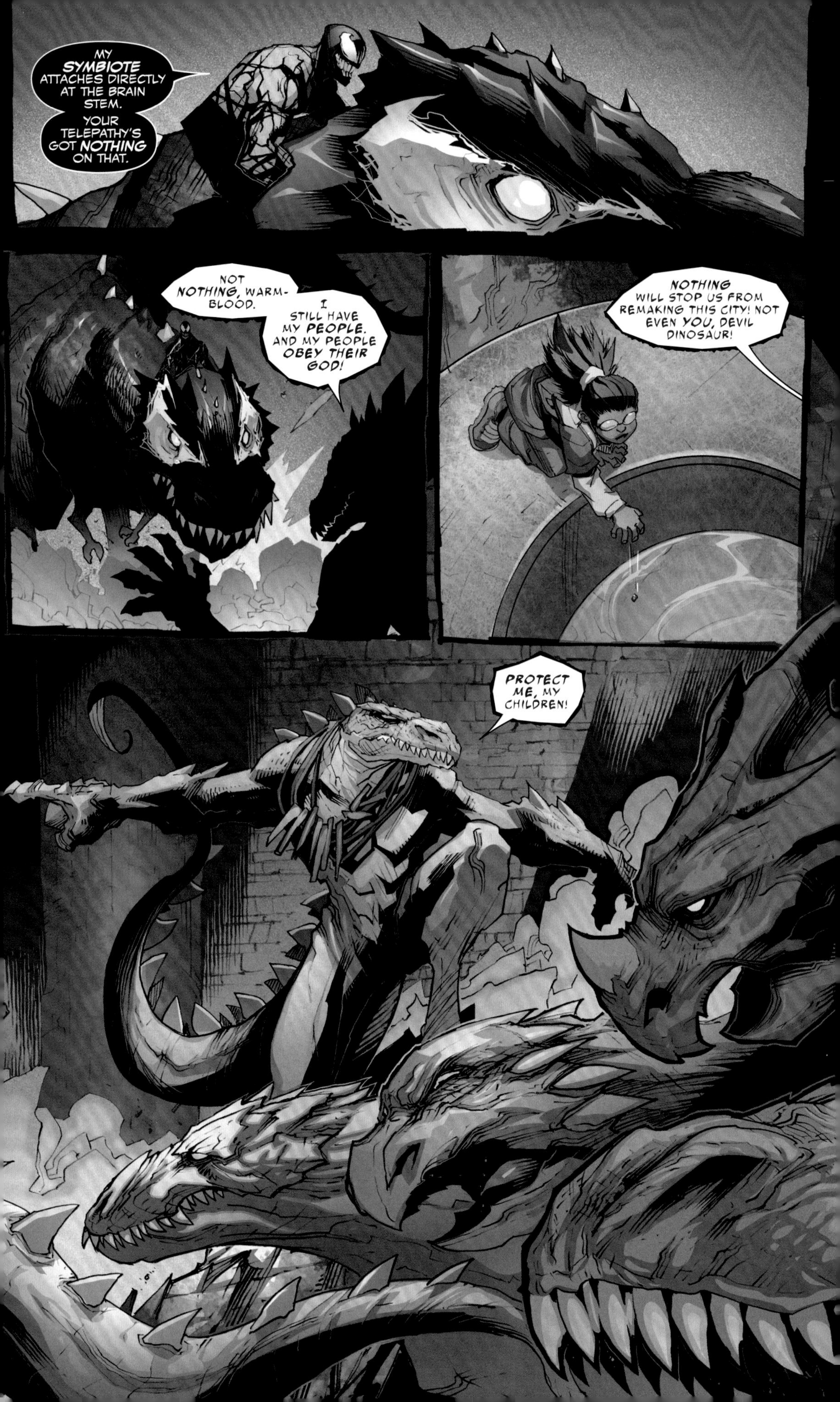
MY SYMBIOTE ATTACHES DIRECTLY AT THE BRAIN STEM.
YOUR TELEPATHY'S GOT NOTHING ON THAT.
NOT NOTHING, WARM-BLOOD.
I STILL HAVE MY PEOPLE. AND MY PEOPLE OBEY THEIR GOD!
NOTHING WILL STOP US FROM REMAKING THIS CITY! NOT EVEN YOU, DEVIL DINOSAUR!
PROTECT ME, MY CHILDREN!

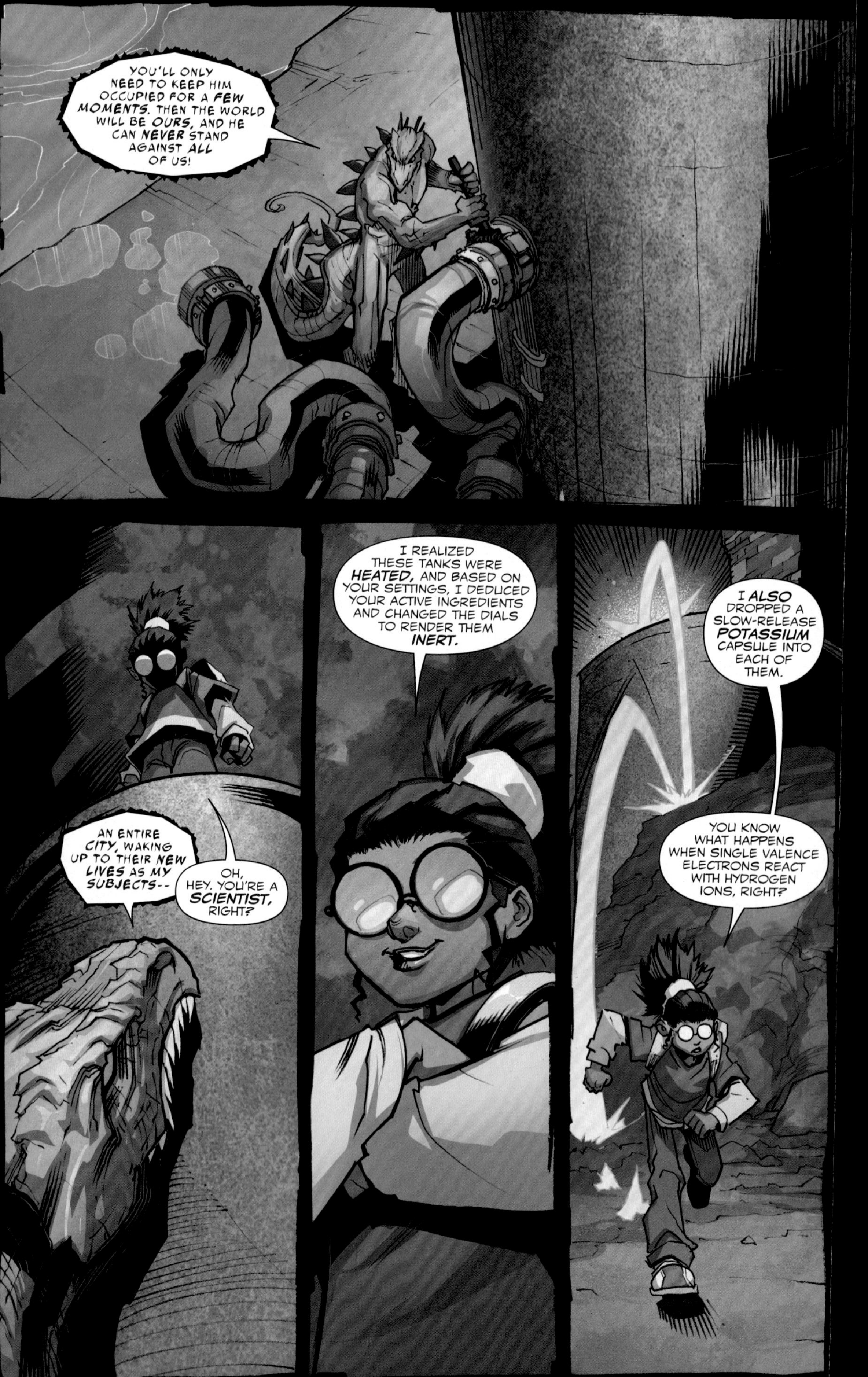
YOU'LL ONLY NEED TO KEEP HIM OCCUPIED FOR A FEW MOMENTS. THEN THE WORLD WILL BE OURS, AND HE CAN NEVER STAND AGAINST ALL OF US!
AN ENTIRE CITY, WAKING UP TO THEIR NEW LIVES AS MY SUBJECTS--
OH, HEY. YOU'RE A SCIENTIST, RIGHT?
I REALIZED THESE TANKS WERE HEATED, AND BASED ON YOUR SETTINGS, I DEDUCED YOUR ACTIVE INGREDIENTS AND CHANGED THE DIALS TO RENDER THEM INERT.
I ALSO DROPPED A SLOW-RELEASE POTASSIUM CAPSULE INTO EACH OF THEM.
YOU KNOW WHAT HAPPENS WHEN SINGLE VALENCE ELECTRONS REACT WITH HYDROGEN IONS, RIGHT?

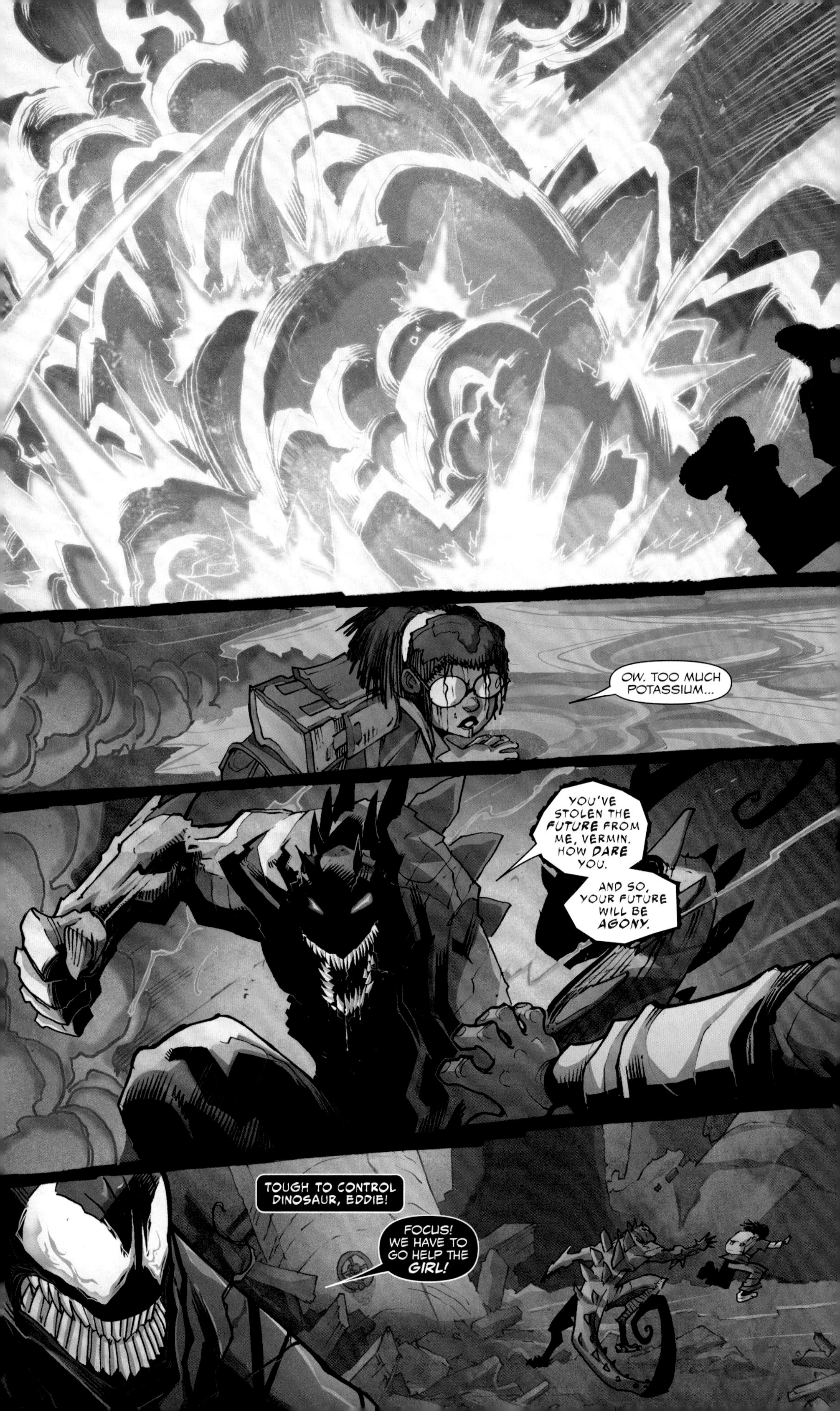
OW. TOO MUCH POTASSIUM...
YOU'VE STOLEN THE FUTURE FROM ME, VERMIN. HOW DARE YOU.
AND SO, YOUR FUTURE WILL BE AGONY.
TOUGH TO CONTROL DINOSAUR, EDDIE!
FOCUS! WE HAVE TO GO HELP THE GIRL!

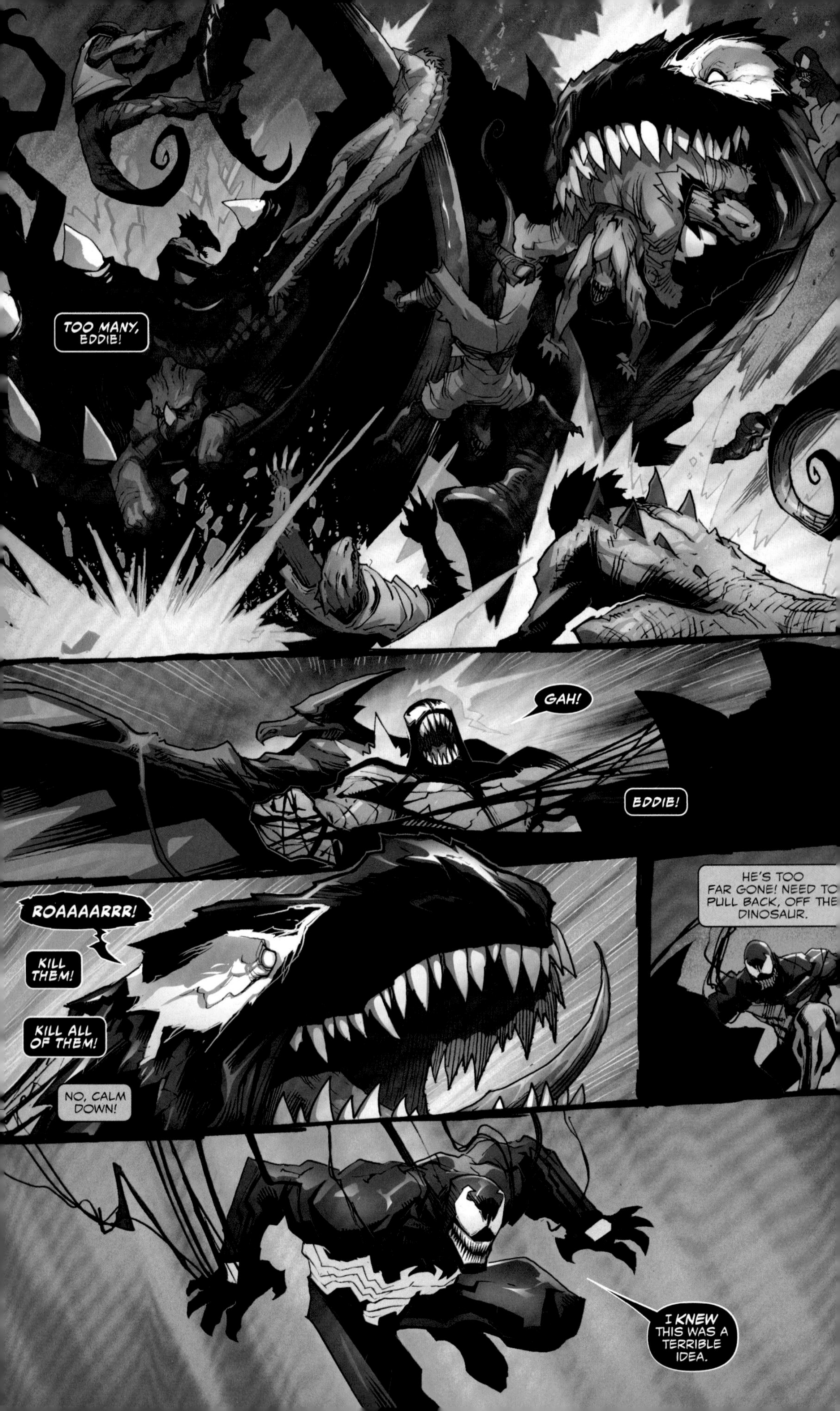

TOO MANY, EDDIE!
GAH!
EDDIE!
ROAAAARRR!
KILL THEM!
KILL ALL OF THEM!
NO, CALM DOWN!
HE'S TOO FAR GONE! NEED TO PULL BACK, OFF THE DINOSAUR.
I KNEW THIS WAS A TERRIBLE IDEA.

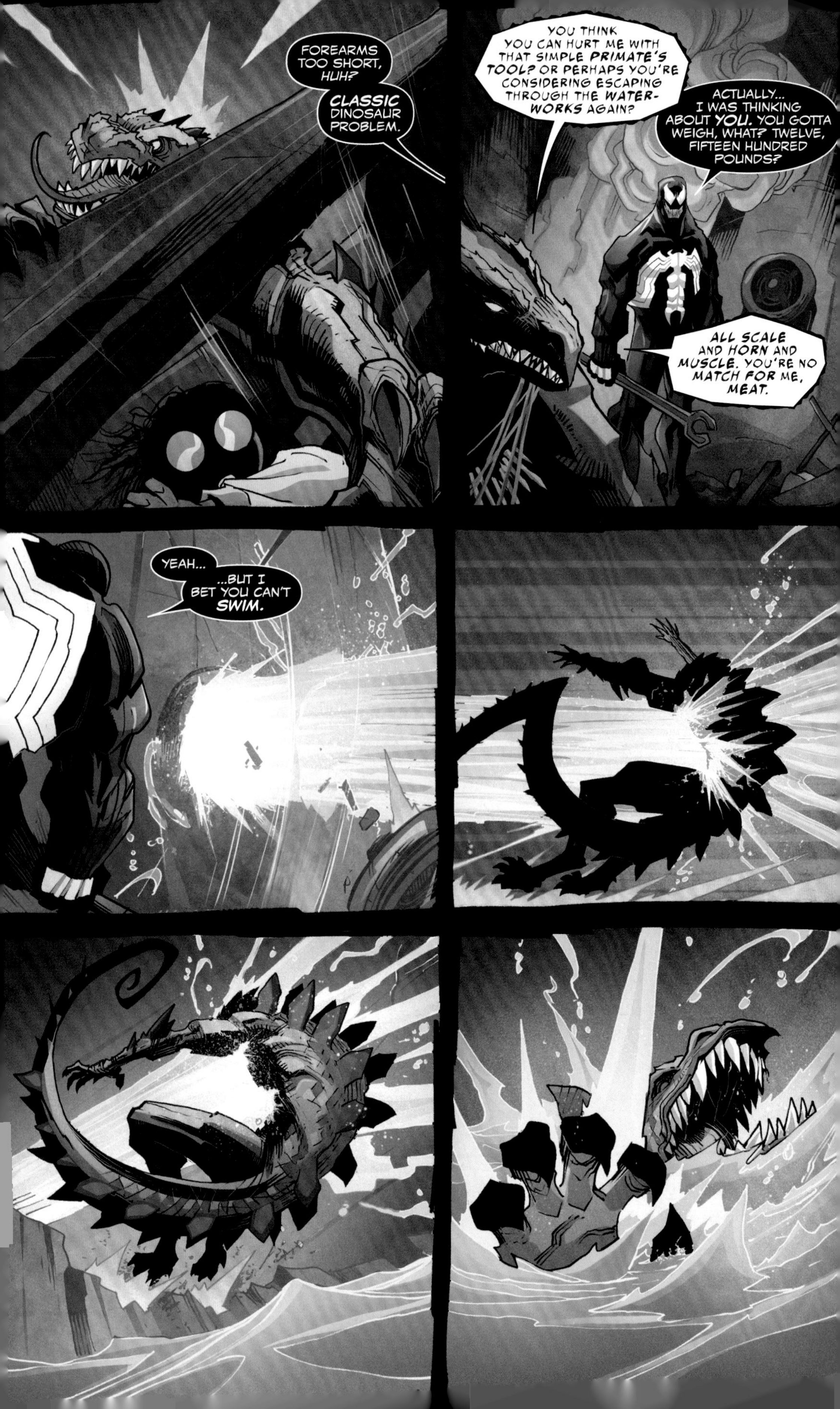
FOREARMS TOO SHORT, HUH?
CLASSIC DINOSAUR PROBLEM.
YOU THINK YOU CAN HURT ME WITH THAT SIMPLE PRIMATE'S TOOL? OR PERHAPS YOU'RE CONSIDERING ESCAPING THROUGH THE WATER-WORKS AGAIN?
ACTUALLY... I WAS THINKING ABOUT YOU. YOU GOTTA WEIGH, WHAT? TWELVE, FIFTEEN HUNDRED POUNDS?
ALL SCALE AND HORN AND MUSCLE. YOU'RE NO MATCH FOR ME, MEAT.
YEAH...
...BUT I BET YOU CAN'T SWIM.

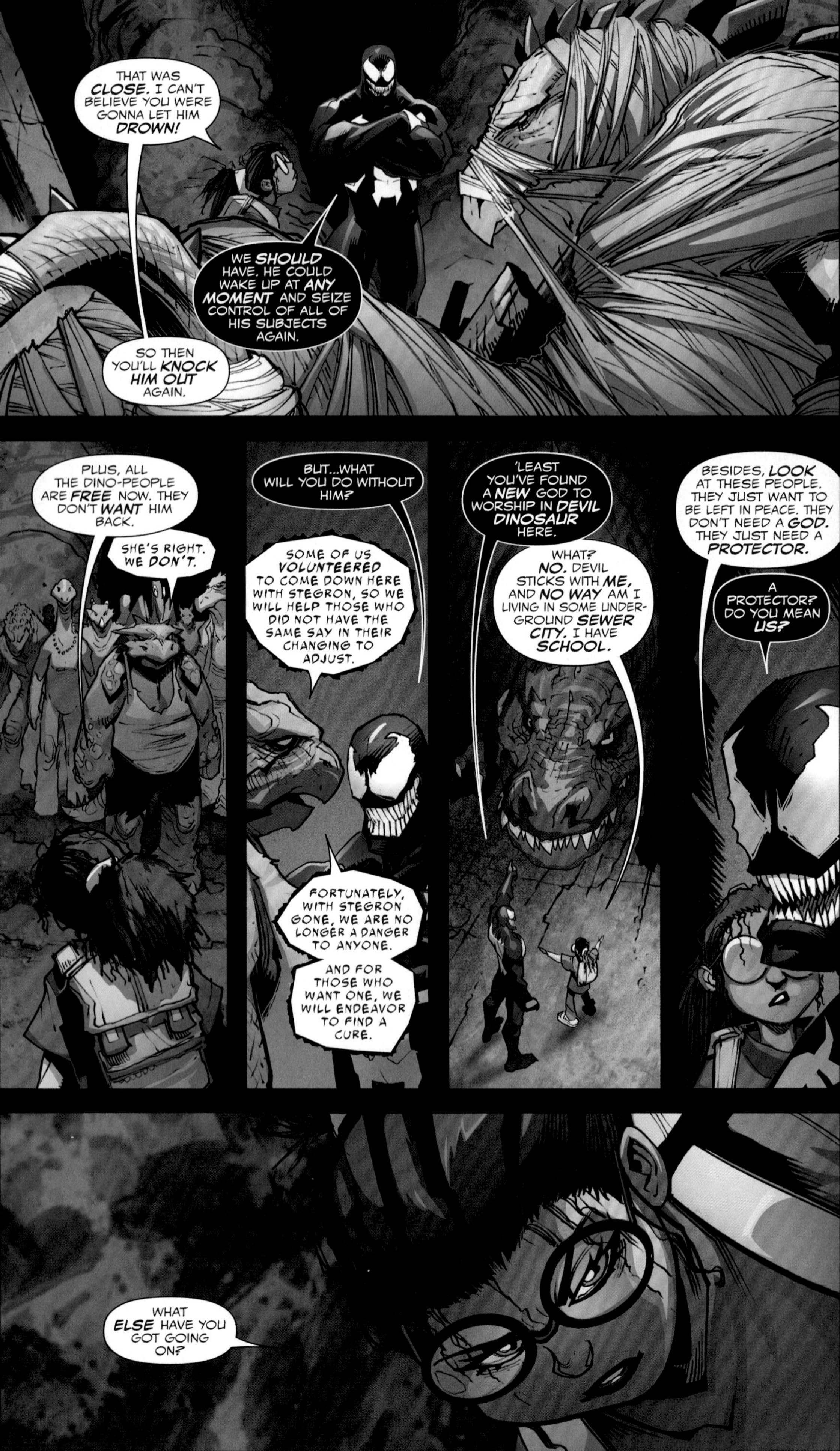
THAT WAS CLOSE. I CAN'T BELIEVE YOU WERE GONNA LET HIM DROWN!
WE SHOULD HAVE. HE COULD WAKE UP AT ANY MOMENT AND SEIZE CONTROL OF ALL OF HIS SUBJECTS AGAIN.
SO THEN YOU'LL KNOCK HIM OUT AGAIN.
PLUS, ALL THE DINO-PEOPLE ARE FREE NOW. THEY DON'T WANT HIM BACK.
SHE'S RIGHT. WE DON'T.
BUT...WHAT WILL YOU DO WITHOUT HIM?
SOME OF US VOLUNTEERED TO COME DOWN HERE WITH STEGRON, SO WE WILL HELP THOSE WHO DID NOT HAVE THE SAME SAY IN THEIR CHANGING TO ADJUST.
FORTUNATELY, WITH STEGRON GONE, WE ARE NO LONGER A DANGER TO ANYONE.
AND FOR THOSE WHO WANT ONE, WE WILL ENDEAVOR TO FIND A CURE.
'LEAST YOU'VE FOUND A NEW GOD TO WORSHIP IN DEVIL DINOSAUR HERE.
WHAT? NO. DEVIL STICKS WITH ME, AND NO WAY AM I LIVING IN SOME UNDER-GROUND SEWER CITY. I HAVE SCHOOL.
BESIDES, LOOK AT THESE PEOPLE. THEY JUST WANT TO BE LEFT IN PEACE. THEY DON'T NEED A GOD. THEY JUST NEED A PROTECTOR.
A PROTECTOR? DO YOU MEAN US?
WHAT ELSE HAVE YOU GOT GOING ON?

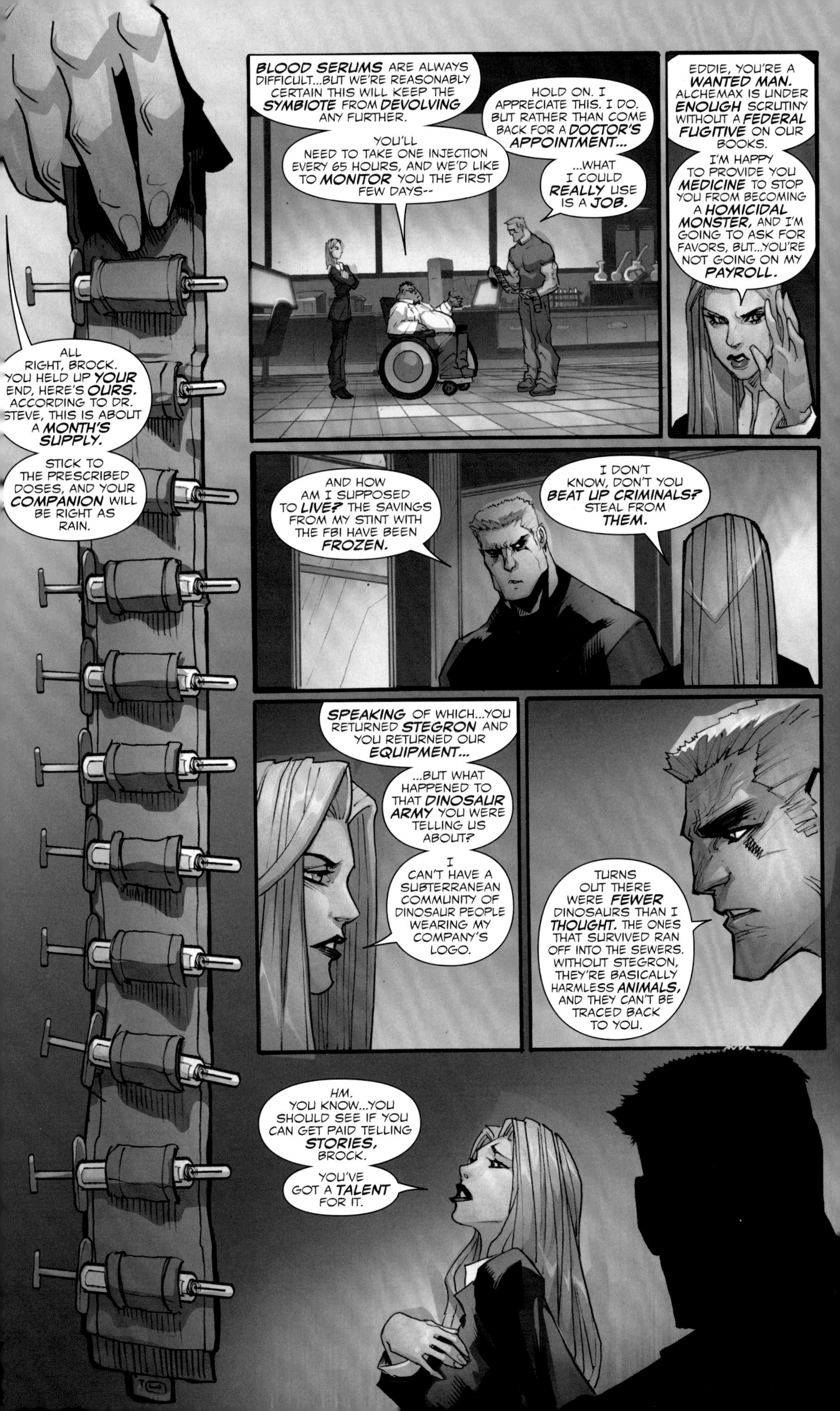
BLOOD SERUMS ARE ALWAYS DIFFICULT...BUT WE'RE REASONABLY CERTAIN THIS WILL KEEP THE SYMBIOTE FROM DEVOLVING ANY FURTHER.
YOU'LL NEED TO TAKE ONE INJECTION EVERY 65 HOURS, AND WE'D LIKE TO MONITOR YOU THE FIRST FEW DAYS--
HOLD ON. I APPRECIATE THIS. I DO. BUT RATHER THAN COME BACK FOR A DOCTOR'S APPOINTMENT...
...WHAT I COULD REALLY USE IS A JOB.
EDDIE, YOU'RE A WANTED MAN. ALCHEMAX IS UNDER ENOUGH SCRUTINY WITHOUT A FEDERAL FUGITIVE ON OUR BOOKS.
I'M HAPPY TO PROVIDE YOU MEDICINE TO STOP YOU FROM BECOMING A HOMICIDAL MONSTER, AND I'M GOING TO ASK FOR FAVORS, BUT...YOU'RE NOT GOING ON MY PAYROLL.
AND HOW AM I SUPPOSED TO LIVE? THE SAVINGS FROM MY STINT WITH THE FBI HAVE BEEN FROZEN.
I DON'T KNOW, DON'T YOU BEAT UP CRIMINALS? STEAL FROM THEM.
SPEAKING OF WHICH...YOU RETURNED STEGRON AND YOU RETURNED OUR EQUIPMENT...
...BUT WHAT HAPPENED TO THAT DINOSAUR ARMY YOU WERE TELLING US ABOUT?
I CAN'T HAVE A SUBTERRANEAN COMMUNITY OF DINOSAUR PEOPLE WEARING MY COMPANY'S LOGO.
TURNS OUT THERE WERE FEWER DINOSAURS THAN I THOUGHT. THE ONES THAT SURVIVED RAN OFF INTO THE SEWERS. WITHOUT STEGRON, THEY'RE BASICALLY HARMLESS ANIMALS, AND THEY CAN'T BE TRACED BACK TO YOU.
HM. YOU KNOW...YOU SHOULD SEE IF YOU CAN GET PAID TELLING STORIES, BROCK.
YOU'VE GOT A TALENT FOR IT.
ALL RIGHT, BROCK. YOU HELD UP YOUR END, HERE'S OURS. ACCORDING TO DR. STEVE, THIS IS ABOUT A MONTH'S SUPPLY.
STICK TO THE PRESCRIBED DOSES, AND YOUR COMPANION WILL BE RIGHT AS RAIN.

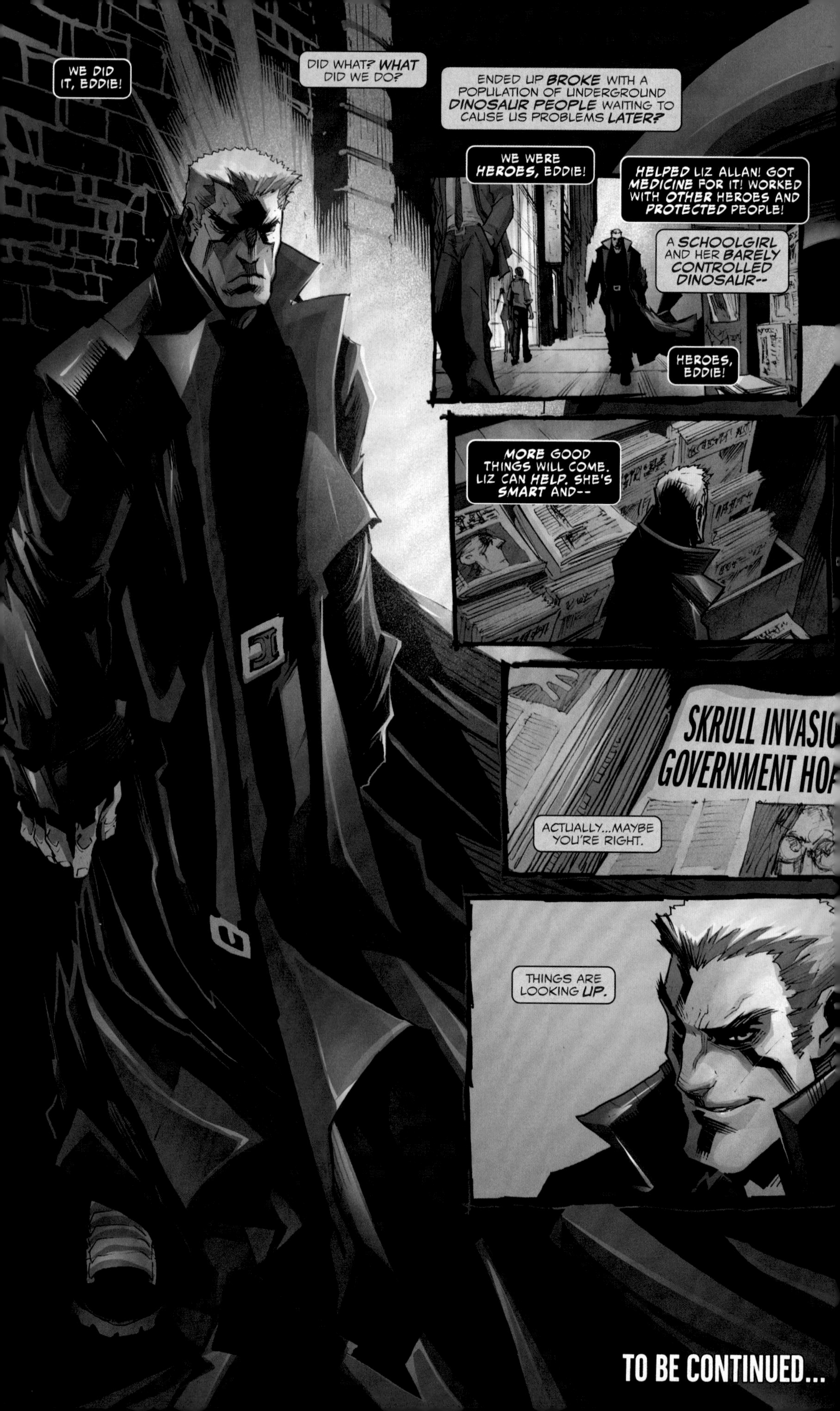
WE DID IT, EDDIE!
DID WHAT? WHAT DID WE DO?
ENDED UP BROKE WITH A POPULATION OF UNDERGROUND DINOSAUR PEOPLE WAITING TO CAUSE US PROBLEMS LATER?
WE WERE HEROES, EDDIE!
HELPED LIZ ALLAN! GOT MEDICINE FOR IT! WORKED WITH OTHER HEROES AND PROTECTED PEOPLE!
A SCHOOLGIRL AND HER BARELY CONTROLLED DINOSAUR--
HEROES, EDDIE!
MORE GOOD THINGS WILL COME. LIZ CAN HELP. SHE'S SMART AND--
SKRULL INVASIO
GOVERNMENT HO
ACTUALLY...MAYBE YOU'RE RIGHT.
THINGS ARE LOOKING UP.
TO BE CONTINUED...

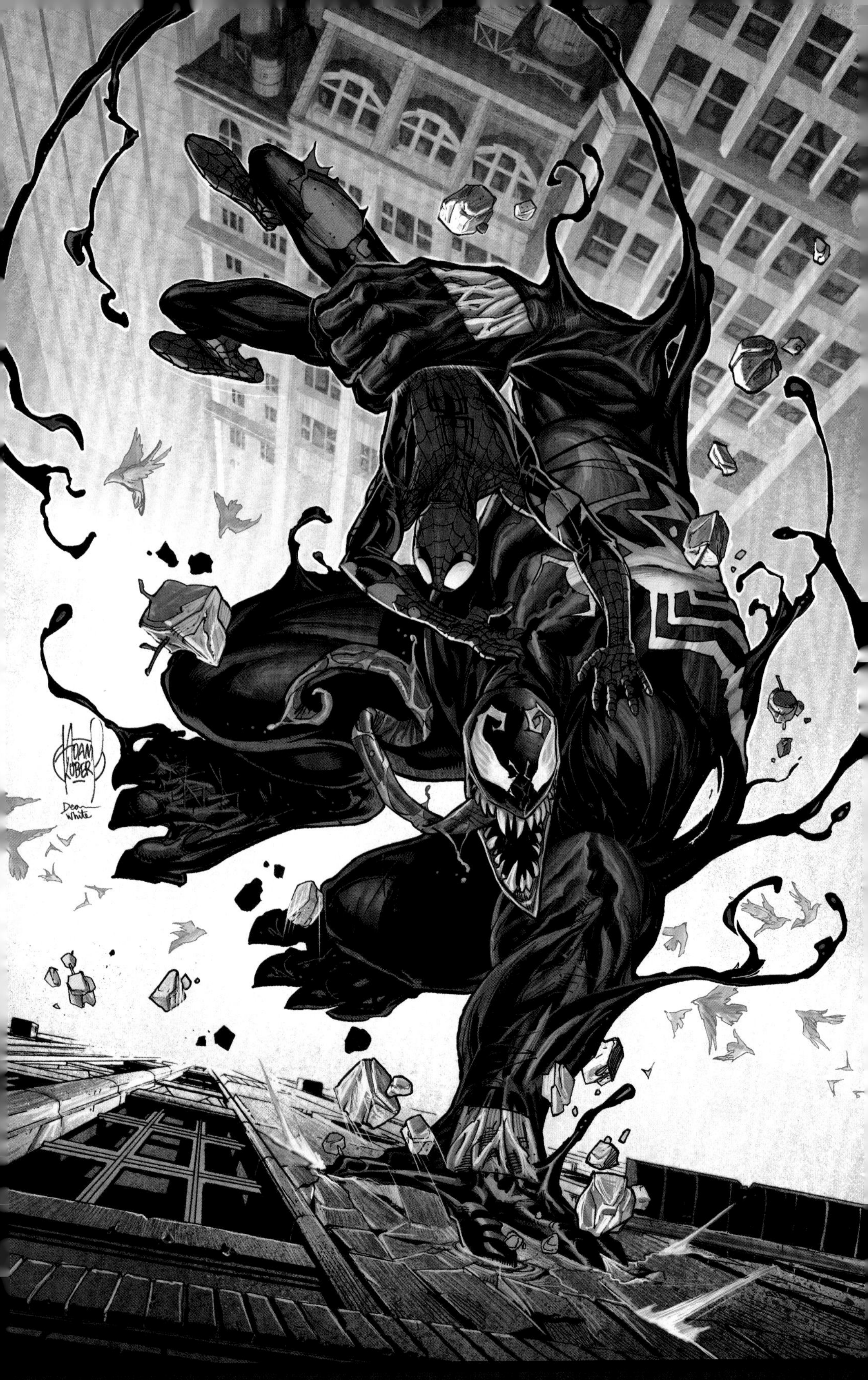
Adam Kubert
Dean White

#150 VARIANT BY ADAM KUBERT & DEAN WHITE

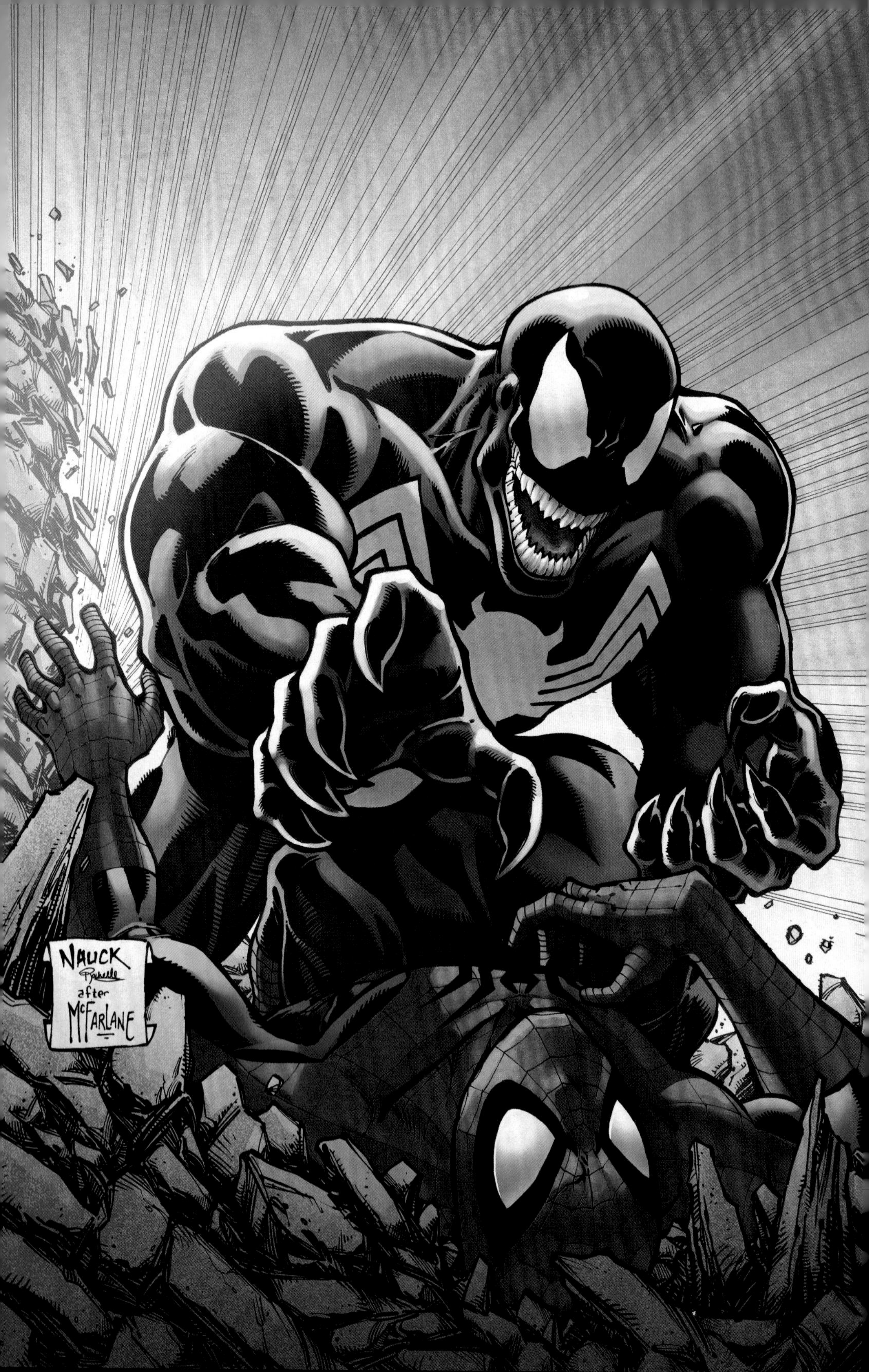
NAUCK
after
McFARLANE

#150 VARIANT BY **TODD NAUCK & RACHELLE ROSENBERG**

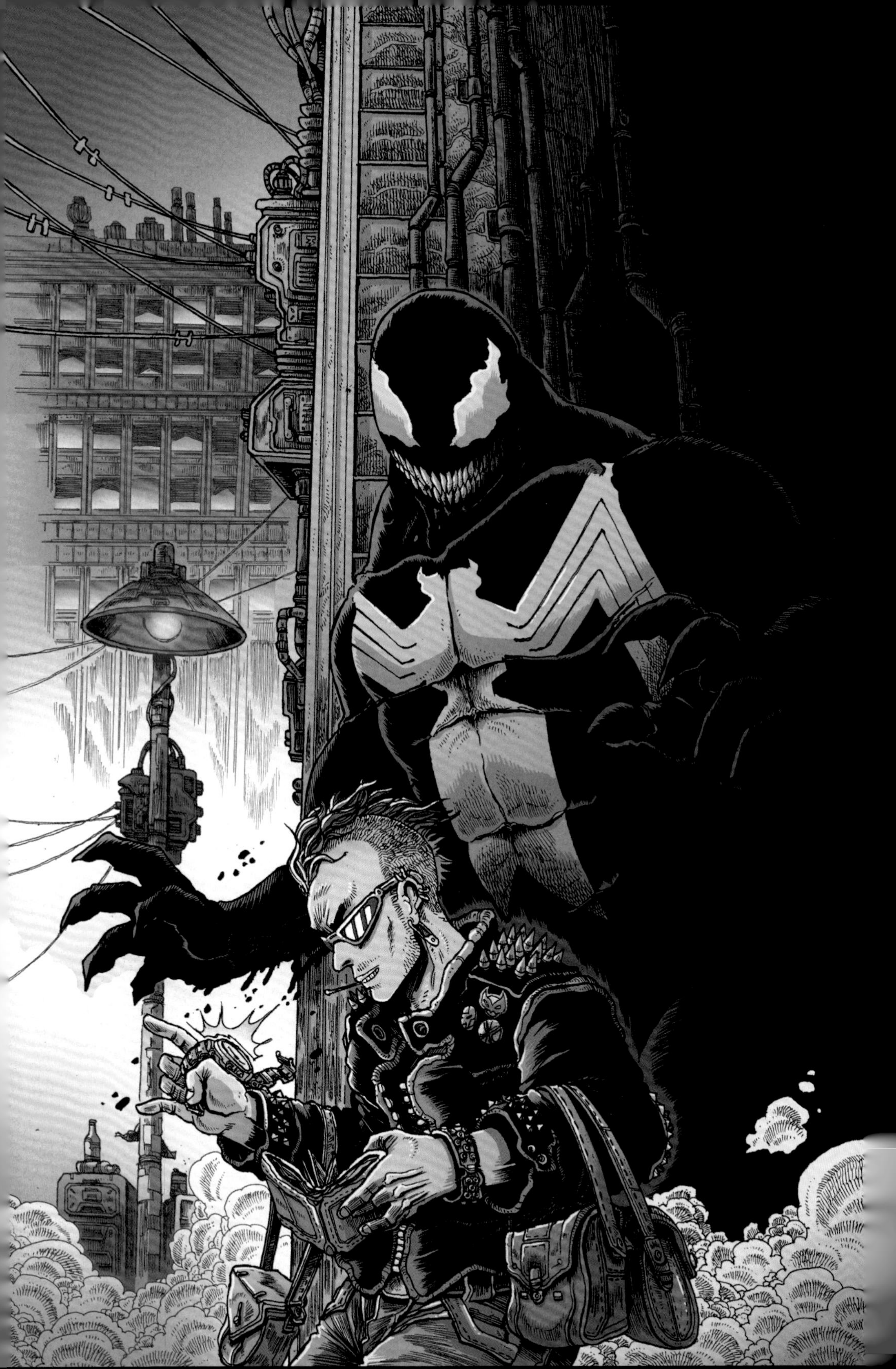

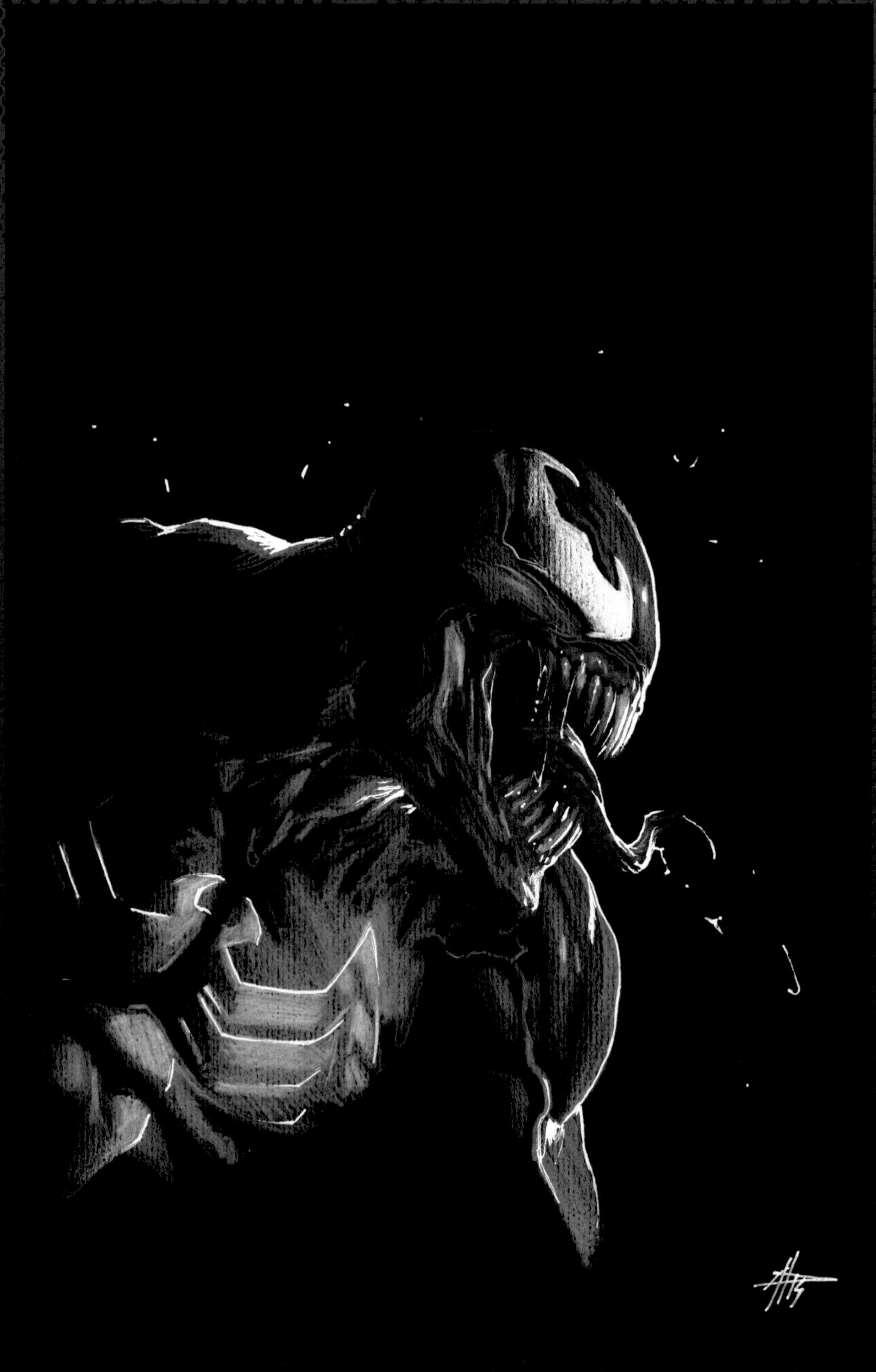

#150 VARIANT BY GABRIELE DELL'OTTO

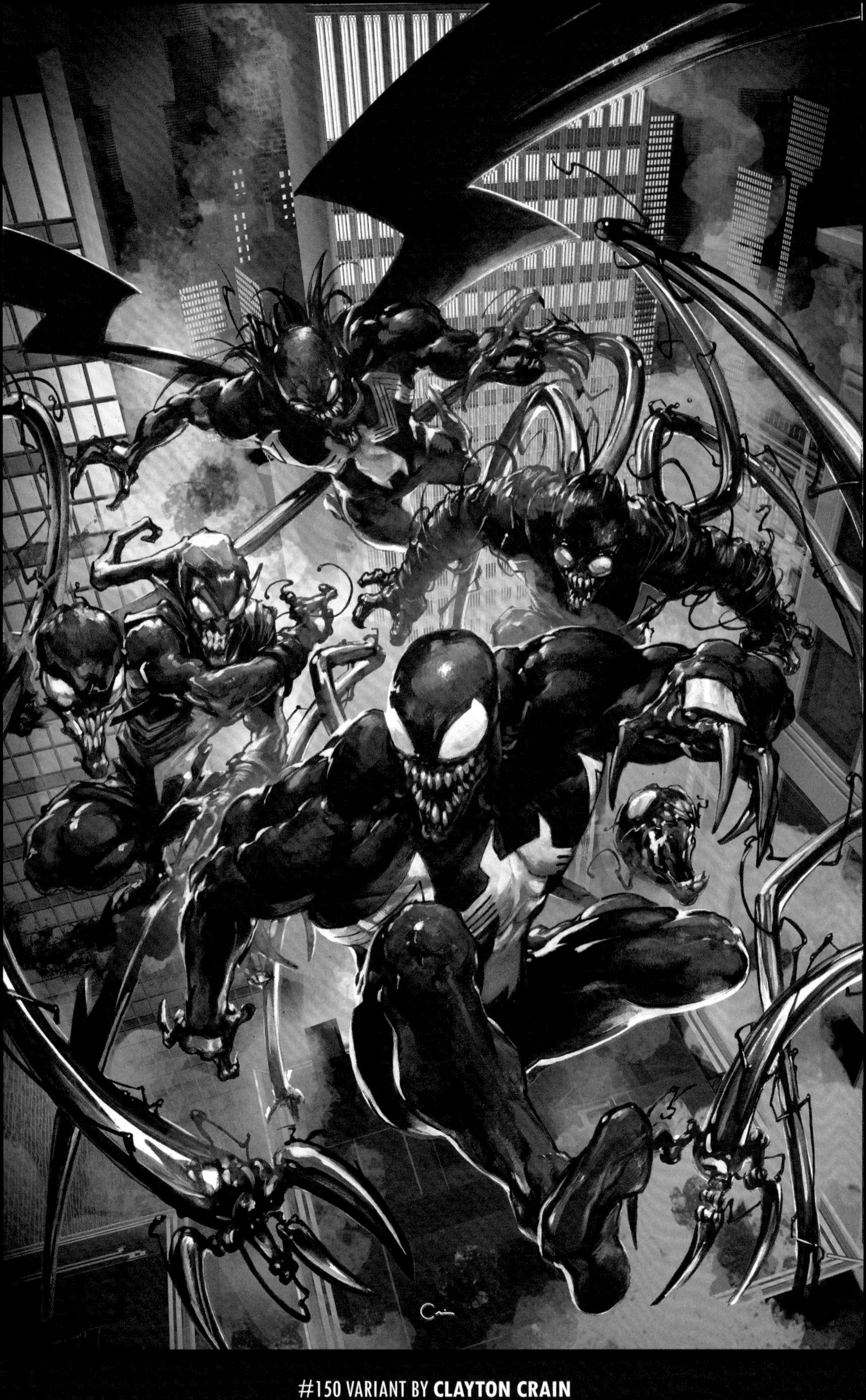

#150 VARIANT BY **CLAYTON CRAIN**

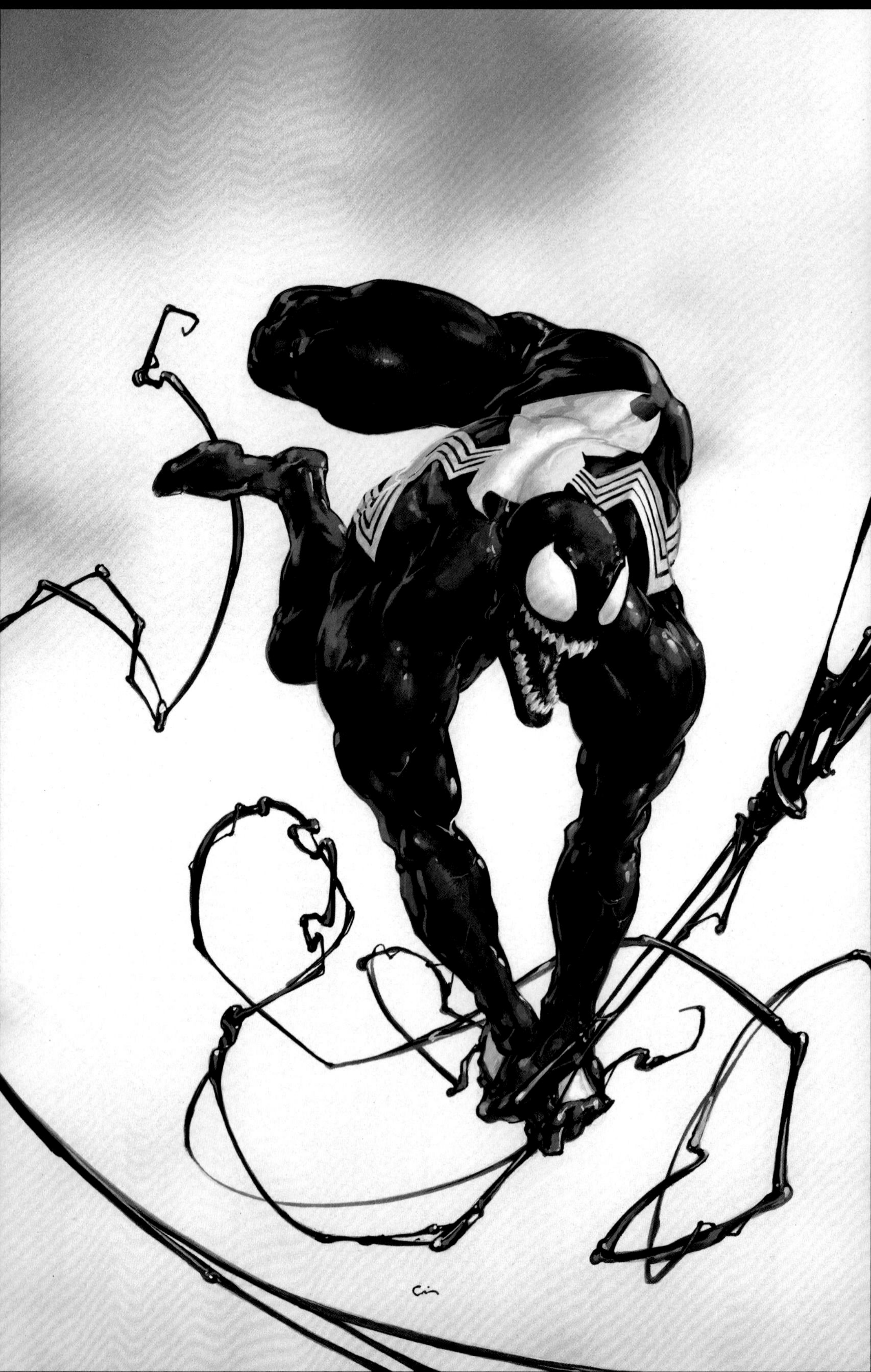

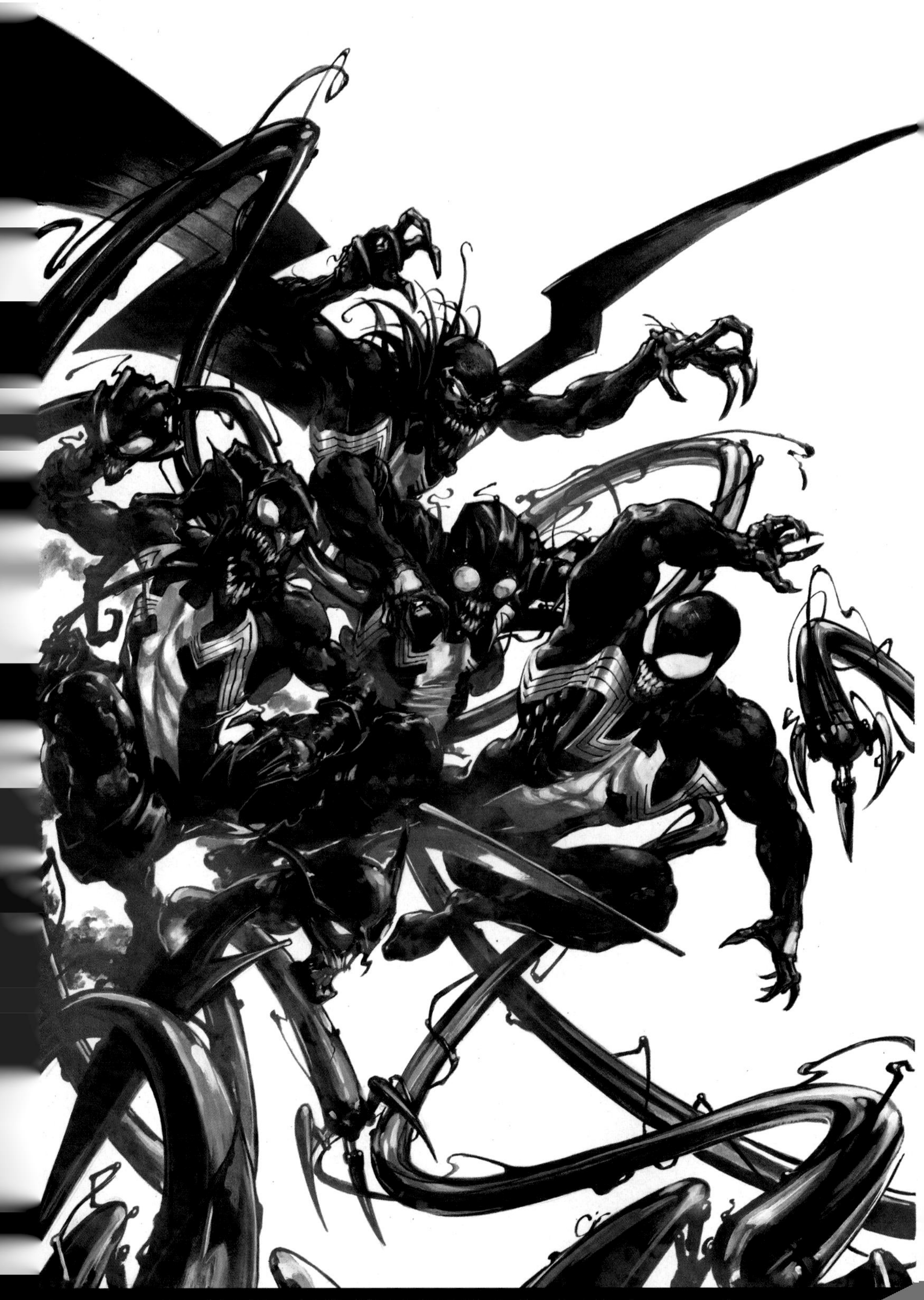

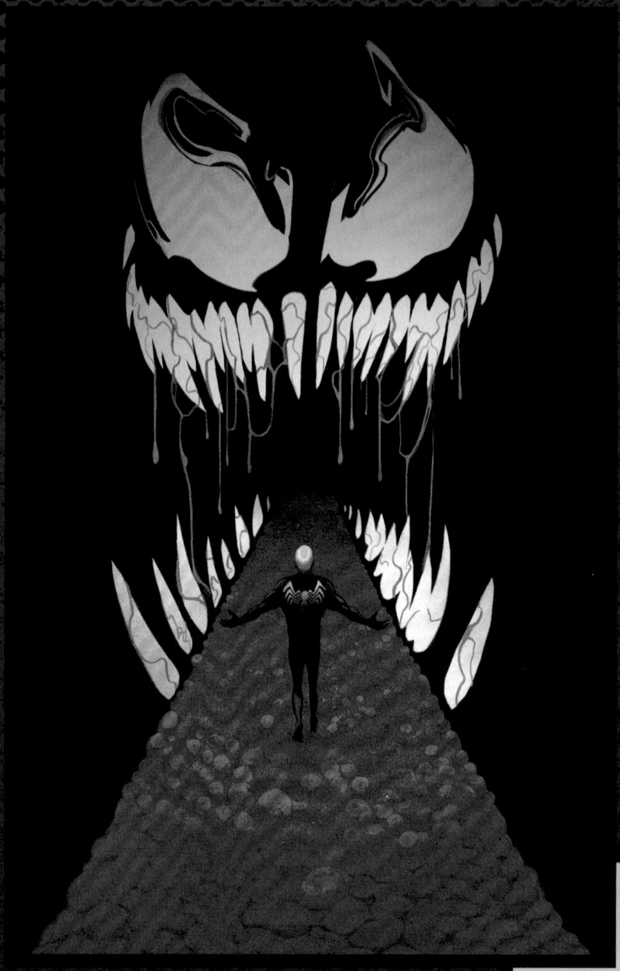

#150 VARIANT BY
MIKE DEL MUNDO

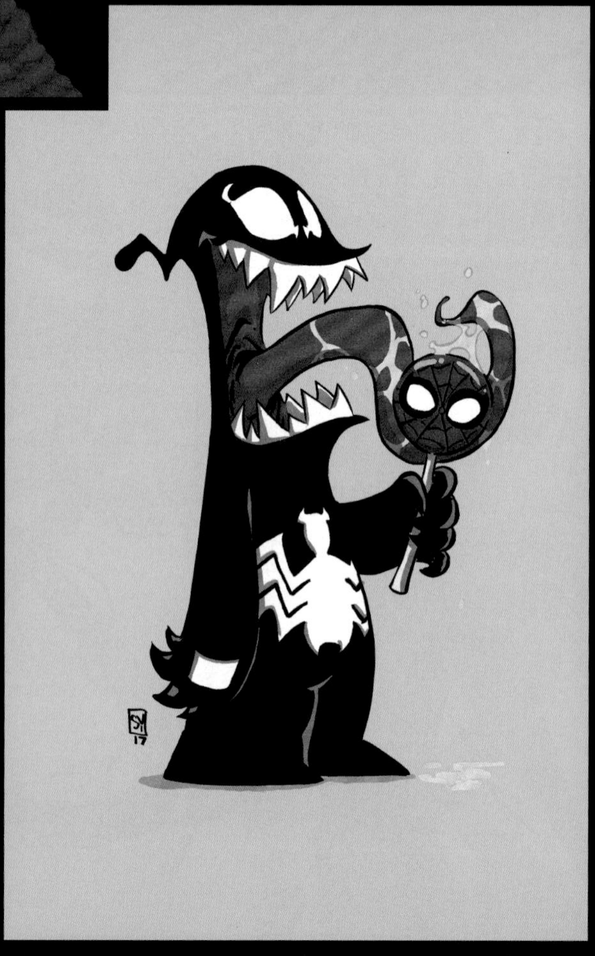

#150 VARIANT BY
SCOTTIE YOUNG

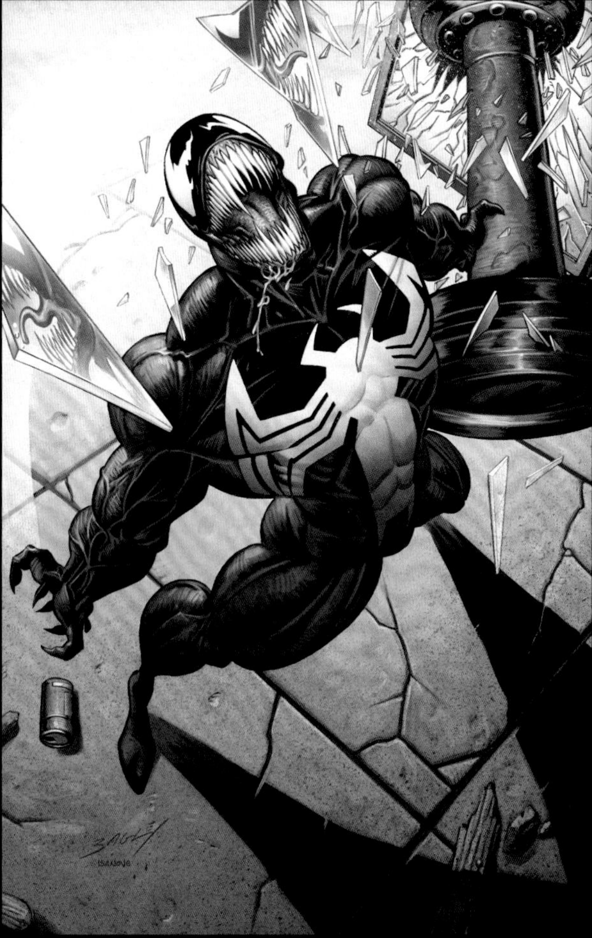

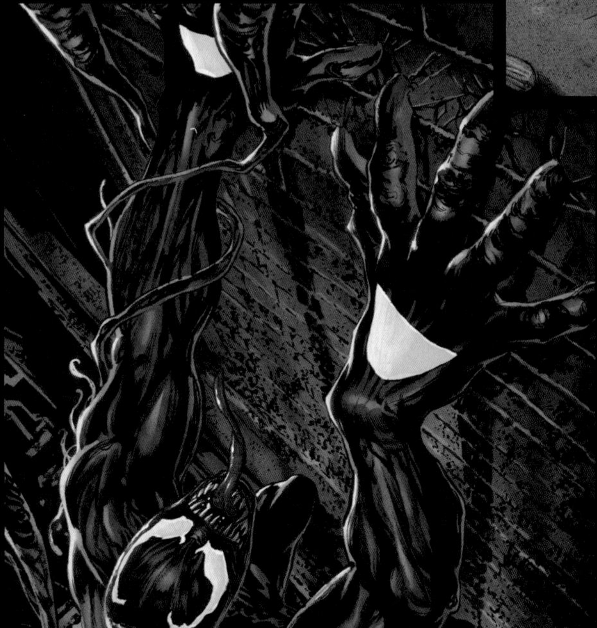

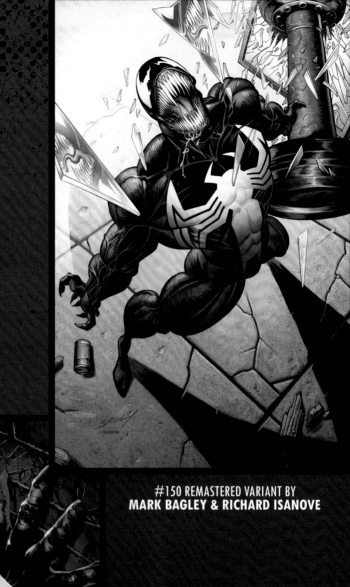

#150 REMASTERED VARIANT BY
MARK BAGLEY & RICHARD ISANOVE

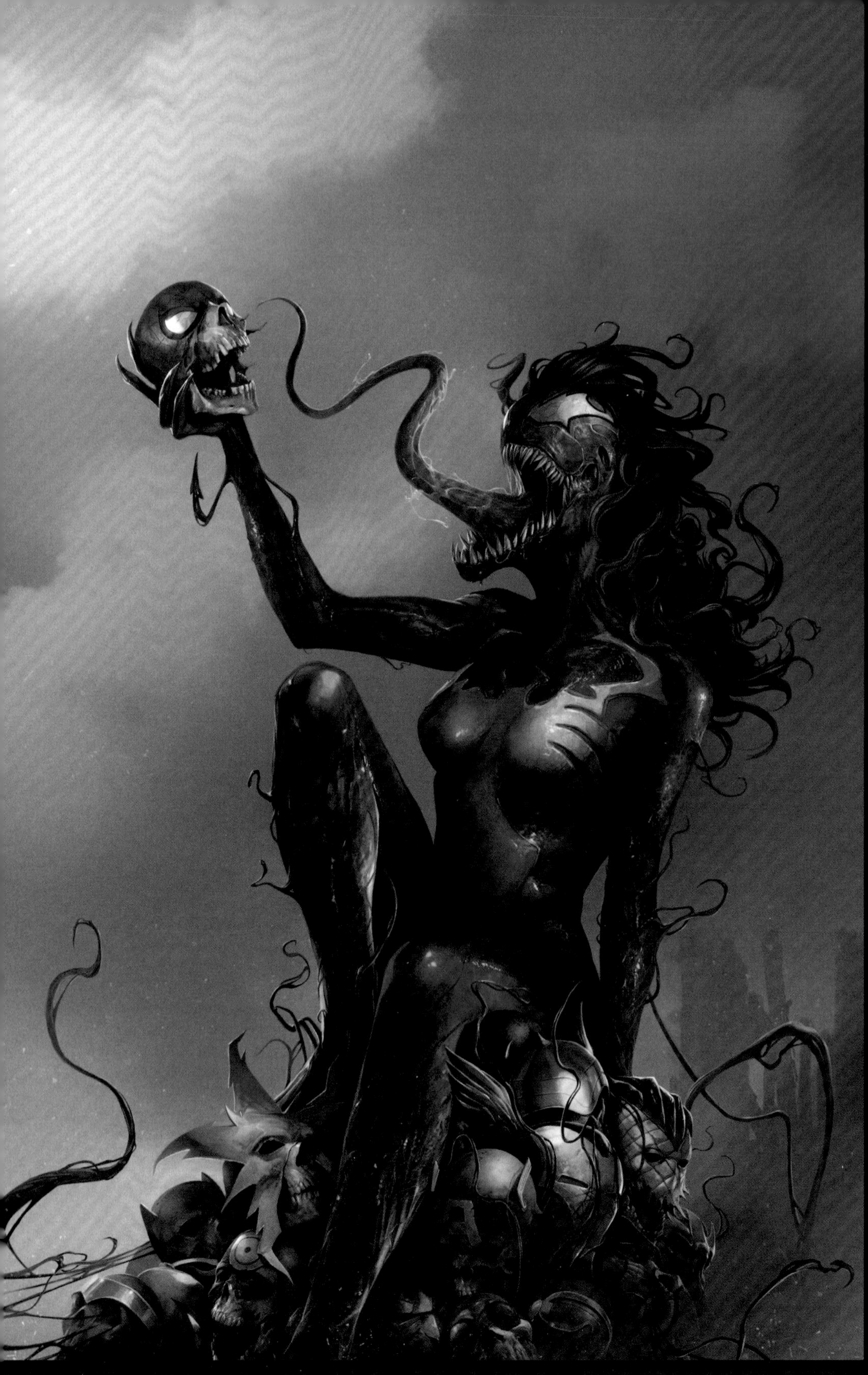

#151 MARY JANE VARIANT BY **FRANCESCO MATTINA**